HOOKED ON
ICE FISHING

SECRETS TO CATCHING WINTER FISH
• • •
BEGINNER TO EXPERT

BY

TOM GRUENWALD

Published by

krause
publications

700 E. State Street • Iola, WI 54990-0001
Telephone: 715/445-2214

Please call or write for our free catalog of outdoor publications. Our toll-free number to place an order or obtain a free catalog is 800-258-0929 or please use our regular business telephone 715-445-2214 for editorial comment and further information.

Library of Congress Catalog Number: 95-77307
ISBN: 0-87341-392-X
Printed in the United States of America

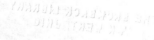

Dedication

*T*o my savior Jesus Christ, for without his unending love and understanding, I would have nothing.

*T*o my wife, Lisa, for standing behind me through countless hours of dedicated hard work-without her this project would never have been possible; to my beautiful little daughter, Alyssa, who has brought Daddy more smiles than even the largest trout; and, to the many of you whose added support and encouragement made all the loose ends come together, I extend my most sincere thanks and appreciation.

Tom Gruenwald

Contents

Preface

Welcome To The World Of Modern Ice Fishing

*M*y ice fishing roots date back to my childhood, in my hometown of Oakfield, Wisconsin. Since I didn't have a driver's license or anyone in the immediate family that ice fished to drive me, and my primary form of transportation—my bike—was garaged for the winter, I did what I had to: I walked.

Thankfully, a small pond just a short hike from my parents' house held sunfish, bluegills, perch, crappies, largemouth bass, pike, and, thanks to the added efforts of the Oakfield Conservation Club, occasional trout. I spent hundreds, if not thousands of hours there, staring through a hole cut in the ice. With ice chips skimmed away and my hands cupped around my face, my nose practically in the icy water, I'd stare into the clear water below, fascinated by the under-ice environment. Sometimes I'd drill a hole over a smooth sand bottom, sometimes over muck with weeds. I could see drop-offs, sunken wood, vegetation, rocks, minnows, and fish. Most importantly, I learned to recognize that certain species had specific areas they tended to hold throughout the winter, even in this small pond ecosystem.

Even more interesting was finding fish, then dropping a lure or bait down and seeing how the fish would react. Sometimes they'd bite hard, sometimes light, sometimes not at all. To catch them consistently required versatility and skill. I also learned that over time, fish seemed to become harder to catch, requiring modified and new, innovative tactics to fool them. I had to be willing to learn how to use various lures, baits, and techniques if I wanted to stay on fish. I didn't realize it at the time, but I was learning the beginnings of some highly advanced ice fishing methods.

By the time I was in junior high school, I discovered that the Oakfield Conservation Club had teamed with the local canning factory and created a small, man-made fishing lake a couple miles out of town.

You guessed it. I walked.

My desire to ice fish was strong. When I wasn't in school, I'd leave before sunup, and proceed to hand-carry my auger, minnow bucket, tip-ups, rods, lures, lunch and extra clothes two miles to this larger, magnificent resource: Raspberry Lake. By sunrise, I'd be fishing. It was there I'd spend the entire day, further exploring and testing the things I learned in previous years, expanding my horizons. Then I'd walk home, take a hot shower and eat ravenously. The next morning, clothes cleaned and dried, and fresh bait purchased, I'd be back on the ice.

This short story may seem trivial, but this experience was instrumental in truly learning the sport of ice fishing. I learned determination. I learned to dress properly and stay warm and dry for extended periods on the ice. I learned to drink plenty of fluids before and during the trip.

I also learned the importance of mobility to find winter fish, and of versatility to catch them consistently. Most fascinating, however, was that by putting these factors together, I learned the basics of winter fish behavior and patterns under the ice, and how to catch numerous species under a variety of conditions on different lake types. I did this without a lake map, modern electronics, super sensitive rods and bite indicators, fancy reels, light lines, or highly refined lures and presentations.

By the time I had a driver's license, I'd learned enough about ice fishing that I was able to travel, explore, and catch fish on a variety of frozen lakes. Blessed with newer, better equipment, I learned even more about the sport and how to modify my approaches for even greater success. On deeper lake trout lakes, for example, I couldn't look through a hole to find fish, or watch fish react to varied presentations. But by learning to use and understand my "underwater eyes"—electronics—I soon learned to accomplish essentially the same thing without physically seeing the fish. I learned to interpret what the unit was reading, match the scenario to a library of fish reactions recalled from past experiences, then make my lure react similarly to the movements and actions applied successfully in the past. The fish reacted positively.

This is somewhat akin to a child learning long division by hand rather than by calculator. Long hand calculations are time consuming; for many, painfully slow. There's also a greater chance of making errors, but ultimately, you gain a better understanding of the method by thinking through each step of the process instead of just pushing buttons.

Today, children learn division, but largely depend on calculators to pull them through. More speed? Usually. More accuracy? Often.

Ice fishing is no different. Today's advanced electronics and equipment make ice fishing more efficient and more accurate. However, while most anglers can learn the basics of how to use this new equipment, if you don't understand the process, the behind-the-scenes methods, or the true capability of each item, you're missing a portion of the understanding and appreciation for what these products can help you achieve.

Electronics for example, provide hundreds of hints that can help reveal winter patterns; in many cases, detailed patterns regarding where fish are holding and what they're biting on. Furthermore, used and maintained properly, today's technologically advanced augers cut holes relatively quietly, and more smoothly, reliably, and efficiently than the dull, inefficient, frustrating cup augers I used as a boy. Improved rods, reels, lines, lures, and techniques offer more options and a wider range of alternatives for fooling fish than ever before. Yet for best results, you must know how and where to use this equipment.

Recent magazine articles have introduced hundreds of new ice fishing products and have somewhat changed the stereotypical image of the ice angler as a simpleminded, grizzled old-timer wearing wool pants and fishing with a broken summer rod doubling as an ice stick. Yet far too many ice anglers still aren't wearing comfortable clothing or using electronics. They are using less than acceptable ice augers, and only one style tip-up. They have a basic jig rod or two, carry only a small selection of ice lures, terminal tackle, and accessories, and don't give much consideration to the specific location they're fishing.

Worse yet, due to the rapid developments in ice fishing products over the last decade, many ice anglers have become downright confused. Regardless of whether you're a confused ice angler, a curious individual in a quest for more knowledge about this intriguing sport, a first-time ice angler wanting to learn how to ice fish, a seasoned veteran looking to pick up a few new tips, or a self-proclaimed expert wishing to compare notes, I ask that you read this book start to finish. You can skim segments or pick chapters, and like using a calculator, come up with some quick answers. If you follow each step, you will learn to better appreciate the process of consistently finding and catching fish in winter, and be a better ice angler for it.

It's been a long time since I fished that little pond in Oakfield, but the knowledge assembled during those years, and in the years of experience since, is revealed within the pages of this book. You will learn to catch more and bigger winter fish, more consistently, no matter what your skill level.

Welcome to the exotic, enchanting, captivating, intriguing world of modern ice fishing.

Acknowledgments

Special thanks to my parents and grandparents who helped me greatly with the pursuit of my dream to become a fisheries biologist, writer and professional angler; to my many teachers and professors, particularly Mrs. Susan Casper, whose support and encouragement to pursue a writing career changed my life; to Mr. and Mrs. Paul F. Grahl and Kenneth L. Grahl, to whom I'm indebted for their endless contributions to this book, including their inspiration, encouragement, and assistance with photos; to Mr. Nate Grahl for his time and patience collaborating artwork, illustrations, and diagrams; and to the many inventors, manufacturers, and innovators of ice tackle for their time, effort, line art, photo support, and information. To you all I owe much gratitude.

Special appreciation is also given to Grandpa and Grandma Gruenwald, my mentors, my wife Lisa and daughter Alyssa, who have taught me more about life than they probably will ever know and inspired much of my writing, and above all, my savior Jesus Christ.

Without your help, support, and love, this book simply would not have been possible.

Introduction

Why I Ice Fish

I sit near the fireplace in my warm living room, sipping a cup of hot chocolate and peering outside, hypnotized by massive clouds of snow swirling past the window. I listen to the howling and whistling of the harsh, unleashed winds slamming against the side of the house. In the background, the weatherman calls this the worst blizzard of the year and posts a warning against travel, explaining more snow is on the way.

Cupping my hands around the warm mug, I realize I'm comfortable inside my cozy, protective home, yet somehow, I don't feel right about staying curled up inside while this immense display of nature is being released. Like a child, the outdoors beckon.

I get up, dress, and, taking one last look out the window, head for the door. Frigid air greets me, and immediately I feel redness forming on my nose and cheeks. I'm surprised by the depth of snow outside the door, where my legs post-hole to my knees, and I squint at the brightness reflecting from the snow's surface. Looking up into the gray sky, I'm bombarded with snow pellets, which rain down onto my Gore-Tex outerwear and sting my exposed face.

Still, the swirling, frigid air is sharp, inspiring. Winter is unleashing a free-falling fury of energy: hardwood branches snap and creak from the force of the gusty winter gale; pines stand covered in white, their upper branches waving, bowing and dancing to the power of the wind. Yet among nature's turmoil, I feel peace.

Turning my back to the raw wind, I find myself facing the lake, and suddenly an unyielding, rushing urge overwhelms me. Smiling, I pick up my ice tackle.

Many have felt such callings. Christopher Columbus. Lewis and Clark. Thomas Jefferson. Ben Franklin. Thomas Edison. Charles Lindbergh. Neil Armstrong. While I, like many others, know I'll never discover a continent, explore a vast wilderness territory, fly over the Pacific for the first time or step foot on the moon, I still feel the need to keep in touch with something unexplored. I thrive on such adventures, and each winter brings hundreds of them. Like me, you can hike to the local pond repeatedly, until the trip becomes mundane. But travel there during or after a snowstorm, blazing a new trail through drifts of fresh, untrodden snow—well, in a sense, you're exploring—going somewhere no one has gone before.

The hike is cold, but I soon arrive at the lakefront, lying before me covered in a sleek, pure robe of white. Thoughts begin flowing. To me, it's not hard to imagine that a peaceful, aquatic world exists below this perfect disguise, hidden from view, awaiting exploration. This is the extraordinary.

Most people have imaginary, extraordinary little worlds to which they can escape, whether they care to admit it or not. For me, it's the aquatic world. During summer, when I stare over the beautiful surface of a lake or bubbling trout stream, I can't help but wonder what magnificent mysteries lie in its hidden depths. Even more awe-inspiring is how the aquatic environment functions beneath a thick layer of ice that seals this unique world of splendor from the mundane, noisy world above.

This seal of ice, just one of the miraculous ingredients of winter, is fascinating in itself. Since ice is less dense than water, the very constituent from which ice is made, frozen water floats on itself. This occurs because when water changes from a liquid to a solid, the distance between water molecules expands. That much we know. Yet to this day, I know of no scientist who can tell us what's in between those molecules.

A tranquil ice fishing view, one of Mother Nature's many splendors.

Air? Nope. There's not enough space in between these water molecules to fit air molecules composed of a mixture of gases such as oxygen and nitrogen within them. Fascinating.

But this is only the beginning. Walking onto the frozen water, thanks to these billions and billions of stretched molecules—I imagine diving through the ice and visiting the world below. Above, a thick gray ceiling of ice. Below, a peaceful, dim green radiance. The water is clear, because runoff and the churning winds are sealed out by the frozen surface. There's little sound— the ice acts as an insulator, shutting off outside noise. Nothing moves, except a slight current that waves tall weeds above the sandy bottom. Peace.

A hard gust of wind whips across the lake, carrying with it a barrage of ice flecks that sting my face and remind me I'm above this protective layer of ice, not below. I draw my collar up and turn my back to the driving breeze. I can't turn back now, I'm obsessed with ice fishing.

I grasp the cold metal shaft of the ice drill. While it's turning, I watch as the auger churns through the ice until I feel the blades break through. Skimming the ice chips away, I lower my tiny, baited silver lure into the dark, cold depths below, doing my best to make its glistening prism flash like a wounded minnow. I lift the rod tip gently, jiggle it, then pause. Nothing. I repeat the action, and the tip jumps slightly. I tense up, ready for a hookset.

Almost instantly the rod tip dips again, and the graphite fibers transmit a definite "tic" to my fingertips. I sense "weight" mouthing my lure and, as if led by a sixth sense, respond instantly. My rod snaps skyward, then arcs into a deep bend as I crank down. He's there.

A few turns of the reel handle later, a thrashing, colorful yellow perch with brilliant orange fins and beautiful iridescent golden-green shine flops from the hole, dorsal fin erect, gills flared. I briefly admire the colors, remove the hook, and gently flop him in my pail. Suddenly I feel a high, which comes from a sense of the mysteries under the surface. My jig creates an almost life-like imitation of a Daphnia, one of the microscopic organisms that supplies an ample food source for both baitfish and panfish during the winter. I can't help but imagine my lure jiggling among the phytoplankton, tiny plants that drift aimlessly through the water's medium all winter, and come in a dazzling array of artistic shapes, sizes, and designs.

The author demonstrates the capability of a sharp hand auger.

The author admires a jumbo yellow perch.

And this is just the beginning. Hundreds of zooplankton, tiny animals that graze upon the hundreds of thousands of species of phytoplankton, also swim freely beneath the ice. Both are fed upon by baitfish, which are in turn eaten by panfish, which ultimately provide forage for the largest predators of the freshwater world. And to imagine, this is just a minute fraction of the fascinating activities taking place under the ice!

My bobber dips under the surface a second time, and my heart races as my rod tip bounces and a plump eight-inch perch twists from the hole. I reach out with childlike enthusiasm to claim my prize. Both happy and excited, I catch several more before returning home to my family, ready to prepare the fresh, sweet fillets into an evening meal.

By nightfall, our stomachs are full and the storm has subsided. Unlike the evening before, the night is still and quiet. Within the yardlight, a delicate, Christmas snow falls peacefully to the ground. My daughter stands by the window, nose pressed to the glass. She, too, feels the calling.

Soon, clad in her miniature snowsuit, my daughter takes my hand as we walk out the back door and into the yard. She stops, sticks her mitten out, and with genuine fascination in her innocent eyes, studies the different shaped snowflakes landing on her mitts before they melt.

I'm equally captivated. It's almost unbelievable that each flake is different. Although it's possible for two flakes to be identical, this is highly unlikely. In order for two snowflakes to be exactly the same, each would have to freeze on exactly the same dust or salt core configurations, fall precisely the same distance through the exact same sequence of conditions for an equal amount of time, and experience similar interactions on the way down. In fact, it's been estimated that a million different weather conditions alone can create ten to the five millionth power of possible snowflake patterns.

Ice fishing is similar to weather. To catch fish consistently, you must understand that an infinite variety of potential conditions exist, and while it's conceivable that the conditions during two fishing trips may be identical, it's unlikely. Successful ice fishing depends upon being on the proper lake, in precisely the right place at the right time with the proper equipment and gear—which is all dependent on the lake type, the species you're seeking, the amount and type of available structure, cover and forage, the progression of the season and the daily weather conditions, among a host of other factors and variables. The number of conceivable combinations creates an infinite number of possible fishing patterns—adventures—the ice angler can experience, explore, and enjoy.

Fried fish and hashbrowns are a tasty meal; reward for a successful trip.

I look forward to unraveling these mysteries with a passion. Each year on June 21, the summer solstice occurs. The sun hangs in the sky longer than any other day of the year. Traditionally, my ice fishing buddies and I sweat through the heat of the day, then commemorate the evening by grilling brats and celebrating that from this point on, the days become shorter and the ice fishing season will begin drawing closer.

Several months later, the jet stream will dip and bring a frigid arctic clipper down from Canada, which will quietly coat the land with a layer of sub-freezing air, and the waters will succumb to the numbing cold. Soon thereafter my phone will ring, a fishing buddy will inform me the ice is solid, and within minutes we'll be on our way to some distant, first-ice bite, more excited than a child in a candy store with a generous grandmother.

I remember such feelings during my school days, especially over Christmas vacation. It was a memorable time, not just because it represented time with family and friends, a break from classes, bright lights, candy and presents—these are things that light up the eyes of any youngster. To me, Christmas break meant more, because with the exception of one unusually temperate December during my youth, the onset of Christmas break paralleled the onset of the ice fishing season. My friends and I would talk, plan, and prepare for the fishing days ahead.

The first day off school, as the sun cracked over the horizon and shed the first dim rays of faint light into my bedroom, I'd hurriedly eat, dress in my warm, comfortable ice fishing clothes, and begin the trek to Raspberry Lake. It was here on the cold, gray ice that I felt solitude without loneliness, and independence in its purest, most innocent sense. At last, freedom.

I'll never forget the excitement and anticipation I felt while watching the small, bright colored styrofoam float, anxiously waiting for it to flaunt the familiar dance indicative of a strike, then slip under the surface. Things have changed since then, however, I still remember these feelings well, because I sense the very same burning, anxious, boyish emotions overwhelming me today whenever I ice fish.

Yes, I'm in awe of the under ice world and the supreme guidance that created it all and will control it for eternity. And through my wonder, I've grown closer to God, and realized that ice fishing is in its own way simplistic, yet when examined more closely, much more complex than I'd ever imagined.

Apparently others agree. Ice fishing appears to be one of the fastest growing winter participant sports in the United States. Why? First, no doubt, because the fish are cooperative, making the sport productive. And if catching a colorful trout, a few fat walleyes, or a bucket full of perch sounds good to you, you're going to love ice fishing.

A second reason for the sport's appeal is the social aspect. As a general rule, I think many ice anglers share their fishing time with other people. I've often seen two or three families fishing side by side—with everybody seemingly catching fish. Most importantly, I see family and friends sharing quality time.

Certainly times have also changed in terms of equipment, which brings me to the third, and main reason in my opinion, for the growth in the popularity of ice fishing. New developments in lightweight, warm clothing have made the sport more comfortable, and better equipment makes catching easier and faster. More resorts and guide services are now open, too.

The beauty of the winter environs also adds appeal to ice fishing, so between the challenging natural elements involved, the generally cooperative fish, the quality time spent with family and friends, the unique, exciting products and available services catering to ice anglers, and the peaceful winter landscape, who wouldn't want to at least try ice fishing? There are numerous wonders waiting to be explored in this peaceful world under the ice. It is a world of which many folks aren't even aware, and many aspects of which none of us, not even the most acute ice angler or biologist, will ever completely understand, but rather, will enjoy.

Why do I ice fish? Superficially because fish taste so good, and after a day in the frigid winter outdoors, few meals can top hot, golden brown fish fillets caught from cold water, served with tartar sauce, buttered rye bread, steaming potatoes and a cold glass of milk. More importantly, ice fishing provides a brief respite from everyday society, a chance to relax, and a break in the normal routine. It provides the opportunity to spend quality time with family and friends, or to revel in quiet solitude. One can enjoy the challenge of finding and catching fish, take in winter's beauty and scenery, relish the outdoors, and explore the unknown. It is a chance to enjoy the adventure of a season in the wilderness, if you will—a chance to feel like a kid again, free on Christmas vacation, with no cares other than to catch a few fish. It brings me back to reality, and provides time to feel and ponder the true meaning of living.

This makes ice fishing worth my time.

Chapter 1

Safety And Warmth, The Foundation Of Success

What seems like many years ago, I went ice fishing for the first time. I had no idea what ice safety meant. I didn't dress properly. My boots weren't insulated, and they leaked. My equipment wasn't up to par. And did I ever catch a whopper! A whopper of a cold, that is—one that lasted several weeks. And that's all I caught. People still laugh when I relay the story.

To someone who has never tried ice fishing, standing on a barren, iced-over lake, gripped in unimaginable cold may seem odd in the first place. "Poor weather for being outdoors," they'll claim. And I have to admit, fully understanding the art of ice fishing can be difficult at first. Furthermore, trying to get started in the sport can be even tougher. Many try, but are unsuccessful because they don't have the knowledge and right equipment. But for adventuresome outdoors folks who have a desire to try something new, there's a great deal of enjoyment awaiting them.

For the die-hard ice angler like myself, ice fishing becomes a deep part of the innermost soul, a winter tradition that cannot be broken or interrupted. "It's not poor weather," I always say, "it's lack of knowledge and poor clothing." I've learned that if the ice angler has the knowledge to ice fish safely, wears the right clothing and carries the proper equipment, ice fishing is one of the most pleasurable and enjoyable sports in existence.

Walking on Water: Ice Safety

Staring over the frozen lake with binoculars, I watch divers in insulated wet suits use their heavy-duty equipment to remove a Chevy from beneath the ice. I shake my head. Every winter

Thin ice/open water signs are posted for the safety of all.

it seems someone tries venturing onto the ice a week or so too early, and ends up with, at the least, an expensive bill from the local wrecking company. Some aren't so fortunate. Last season I had the sad experience of hearing a paramedic discuss how he removed the body of an elderly gentleman from beneath the ice.

The problem, I believe, revolves around the ever-growing popularity of ice fishing each year, and while veteran ice anglers know what to look for to make sure the ice is safe and are cautious when venturing out, beginners often aren't sure what warning signs to look for.

Ice fishing is supposed to be fun, but breaking through the ice and becoming submerged in icy water is not amusing. Such a fall can and has taken lives, and in most cases, these mishaps could have been avoided entirely by following some simple safety tips. The key? Common sense. Never take unnecessary chances. The best advice is, "when in doubt, don't go out."

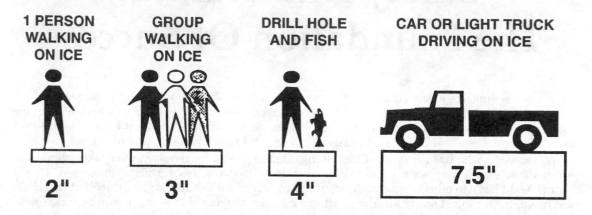

1 PERSON WALKING ON ICE — 2"
GROUP WALKING ON ICE — 3"
DRILL HOLE AND FISH — 4"
CAR OR LIGHT TRUCK DRIVING ON ICE — 7.5"

A safety guide for minimum ice thickness during clear blue ice conditions (Bill Mitzel)

It's a chemical principle that ice floats on water, but trucks, cars, snowmobiles, ice shelters and people don't. If you don't have the right type of ice conditions, you'll take a cold water plunge that may cost your life, which is something far too valuable to risk. So when planning a trip, the first hard-fast rule is to check with knowledgeable, reliable sources. Local chambers of commerce, resource agencies, resorts and bait shops in popular ice fishing areas are continually in touch with people monitoring ice development. Phoning ahead to them may not only save a trip, but a life.

Of course, never take anyone's word for the truth. Any knowledgeable source will warn you that walking on ice is a risk, and they won't use the term "safe," they'll just warn you when it's unquestionably unsafe.

So how do I tell the ice is safe? To be honest, I can't. I can only look for clues that indicate it may not be. I've addressed this question to other anglers. Some will respond the ice is safe when they see others on the lake. Nope. Not good enough. I've read too many articles about people that have fallen through, and seen too many pictures of vehicles gripped in ice as they're removed from a frozen lake. I therefore cannot reliably use other people's judgment as a means of determining safe ice.

Others will have ice thickness guidelines. "Two to three inches of new, clear ice is generally considered safe for one person walking. Four is safe for a person to drill a hole and fish. Add two more inches, and the ice is safe for snowmobiling, and seven and a half is considered safe for a car or light truck," I heard a speaker reveal at a recent ice fishing seminar. I cringed, knowing that while these words were true, they were also misleading, because this isn't the whole story. Ice develops at different rates and into a variety of conditions, factors which must be considered before walking onto a frozen lake.

A good place to start is using common sense and checking around the shore. If shoreline ice appears gray and mottled or broken up, stay off. But other factors are even more important. Geographical location, for example, makes a difference. It's no secret that the further north you travel, the earlier ice forms. Thus, people can be in the midst of the first ice bite around mid-

Currents in channels and other inlets may lead to open water periods.

November in northern Minnesota, while folks in northern Illinois may be enjoying days they don't need a jacket. Elevation and proximity to the moderated temperatures of the Great Lakes and the ocean are considerations, too. Ice anglers may be walking onto the ice in higher elevations in the mountain ranges in and along the eastern and western United States, while anglers at lower elevations may be casting in relatively warm, open water. At the same time, anglers in western Wisconsin may be ice fishing for several weeks, while those in western Michigan, where air temperatures are moderated greatly by the prevailing westerly winds and "lake effect" from Lake Michigan, may still be awaiting ice cover.

Once ice does form, it's easy to assume the ice cover is uniform throughout a geographical area, but ice conditions may vary greatly. In fact, ice is seldom of uniform strength and thickness even on lakes within the same geographical region. Shallow lakes, which feature a greater surface cooling area to volume ratio, freeze sooner than larger, deeper lakes holding a greater water volume, which take longer to cool. Thus, you might fish a shallow lake featuring six inches of ice all morning, then, assuming the ice is safe, cross the road to a deeper lake in the afternoon, only to find less than an inch.

For that matter, different parts of a single lake may freeze at different times. This is especially true of larger, irregularly shaped lakes. Shallow areas protected from the sun and wind by high banks are more likely to freeze earlier and more solidly than deep, open expanses of water being beaten by the wind and sun. Other factors enter in, too. Ice beneath a snowdrift, for example, is insulated and won't be as thick as an exposed area nearby.

Inflowing springs or channels also bring in relatively warm, moving water that creates areas of thin ice, perhaps even pockets of open water. Examples would include channels between lakes and the mouths of inlets or outlets, because the underlying currents of relatively "warm" water erode the ice pack. Another example is ice covering underwater springs, which generally feature thin patches of ice throughout the winter because spring water remains a consistent fifty-some degrees year around. s, often placed by fisheries agencies trying to maintain oxygen levels in lakes to avoid winterkill problems or by property owners trying to protect docks or boathouses, create artificial currents which have the same end results. Even fish, muskrats and other animals swimming under the ice can weaken the ice pack.

Shallow, vegetated areas don't freeze as solidly, either, because the weeds attract sunlight, warming the area and melting the ice. In fact, any solid object—an emergent stump, rock, fallen tree or dock are good examples—carry out this process of conduction. Objects on the ice create similar results. Ice shanties, for example, should be moved a minimum of every ten to fifteen

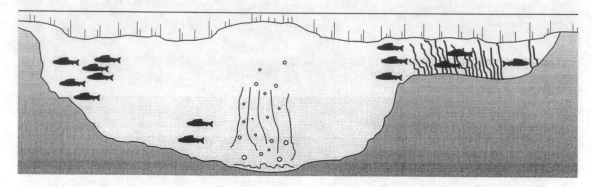

Ice overlying a spring will be much thinner than the surrounding ice.

days, as they will conduct the warmth of the sun and weaken the ice around them during the day, settle in, then refreeze down into the pack at night. Many shanties have been destroyed by anglers failing to recognize this process, allowing it to continue for extended periods of time.

Pack ice is another danger, especially on larger waters. Pack ice is formed when certain bays, shorelines or regions of a water body freeze, then due to wind action or pressure crack formation, chunks of varying thickness break free, drift to another area and refreeze together. Often these chunks plow together at different angles, resulting in tremendous variations in ice thickness throughout the pack. Certainly the ice forming between chunks isn't nearly as thick as the ice blocks themselves.

Ice on reservoirs or flowages, which often feature fluctuating water levels, must also be monitored closely. If water levels rise, they can create unsafe conditions by pushing the ice upward, leaving shorelines open. Often, to unknowing anglers, these shorelines quickly refreeze, but not to safe thickness. Given such conditions, you may leave the lake one evening on twelve inches of shoreline ice, and unknowingly trod over less than an inch the next morning. If the water

Ice shanties are very vulnerable during mid-winter thaws. If not tended to and moved after these warming trends, this may be the result.

drops, shoreline ice heaves may form and jut up at steep angles, again creating poor shore ice conditions.

Another bad ice situation often occurs at first ice. Early cold snaps often form thin, one- or two-inch layers of ice; then a heavy snowstorm will dump several inches of snow. This snow insulates the ice from further freeze up, and may even weight the ice down, pushing it below the waterline. The snow then acts as a sponge, absorbing water and creating slush, which makes ice conditions poor and travel difficult. Cold weather may partially freeze this slush, but this is mottled ice with numerous air pockets, with only a thin layer of solid ice below. Cross a spring or current-influenced area now, and you're in over your head. Which brings us to another topic: ice condition. Without question, new, clear, blue-colored ice is much stronger than old gray or blackened ice that has been partially thawed and refrozen. Two inches of new, clear ice will normally support an average size angler, but twelve inches of honeycombed ice may not. Be aware of such idiosyncrasies.

Even thick, solid ice can develop cracks or thin spots called pressure ridges. Pressure ridges are formed by the force of expanding ice. As winter progresses in a typical year, ice thickens and expands, but since the surface area covered remains the same, the expanding icepack causes pressure heaves to occur in the areas of greatest stress, ultimately causing the ice to crack and heave, sometimes even forming pockets of open water within the cracks. Often, due to lake shape, these ridges form in the same areas each winter.

Strong winds may also cause a "pumping" action on the surface of the ice regardless of its thickness, which forces water up through fishing holes and pressure ridges, enlarging openings in a short time. Although this phenomenon may occur on solid ice, this is especially common in areas where open rivers enter large frozen bays, and water is blown from the river under the icepack.

Finally, late ice presents another bad ice situation. Dark, honeycombed ice is by far the weakest ice, followed by shoreline ice, when the warming ground warms the shallows and begins weakening the ice pack above. Being the shallowest water to begin with, shoreline ice remains the thinnest ice on the lake. Ice around emergent objects such as vegetation, trees, rocks, or piers is the same. As the warming spring sunlight shines on these objects, they absorb heat and transfer it to the ice, weakening and melting the pack in the process. Of course, there are other such conditions that may cause poor ice formation or poor quality ice. Consider for example, a combination of the above conditions. Be cautious.

Approaching a Lake

When unsure of the ice conditions, be sure to check with locals for information. When you reach the lake, travel in pairs for safety, spread out, and try to follow old trails if possible. Walk onto the ice slowly, taking each step carefully, and test the ice by chopping ahead with a chisel and drilling a test hole every ten or fifteen feet. If the chisel breaks through, the ice cracks or a hole reveals thin ice, slowly follow your path back to shore.

Wearing a life jacket outside your clothing is also a good idea. I'm not talking about the big, bulky, bright orange "horse collar"-style life jackets, but today's thinner, warm and comfortable flotation jackets and matching bibs. These are type 3 PFDs (personal flotation devices) made of

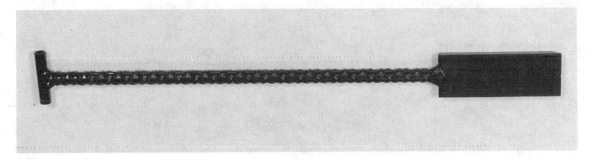

A standard chisel is an essential tool for an ice fisherman's arsenal when checking early ice.

A pressure crack is caused by expansion and contraction during freezing.

Shorelines often melt early during warming periods, partly due to the ground's ability to retain heat.

closed-cell PVC foam. While not yet Coast Guard approved, they're designed to keep you afloat should you fall in, and at the same time provide insulation between your body and the water.

"The next generation of PFDs for ice fishing application will likely be inflatable life jackets, fitted with a self-activated carbon dioxide cartridge," said Garry Spurlock of Stearns Manufacturing. "The jacket stays flat and virtually unnoticeable, until you fall through the ice. When the jacket becomes immersed in water, a water-activated soluble pill causes the plug to dissolve, triggering the cartridge to inflate the device." Several companies, including Stearns and the Canadian based Buoy O Boy, are also developing flotation, or "anti-hypothermia" style snowsuits.

This practice may sound strange, but you could unknowingly be facing an under ice current or spring, a pack ice situation or old thawed and refrozen ice, and such safety precautions could save your life.

Weather such as sun, rain, heavy snow and wind can change ice conditions rapidly, causing slushy and wet surroundings.

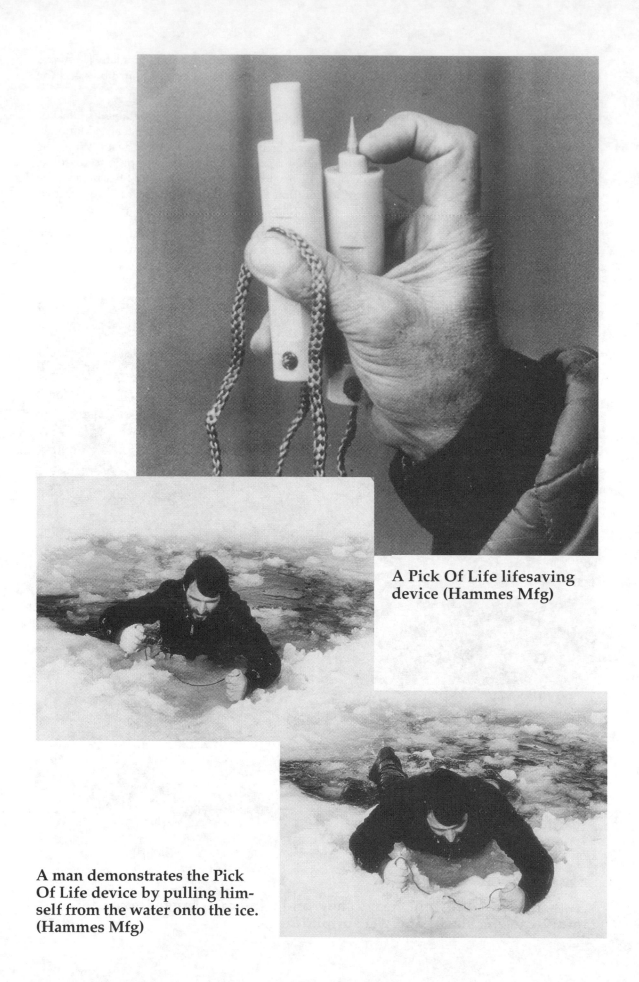

A Pick Of Life lifesaving device (Hammes Mfg)

A man demonstrates the Pick Of Life device by pulling himself from the water onto the ice. (Hammes Mfg)

In addition to wearing a PFD, carrying a set of screwdrivers, Strikemaster's Ice Studs, or Pick Of Life ice picks is an outstanding safety precaution. "Currently there is no state law requiring people to wear life jackets, or more importantly, carry safety picks when traversing the ice," stated Bob Hammes of Hammes Manufacturing, makers of the Pick Of Life. "But the future may see it happen. If you fall in the water during summer wearing a life jacket, you'll stay afloat and survive. But if you fall through the ice, you need to accomplish more than just staying afloat—you have to get out of that icy water. Time is of the essence. You've got fifteen to twenty minutes before hypothermia sets in, and the Pick of Life helps shorten your time exposed to water—and believe me this is important. I developed the Pick Of Life after two snowmobilers on my home lake drowned several years ago. I feel if the picks save just one life, it's worth the effort."

The Pick Of Life consists of two four-inch plastic cylinders, connected by a cord, that easily fit in an accessible pocket. Each cylinder contains a sturdy pick that is protected by a retractable, spring loaded guard. When plunged into the ice, the guard retracts, allowing the pick to penetrate the ice. If you break through, use the picks, one in each hand, with an alternating hand over hand action to pull yourself to safety. Each Pick Of Life is bright orange for easy visibility, and the cord keeps the units together. The unit also floats, as does the attached cord, so if they slip from your grasp they can be retrieved easily. Carrying a length of rope is a good idea as well. Should you or your partner fall through, the rope can be tossed to the victim from safe ice and used to pull him or her out. As Bob Hammes said, "It's better to have them and not need them, than to need them and not have them."

By the way, if you do fall through, leave your clothing on. In addition to conserving body heat, layers of clothing trap air that will help keep you afloat. Get out of the water fast, unless help is near, then you're better off not to move. Some studies have revealed that remaining motionless in a fetal position doubles the amount of time an individual can survive when submerged in cold water.

If you're on your own, you must get out quickly, and the best way to do so is to get your body parallel to the surface by turning on your back or stomach and kicking your way out of the hole. Once out, don't stand up, but rather, slide across the ice to distribute your body weight and get as far away from the hole as possible, using your screwdrivers or Pick Of Life spikes to pull yourself away from the icy water. When you're back on safe ice, access your car keys and move fast. Your clothes will quickly freeze, and if you don't reach for your keys and move quickly, you'll find yourself rigid as a 4x4 post, unable to access your pockets, or for that matter, move at all.

If assisting someone else who has fallen through, stand back and shout instructions while "extending yourself" to the victim. Throw a rope, or try tying items together to make one. A drill, chisel, belt, shirt, your pants—tie them together and you'll find most anglers have a good thirty feet of extension material available. Just remember, don't panic and never get too close. Two people in the water can't help each other.

Once you have the victim safe in hand, handle him or her gently; cardiac arrest is a danger to someone suffering from hypothermia and possibly, shock. I'm not trying to scare you, just warn you, and while offering safety tips for avoiding trouble, also trying to go a step further and provide information about what to do in the event an emergency would happen. You may never use the information listed here, and I sincerely hope you don't, but being prepared with a plan can save lives, and no one can argue the importance of that.

Driving on the Ice

Driving vehicles on the ice can be dangerous at any time. Snowmobiles and ATVs are a safer bet than a car or truck, and are a good source for ice travel, but there are still some safety concerns to keep in mind. First, understand that most problems with these machines occur at night. Of course, never drink alcohol and operate a snowmobile or ATV. I don't have any statistics, but I'd guess the majority of snowmobile and ATV ice accidents are drinking related.

Secondly, with any vehicle, avoid excessive speeds. It's tempting to race at high speeds across a frozen lake in search of a hotspot, especially at night. However, many anglers have dropped their machine through the ice because their speed overran their headlight. In other words, their stopping distance was greater than the distance the headlight penetrated the darkness ahead. Also keep in mind that as a vehicle moves across the ice, it pushes a "wake" called

Avoid excessive speeds when driving on the ice.

a shock wave through the ice pack. Driving fast, especially with heavier vehicles, can be dangerous when two or more vehicles are going at the same time because these shock waves may meet and weaken or fracture the ice. Sergeant David Branley, a gentleman from the Dane County sheriff's department here in Wisconsin, is involved with ice rescues and claims to be able to see this wake, much like a boat wake, when crossing thin ice.

He recommends that if you drive a car or truck on the ice, leave your seat belts unbuckled, keep the windows rolled down, remove any heavy clothing, turn your heater wide open and be ready to bail out. Reasoning? "Leaving your seat belts unbuckled saves a few precious seconds when you're trying to escape the sinking vehicle," David emphasized. "Having the windows open and heavy clothing removed, you'll be able to escape out the window quickly, otherwise, you'll find water pressure makes opening windows and doors under the ice difficult, and squeezing through the window with heavy clothes on next to impossible." The heater, of course, keeps you comfortable until you reach your intended destination. "By the way, if you should go through, remember that the ice pack will appear gray, whereas the hole you fell through will appear dark in contrast," according to the Minocqua Fire Department diving team.

Finally, those groans and creaks in the ice pack—the eerie sounding ones that echo beneath your feet like a muffled version of laser fire from starships in an old science fiction movie—are normal. Ice packs continually expand and contract, a natural process that given typical conditions and solid, thick ice, causes no major problems.

Ice Strength

I certainly don't say these things to make ice sound unsafe. Good ice will easily hold anglers and vehicles, and most good ice packs are even somewhat flexible. If you actually measured it, you'd notice that several heavy vehicles parked close together on the ice can actually sink the icepack below water level, causing water to collect on the surface. When the vehicles are moved, the ice will rebound back to its previous level.

While no ice can ever be considered 100 percent safe, good, thick ice is strong. When the Trans-Siberian railroad was completed across southern Siberia, train ferries that carried entire freight trains across Lake Baikal, the world's deepest inland lake, were replaced in winter by railroad tracks laid directly across the ice; so ice can be more than safe enough for foot or light vehicle travel. It simply demands knowledge and respect.

Ice Creepers

Whenever traversing slick ice, especially slick ice with a thin layer of wet, heavy snow atop, I highly recommend use of ice creepers. Slick ice or a thin film of snow on ice is treacherous, especially when pulling a sled or carrying gear. Ice cleats come in a variety of types, ranging from adjustable belts with a piece of toothed metal underneath, to complete creepers that look like the sole of a baseball shoe with sharp spikes.

From personal experience, I've narrowed my selection down to Pat O' Grady's "Real Feel Ice Spider" cleats, a comfortable, durable, highly effective design that works. They slip on over even the largest pac boots, and attach with two easily adjustable, heavy-duty velcro strips. The rugged logger points grab hold, and don't collect snow, which can form a slippery ice pack beneath your boots, causing them to slide better than a new pair of roller blades. Last time I checked, they were available through Cabela's mail order catalog. If you don't get Real Feel cleats, at least get a good pair. One fall on the ice that leads to a broken arm can put a damper on any ice fishing season in a hurry.

Reel Feel Ice Spider cleats

The bottom line to ice safety? Use common sense, be cautious and responsible for yourself. Again, there's no need to fear the ice, but there's no question that you must respect it.

Staying Warm

Folks often question how I manage to remain on the ice in blistering cold weather all day long, day after day, without becoming cold, uncomfortable—or often in my case, almost dying of hypothermia. The trick is diet and proper dress. That's right. Diet. No, I'm not here to preach and discuss a cutback in caloric intake. In fact, I'm talking an increase! While I'm not implying that an increase in caloric intake is healthy, I can tell you that when it comes to ice fishing, you can and should temporarily break the rules.

The trick to staying warm is to drink and eat a lot and often. Drinking fluids is most important, as dehydration is a significant concern in cold, dry air, and without adequate liquids your body's metabolism slows, producing less heat. For best results, drink a lot of liquids of the non-alcohol and non-caffeinated variety. Alcohol cools the body, certainly an undesired result and caffeine is a diuretic, which triggers the bladder to release, causing the body to lose vital liquids. Hence, avoid alcoholic drinks, cocoa, coffee, tea and caffeinated soda. Rather, stick with water, juices and non-caffeinated herbal teas.

Often, ice anglers ignore this general rule, and begin suffering dehydration without even knowing it. Symptoms of dehydration include a nagging headache, dizziness and listlessness, and most people shrug this off as a headache from bright sunlight, a cold or the flu. Often a simple six or eight ounce glass of water or fruit juice will solve the problem in a matter of minutes. By the way, avoid eating snow as a source of moisture. This can actually be dangerous, as it can cause severe stomach cramps. Melting small chunks in your mouth and then swallowing the melted water, however, is okay in an emergency.

As for food, go against the rules: eat a lot, often. I haven't seen anyone gain weight while ice fishing. Eat as much as you like, drink and snack frequently and shift to a diet rich in fatty foods. Remember, fat has three times more calories than carbohydrates or sugars. Furthermore, fried, hi-calorie fats provide more energy with less volume than other foods, plus they burn slow and steady as opposed to carbohydrates, starches or sugars, which offer quick bursts of energy and heat, but burn fast.

Pre-fishing meals should be hearty. Before a trip I enjoy rich food such as fried bacon, sausage, scrambled eggs, meats, potatoes with gravies or real butter, stews and soups. I supplement this with heavy bread, butter, doughnuts, non-caffeinated hot drinks—and carry along frequent snacks comprised of beef jerky, cheese, cookies, hearty meat or peanut butter sandwiches, hard candy, dried fruit, caramels, instant oatmeal, freeze-dried foods and hot, non-caffeinated beverages. Such a diet aids your body's metabolism. One offshoot of this is heat production and increased blood flow, which ultimately helps keep you warm. And don't worry about gaining weight. I have yet to see any active ice angler who spends hours at a time on the ice gain weight.

Your body works hard while ice fishing, burning a massive number of calories just to stay warm, in addition to the calories burned while trudging through deep snow to and from fishing hotspots and pulling sleds heavy with gear, not to mention drilling holes. Don't get me wrong, I'm not recommending a rich, fatty, heavy diet. That's not good. But while ice fishing, you must keep your metabolism churning and your body warm, and eating the proper food can help you in both respects.

Clothing

In addition to fluids and diet, the secret to comfort and warmth is proper attire. There was a time when I didn't know how to dress properly for winter, and judging from experience, I suspect many of those who haven't spent much time on the ice probably dress more for looks and general comfort than for the purpose of staying warm. While today's cold weather clothing looks an awful lot nicer than ten years ago, it still must serve the primary function of being insulating and warm rather than fashionable. But so what? Ice fishing isn't a fashion contest, and I'm not a model. After spending many long hours on the ice, my primary considerations are warmth and catching fish, and if I don't fit the bill of Joe Fashion and I smell like walleyes, so be it. I'm happy.

The first concept to understand when considering staying warm is that body heat is lost in percentages, approximately 40 percent from the head, 30 percent from the body torso and legs, 20 percent from the hands, and 10 percent from the feet. Thus, keeping the head and body core warm are more important than most people realize. Many beginning anglers are concerned about keeping their hands and feet warm, but do not understand that the heat for their hands and feet comes from the body core. Indeed, if your hands or feet feel cold, try zipping up your jacket and pulling your hood up. Your extremities will warm.

How do you accomplish keeping the torso and head warm? Simply by using a system called the "three W's": Wicking, Warming, and Wind resistance. Essentially, this system keeps your skin dry, and traps pockets of warm air between your body and the cold outside air and wind, providing the best insulation available.

Fortunately, with winter clothing designs being dramatically revolutionized in recent years, numerous exceptional choices in lightweight, warm, comfortable, high quality winter clothing are now available. In many cases, they don't look bad either. That's a much different picture than years ago, when ice fishing proponents basically had two choices: cotton or wool, usually in lumberjack plaid. Not that these are bad choices, as both materials are warm and do an acceptable job of insulating, and I kind of like looking like a lumberjack.

Yet the most important aspect of winter dress is to dress with as few (that's right, few) clothes as possible. Modern ice fishing involves a great deal of movement and physical activity,

Numerous exceptional choices are available for warm, lightweight layering.

and the ice angler's greatest enemy is perspiration, which leads to chilling. The key to winter comfort is to remain "comfortably cool," never breaking the point of perspiration. No one likes to be cold, and hence, clothing choice is critical to the modern ice angler. While cotton is warm and comfortable when dry, once you begin to sweat, it also draws moisture against the skin, cooling the skin's surface and counteracting any insulating properties when damp.

Wool is an excellent insulator and even stays warm when damp, but dries slowly and becomes heavy and scratchy when wet. Any true-blue ice angler that has worn wool or cotton clothing while dragging ice tackle around a lake, drilling holes and experiencing periods of both intense exercise and inactivity, has certainly figured there must be a better, more comfortable way of doing things. After all, during periods of activity such as walking or drilling holes, you'll likely perspire. When you stop to fish, perspiration begins evaporating from the skin. This causes chills, especially in wind, because evaporation is a cooling process, but also requires energy, which tires the body quickly. Thus, trying to stay warm and comfortable in wet clothing is nearly impossible.

This is where today's fabrics come into play. Rather than absorbing moisture and packing down, modern synthetic materials maintain their loftiness by transferring moisture away from the body and transmitting it to the outside of the fabric where it can evaporate away, and at the same time, trap a layer of warm air against the skin. As a result, your body stays dry and warm even if your clothing becomes damp, and you'll retain more energy.

Underwear Basics: Wicking

Since the first step of staying warm in cold weather is keeping the layer of clothes next to your skin dry, the right underwear is the first major consideration. Over the last several years, a variety of advanced synthetic fabrics have appeared on the market, increasing the options available to winter anglers in terms of comfort and protection. This revolution continues today as more high-quality cold weather materials become available.

The secret formula in creating these new designs? Again, the material must retain body heat, yet still have the capacity to wick away moisture from the body and its insulating environment, because moisture conducts body heat away. Polypropylene was the first material available to the ice angler that accomplished this feat. While early versions of this fabric were somewhat scratchy and irritating to the skin, modern versions are quite comfortable and best of all, relatively inexpensive. Unfortunately, anyone who has spent a small fortune on quality cottonwear only to see it shrink into oblivion after being washed, won't be happy to learn that polypropylene garments are also prone to shrinkage, so use care and follow instructions when washing.

While more costly, polyester is now considered the highest technological advance in winter clothing materials, and is the first choice of most leading outdoor clothing manufacturers. Unlike polypropylene, polyester clothing is shrink-resistant and often provides years of service, even after hundreds of washings. In addition, polyester clothing is soft, comfortable, and available in various thicknesses or "garment weights," depending on the insulating qualities you demand.

Most manufacturers provide several "weights" of clothing, particularly in regard to underwear. A lightweight classification, for example, provides lots of wicking action, but minimum insulation. Mid-weight garments provide more insulation, yet will still keep you dry, and are generally the best all-around choice. If you intend to move very little, or only slowly, heavy weights provide heavy insulation and still keep you dry.

Incidentally, polyester is marketed under several private label names, including DuPont's Thermax™ or slightly improved Thermostat™. Polyester can also be made into a fleece-style fabric, and while this form doesn't wick away moisture easily, it does provide considerable insulation.

Other comparable materials such as chlorofibre are also available and are designed to be both functional and comfortable. I've been extremely impressed with this material in the hand-crafted Blue Johns™ long underwear I've been using over the last three seasons. Blue Johns are a product of British Columbia, Canada, a world leader in hypothermia research, and their design was based upon these research findings. Blue Johns are made of "mid-weight" rated chlorofibre, which I've found durable, comfortable and highly functional under a wide range of temperatures, and they've kept me warm under even the most extreme winter conditions. Da-Mart offers a similar line of long underwear.

Of course, some clothing manufacturers have opted to create combinations of the above materials to capture their primary characteristics and gain other ulterior motives. For example, two-layered garments can be formed by laminating polyester clothing to wool. These items feature all the exceptional insulating qualities of wool, plus polyester's ability to insulate and wick moisture away from the skin and the use of wool brings down the price of these garments considerably.

Just a word of caution. To maximize the longevity of thermal garments, regardless of the material, wash them in warm or cold water, and air dry them away from heat. It's also recommended that today's thermal materials not be ironed. Also, don't defeat the purpose of the polyester by adding cotton underwear beneath the polyester layer. Be sure the polyester is against your skin so the material can fully complete its purpose of wicking away moisture.

Insulation Layer

Once the proper undergarments are in place, next comes the insulating layer, which essentially traps layers of warm air between the body and your outside wind layer, something we'll discuss shortly. For now, understand the insulation layer is largely a matter of high versus low density materials. For example, a two-inch-thick plate of steel has a high density, and makes a poor insulator. But if the same piece of steel is stripped into fine coils of steel wool then stuffed into a layer two inches thick, you create a low density material that would make a fine insulator.

It is the same with clothes. The more porous or "fluffed" a material is, the better the insulator. Goose down, for example, is low density material and stays fluffed, providing good insulation value. Low-grade fillers such as cotton, however, compress over time as they're worn and washed, thus reducing their insulation value considerably. To further complicate matters, human skin normally releases more than a pint of water every twenty-four hours above and beyond perspiration, and as such materials compress, this moisture reduces the insulating value of the material further yet.

What is the key to providing a good insulation layer? Purchase insulating materials that are thick, fluffy, and low density porous (and will stay so). The material should also transfer moisture through to prevent dampness. If air is trapped, condensation will build, causing chilling by evaporation. However, an exchange of this moist, warm air with the colder, outside air eliminates this process. The problem is, this must be a slow exchange; if it's too fast you'll chill, if too slow, you'll suffer the consequences of condensation. Modern insulating materials accomplish such a feat.

Once you've chosen suitable underwear, you'll need to consider the concept of layering, or wearing numerous layers of lightweight clothing. Start with good polypropylene or polyester long underwear, then add a set of cotton-wool blend long underwear. Simply put, wool or cotton garments worn over the thermal insulator greatly enhance the drying speed of the underlying material, and take advantage of the insulating value of the wool.

Next, add an oversize T-shirt or two to keep the moisture moving outward, then add layers including bulky wool sweaters, chamois type flannel shirts, down vests or light down jackets as necessary and the insulating layer will be complete.

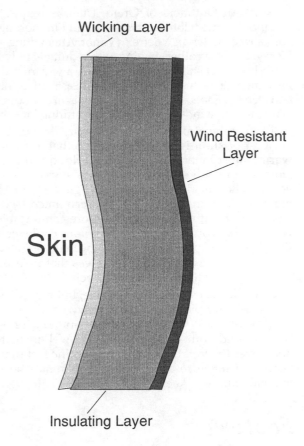

The WWW layering system

Outerwear: The Wind Resistant Shell

This system should be topped with a two-piece nylon rainsuit, preferably with a pair of Gore-Tex™ or Thinsulate® lined units, which transfer moisture yet provide a barrier to the wind. This overall concept traps layers of warmer air between each layer of clothing. The wind and water-resistant shell provides exceptional insulating qualities, yet the outer layers will still "breathe" and allow an exchange of air and water vapor between your clothing and the outside. This helps keep you dry, all the while blocking the chilling effects of the wind.

Of course, there are wide variations in temperature and personal activity, so a two-piece, water repellent breathable suit made up of bibbed overalls and a waterproof, warm coat are always an excellent choice for the mobile angler. This makes it easy to open to cold air when performing strenuous exercises such as walking and drilling holes, yet makes it possible to close up the suit when sitting still or facing wind, rain, or snow. Otherwise, for snowmobiling to and from hotspots, for more lethargic, relaxed anglers, or for those on a large school of fish, a one-piece snowsuit such as those produced by Wall or RefrigiWear are excellent choices.

As for specific products, Gore-Tex™ fabric is a highly innovative, lightweight, weatherproof outerwear material which has been assimilated into a variety of clothing lines. The material is both windproof and water repellent, which is important, because with most waterproof materials, trapped body heat and moisture make you feel clammy and uncomfortable. However, with Gore-Tex, water is kept out and you're protected from the natural moisture vapor your body produces, again, because it's breathable and transfers moisture from the inside out. Thus, you always stay dry and comfortable, no matter how wet or cold the conditions. And Gore-Tex is virtually unsurpassed in cutting the wind. Similar materials are also being developed by other manufacturers, improving on the same principle.

Northern Outfitters of Orem, Utah, is unquestionably one of the leaders in technologically advanced winter clothing systems, and I'm thoroughly impressed with this line of products. Their specialized material, Vaetrex (Vapor Attenuating and Expelling, Thermal Retaining clothing for EXtreme cold weather) begins with a durable polyurethane foam that stabilizes insulating air next to the body, yet still transfers moisture away from the skin through a hydrophobic (water repellent) insulation. The insulating layer consists of a high-efficiency insulating material sandwiched between this inner surface layer of moisture-conducting material and an outer lining composed of a tear resistant, wind-breaking fabric featuring low air permeability, but still "breathes".

This combination works just like the "layering" concept described earlier, all in one garment, but best of all, it is also designed so that a differential vapor pressure is formed between the warm, moist inner lining and the cold, dry outer shell. This clothing not only does a superior job of retaining body heat, but also allows an exchange of moisture with the outside air to keep you dry. Best of all, the material is lightweight and comfortable and again, all found in one garment. In fact, the manufacturer recommends wearing nothing but the Northern Outfitters clothes, but if it makes you feel more comfortable, a set of polypropylene or polyester underwear can be worn beneath this fabulous cold weather clothing system. Numerous company testimonies and experiments have repeatedly iterated the effectiveness of Northern Outfitter's line of clothing. The company guarantees that their boots and clothing will be the warmest you've ever owned, or they'll buy them back.

Other such systems are available, but regardless of the assortment you choose, make sure at least one outer piece features a heavy hood large enough to be placed over a Thinsulate-lined, polypropylene stocking cap. In my opinion, a non-hooded snowsuit is useless. Rather, wrap a scarf around your neck, add a thick, well-insulated polypropylene stocking cap, and tie your hood over the top. It's a proven scientific fact that most body heat is lost through the top of the head, and such dress will virtually eliminate heat loss. The hood may look strange, but it cuts the wind and will keep you warm.

Footwear

As for footwear, start with warm socks, such as polypropylene or silk-wool blends, and when fishing in really cold weather, also try a pair of Gore-Tex fabric outer socks. Just be sure to leave extra space in your boots to provide an insulating layer of dead air between the boots and your feet. Remember, a tight fit equals cold feet. Of course, bootwarmers can also be helpful.

In boots, scrap the old four-buckled uninsulated, leaky rubber boots—they're history within the realms of modern-day ice fishing because today's Pac boots are far superior products. Heavily-lined felt Pac boots with thick rubber soles such as those produced by Sorel, La Crosse Footwear, Northern Outfitters and Red Ball are all excellent choices.

Sorel® is a name any ice angler is sure to recognize, as this company pioneered the use of removable boot liners. Today, with more than 125 models in the Sorel line, a wide range of boot designs exist. However, for a high-tech approach to ice fishing, Sorel's Pac boots are top of the line. These boots feature Sorel's Thermoplus™ system, a unique revolutionary design that provides extreme protection against cold. A three-eighth inch inner liner of non-absorbent felt draws moisture away from the foot and a three-eighth inch outersole of non-absorbent felt prevents cold transfer from the bottom of the boot to your foot, yet absorbs transferred moisture, while a middle layer of Radiantex™ insulates between the two. A one-fourth inch DuPont Thermax inner sock also adds further insulation.

La Crosse's Iceman boots pioneered the concept of double insulated Pac boots, and their triple insulated Maxim™ are revolutionizing ice fishing footwear a second time. These boots are specifically designed to wick away moisture in cold weather and keep feet warm, even while participating in high-level activities on the ice. The design consists of a 100 percent waterproof natural rubber bottom featuring a one-fourth inch polymeric foam insulation and B-400 Thinsulate. A one-half inch wool felt midsole is also built into the rubber bottom, a removable polypropylene/wool felt liner surrounds the feet, and a removable "moisture trap insole" retains perspiration wicked from the liner. La Crosse's Pac boots are similar in design and function.

Other designs have also been introduced. Take Red Ball's -65 Boundary Boots, for instance. While somewhat heavy, I can honestly say I've never gotten cold feet while wearing these boots, even when spending ten or twelve hours on the ice in below zero temperatures with a wind chill over -30°F. A five-eighth inch thick Ensolite® midsole is a closed cell construction

Red Ball Pac Boots (photo courtesy Red Ball)

and won't absorb moisture, yet also totally seals out cold. A polymeric foam liner encompasses your feet within an insulating layer of dead air, and this is surrounded with quilted insulation sandwiched between layers of polypropylene and a high density layer of B-400 Thinsulate.

Better yet are Red Ball's Quad-Pacs, a highly sophisticated boot that provides outstanding cold weather protection. The boots feature seven separate layers of insulation, one-fourth inch felt insulation, one-half inch Ensolite midsole, polymeric foam insulation on both sides and top of the foot, a 100 percent waterproof 1000 denier Cordura® Nylon Upper, and roller-lace lock, a unique system that allows the wearer to adjust upper and lower lace tension independently for maximum comfort—all in a compact, lightweight boot design.

Quad Pac liners feature a 400-gram Thinsulate layer and Alpha™ Pile, a new "miracle" fiber-pile insulation. This design enables your feet to stay warm in extreme conditions, regardless of whether you're sitting still or walking for a long distance, and the comfort level rivals any other boot liner on the market.

As improvements in footwear continue to develop at a rapid rate, we'll no doubt see lighter, warmer, more comfortable designs continue to appear.

Mitts

As for the hands, start with neoprene gloves such as those produced by Glacier Gloves or HT Enterprises for drilling holes and handling bait. These provide waterproof hand protection without sacrificing a good sense of touch when needed. The rest of the time, however, use a pair of well insulated mitts. Five-fingered gloves only serve to separate the fingers and disperse body heat, causing them to become cold more quickly. Also make sure your mitts cover your wrists, and always be sure to carry an extra pair (or two) just in case the first becomes wet, or choose waterproof mitts such as HT Enterprises' Eskimo Mitts, comfortable, fleece lined mitts that feature a seamless, molded PVC shell that is 100 percent waterproof, nice when handling bait or pulling in line from a tip-up.

For most other applications, water-repellent nylon or leather gloves with good, fluffed insulation are excellent, especially when waterproofed. I'm particularly impressed with the mitts offered by Northern Outfitters, and Wells-Lamont's "Grippers," a Thinsulate based mitt. Both are contoured to fit the natural posture of the hand in a relaxed position, and offer superb insulating qualities. Of course, on exceptionally cold or long trips, dropping a heat pack in your mitts for added warmth is an excellent idea. Finally, be sure your mitts allow free action of the hands. If there is any bind at all at the back of the hand when your hand is clenched, go bigger. Binding reduces the insulating value of the mitt.

In fact, once you've chosen your clothing, an important consideration is fit. For today's modern, mobile ice anglers that are moving and drilling numerous holes, today's clothing must fit loosely enough to allow free movement, yet be tight enough to stay in place, particularly around the wrists and ankles. In other words, a proper fit must be comfortable, yet still be somewhat snug in order to be effective.

Fit also applies to footwear. Often, ice anglers wear too many socks, lace their boots too firmly, or wear mitts and gloves that fit too tightly, all of which constrict blood flow and reduce warmth to the extremities and the pocket of warm air insulation surrounding the feet and hands. Just remember, mitts and boots should fit comfortably, but not overly tight. Also be sure your wicking layer fabric doesn't extend outside your wrist or leg cuffs to the outer layer of waterproof clothing, as the wicking action of the underlying fabric may move water up your arm or leg.

By the way, all clothing, once it's been worn for a period of time, will accumulate moisture and body salts in the material. To make it continue to work, it must be washed and dried after a specific number of hours of use, usually at the end of a fishing day. Northern Outfitters clothing, however, is designed to keep you warm and resist moisture buildup for unlimited amounts of time, making it highly efficient if you're an all-day angler on a several day outing. Good stuff.

Outerwear should always fit loosely, because you'll have to fit these items over several layers of underlying clothes, but be sure these garments cover and fit snugly around the legs and cuffs and feature both water-repellent and "breathing" qualities.

The chill factor is based on air temperature, wind, and humidity, because each causes complications with the clothing system you choose, but by following this system, you'll remain comfortable for extended periods of time, in even the coldest weather.

Other Factors

The other intrinsic factors affecting warmth on the ice include the quality of your blood circulation, and the degree of physical activity you're involved in. Consider each when dressing. Blood circulation, for instance, varies between individuals, especially men and women. Yes, guys, if your wife complains she's cold before you feel chilled, she probably isn't kidding. Blood circulation in women is poorer than men, largely because they have smaller blood vessels than males. An extra layer or two of clothing should remedy the situation.

As for the degree of physical activity, think. If you walk two miles to Raspberry Lake carrying all your gear, strip down to just your initial underwear layer and perhaps a light wind-resistant layer, or you'll perspire and become chilled. Upon arrival, open the wind-breaking garments for lake exploration and hole drilling, and when set up to fish (meaning the level of physical movement stops), add more undergarments, insulating layers, and close up the wind-breaking layer, one step at a time, as your body cools down and as dictated by the conditions. This way, you won't sweat and you won't be cold, either.

Remember, in addition to adding or subtracting layers of clothing to adjust insulation, clothing can be loosened or tightened to adjust heat flow. Since heat rises, the human body acts as a chimney. Opening a flap somewhere near the neck or head, even wrists—can allow heat escape and a consequent cooldown. The trick is to do so before perspiration becomes a problem.

One final point to consider: cosmetics, perfumes and colognes. They're great for looking and smelling good, but increase the possibility of facial frostbite, and the alcohol content can decrease skin temperatures. Even hand lotions can reduce hand warmth. Forget such things on the ice. The fish don't care what you look like, and no matter how much your date or spouse may like it, the fish may be repelled by your otherwise irresistible fragrance.

In summary, when traveling from place to place on the ice consider wearing a PFD, carry warming and nourishing food and drink, dress properly using modern clothing technology and the three W's system, always being prepared to add, remove or loosen layers of dry clothing as necessary to suit your body, and avoid using cosmetics. You'll be glad you did.

Hypothermia

Winter tragedies caused by improper preparation for cold have not been few. Your body temperature should be 98.6°F That's a far cry from the subfreezing temperatures you'll be exposed to when ice fishing. Should something happen that you do get cold, you risk hypothermia.

Hypothermia starts with chills and uncontrolled shaking, and severe fatigue. Next, muscles become rigid, the victim becomes sleepy, and eventually loses consciousness or experiences heart failure. However, recognize the signs early, and hypothermia is easy to counteract. Start by getting out of the wind, adding more clothes, and finding heat. Supplement this by drinking warm liquids, eating warm foods, and taking a hot bath or shower if possible. You'll recover.

Advanced stages of hypothermia resulting in unconsciousness for a fellow angler can be a scary experience. Should you face such a situation, remain calm, handle the victim carefully, and call for a doctor quickly. Under the supervision of a doctor, even if in advanced stages of hypothermia, many victims who may appear dead actually survive, thanks to a condition called "Mammalian Diving Reflex" that causes the body to lower its rate of metabolism and hence, lowers the need for oxygen for a temporary period of time without serious consequences.

One of the members of the experienced Minocqua, Wisconsin Fire Department Diving Team explained, "When the body cools, its metabolism slows, and requires less oxygen, close to 50 percent of what is normally needed. Some hypothermia victims have been submerged for fifty minutes underwater, and not only lived to tell about it, but showed a complete recovery." Consequently, never give up on a hypothermia victim. Rather, act quickly, follow the proper safety measures, and above all, don't panic. Most victims of ice fishing related accidents can be saved if you act quickly and maintain a level head.

However, such things shouldn't happen in the first place if you prepare for the cold and remember the clothing layering concept; in fact, if you layer your clothing according to the recommended system outlined here, you'll be able to spend hours at a time on the ice with little or no discomfort. And by following the proper safety measures, you reduce your chance of falling through the ice tremendously.

So despite questioning of your sanity by others, you'll just smile, because you know the secrets of remaining safe, warm and dry, even while fishing under the most extreme conditions. Consequently, you'll be able to spend more time concentrating and focusing on more important things when ice fishing—like catching fish.

Chapter 2

Basic Ice Fishing Equipment

*O*ne of the most wonderful aspects of ice fishing is its simplicity. Just check that the ice is safe, choose a spot, cut a hole in the ice, and fish.

Ice fishing is also relatively inexpensive. You don't need a $20,000 bass or walleye boat, or the gas, maintenance and repair that such a boat requires. Instead, knowledge of ice safety, warm clothes and a basic assortment of gear will equip you for fabulous catches.

Of course, successful ice anglers don't just wander onto the ice and chop a hole. They follow basic strategies to find areas that will likely hold fish, try to determine the best access to these spots, then use proper equipment and tackle to meet the situation.

Reviewing a lake map can be a successful plan of attack.

Lake Maps

The first tool you'll need is a lake map. Often, such maps are distributed free by local businesses. If not, for just a couple of dollars an accurate lake map will depict your target lake's size, layout, depth, water clarity, inlet and outlet locations (areas of potentially dangerous ice), and prominent bottom contents. It will also show which areas feature fish-holding cover such as weeds, rocks, and flooded timber, and will indicate access points, parking areas, and shoreline landmarks. Other map features might include marinas, campgrounds and resorts, fish species present, and fishing tips, among other things.

If you take your map to a natural resource agency, fisheries management office, or a resort or bait shop, the staff may suggest the best access sites, provide directions, point out areas of bad ice, note productive fishing locations, and recommend productive fishing techniques. This will save time on the ice and maximize your fishing time.

Sleds

Of course, you'll need something to tote your gear across the ice. Many portable shelters double as sleds, but for the ice angler who would rather save money and fight the elements, a sled is the answer. You can store all your gear inside, and simply slide the unit out of your truck or car trunk as needed.

Many ice anglers build homemade sleds such as this.

When weather and ice are accommodating, I load my ice drill, bait, tip-ups, rods and tackle into a crate or 5-gallon plastic pail (that may double as a seat), set the equipment on a sled, walk out, set up, and turn my back to the wind.

Many anglers build their own sleds. These are usually works of art featuring a gas lantern or catalytic heater to keep the seat warm, as well as storage for ice drills, chisels, skimmers, five-gallon pails, portable shelters, and more. I'd rather fish. (Actually, a child's toboggan rigged with bungee cords will do the trick.)

Here are some of my favorite commercially-made ice fishing sleds:

*SnowTote from USL is the most rugged sled I've seen. It's a one-piece, molded plastic sled with an optional hitch for towing behind a snowmobile or ATV. It also features tie-down holes along its edges.

*Otter Sled from Otter Sales features deep, high sides and a windbreak/ice shelter option.

*Equinox, a Canadian based company, offers five "boggan"-style ice sleds.

*Polar Sled from HT Enterprises is made of lightweight, durable, high impact polyethylene with a three-runnered base. Designed to be pulled manually when walking out, it sports compartments and space for all necessary equipment.

Chisels

Once you've determined a place to fish, you'll need to cut through the ice. A chisel (a heavy metal bar with a beveled blade on one end) works well for chipping through just a few inches of ice. Handles ranging from 50-70 inches long are best for an average-height angler, although longer and shorter models are available. Brand names include HT Enterprises, Lakco and Strikemaster. HT also offers a handy 20-inch bucket chisel, as well as a 9-1/2" pocket chisel.

Heavier models with medium-size blades chop ice best. Narrow blades chip too little ice with each blow, large blades focus too little force per square inch (and are cumbersome). Always strap the chisel to your hand or wrist so it won't sink to the bottom if you lose your grip. A chisel also can be used to test for thin ice as you walk out.

Look for a heavy-duty chisel with a strong weld and a sharp heat-treated point. Protect the chisel point (and yourself) with an old carpet scrap, waxed cardboard and duct tape, or a slit tennis ball.

On a few inches of ice, use a chisel.

Ice Drills

The old-time hand ice augers are no longer manufactured. Those clumsy, often-dull contraptions cut a "plug" that had to be pulled out from the ice. They've now been replaced by ice drills.

A sharp hand drill will cut through a foot of ice in no time. It requires only a strong arm and some energy. Simply hold the auger perpendicular to the ice and start drilling.

A variety of manual ice drills are on the market:

*Jiffy offers hand drills in six and eight-inch diameters, and feature nylon bearing handles and replaceable blades.

*Strikemaster produces the popular Mora line of hand drills. Their Lazer model, however, is one of a few that will drill through thick ice in seconds, almost effortlessly. The Lazer can be equipped with a special handle for drilling with both hands rather than just one.

*Normark, a Scandinavian brand, also is an excellent drill.

*HT Enterprises recently introduced "The Edge" ice drills that bite an amazing amount of ice with each turn. Their European two-hand design offers twice the cutting power of a standard drill, and the blades are made of a specially hardened steel to eliminate frequent sharpening.

A sharp hand auger can handle even the deepest snow and ice conditions as long as you keep the hole clean while drilling.

A Jiffy Power Ice Auger at work

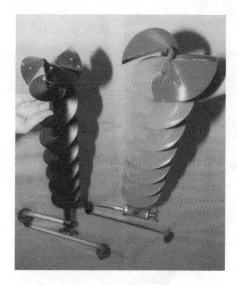

European auger heads

Hand drills usually are offered in diameters of 4 to 10 inches, though some smaller and larger models are available. Obviously, the size of fish you intend to catch will determine the size of your drill.

Keep your blades sharp, as cutting a hole with dull blades is almost impossible. Restore the edges with a sharpening steel. Simply remove the blades from the drill, grasp one with a Vise-Grip pliers, then sharpen the edge by pushing the blade down and across the steel as if trying to cut off a thin slice of the steel. Repeat the procedure several times, switching sides of the blade after each stroke. (You also can shim the blades on some models to increase the drill's "bite.")

The author drills a hole with a hand auger.

Once sharpened, be careful to maintain the edge by taking the following precautionary measures:

*Prevent rust [which reduces cutting power] by greasing each blade. Also, try packing a layer of grease or petroleum jelly in each plastic blade guard.

*Wipe the blades dry after drilling a hole. Otherwise, ice buildup will cause poor or no cutting action.

*Never attempt to open an old hole unless you have Strikemaster's Lazer or HT's Edge, which can cut through old holes without blade damage.

Power Augers

At the request of a fellow volunteer fire fighter at the Plymouth, Wisconsin Fire Department, inventor Marvin Feldmann attached a small gasoline engine to an ice drill. The prototype worked, and by 1951, the Feldmann Engineering and Manufacturing company was producing and selling the Jiffy ice auger. The machine changed ice fishing forever. (Notice in the photo on page 42 the absence of the modern spiral auger that removes ice chips!)

If you plan to drill numerous holes, or if the ice is thicker than 12 inches, there is no substitute for a power auger. There are two types, electric and gas.

Electric:

Electric augers are quieter, don't require mixing of gas, and don't release noxious fumes inside a fish house. **Strikemaster**'s Electra Lazer is the only electric model I'm aware of. When powered by a 105 amp marine battery, it will drill approximately thirty holes through two feet of ice. Its main drawbacks are low speed and the cumbersome battery.

Gas:

Gas-engine augers are far more common than electric models. Though they're available in numerous diameters, I prefer the 10-inch models. My manual augers take care of the smaller diameter holes. Several companies offer quality gas-engine augers:

*Jiffy makes augers with up to 3.5 horsepower, with cutting depths that can stretch to 36 inches. The broad range of models offers many features.

*Strikemaster, another leader in power augers, offers several models with high torque and stainless steel blades. Its Lazer Mag is one of the lightest power augers on the market.

*The Country Store offers the Ice Sabre power, which features an exceptionally lightweight, high rpm engine. The maker claims it can drill 15 percent faster than any other lightweight-class power auger.

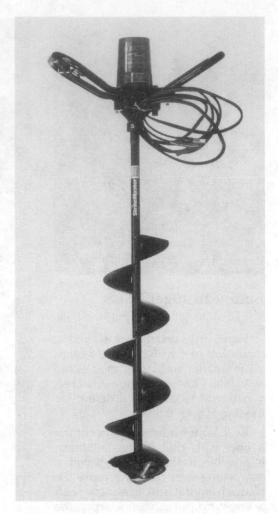

An electric auger (Strikemaster)

*General Equipment Company offers a lightweight two horsepower auger with a limited lifetime warranty on major components.

*Ardisam is known for its popular line of Eskimo power augers.

Buying tips

What should you look for in a good power auger? Features, horsepower, weight and cutting head design. Once you've purchased it, follow the manufacturer's instructions for use and maintenance religiously. Remember, this is an expensive, precision machine, and with proper care it will last a lifetime.

Accessories

Auger extensions from makers such as Jiffy and Strikemaster will enable you to go further if the ice reaches an extreme

A Jiffy power auger ad circa early 1950s (Feldmann)

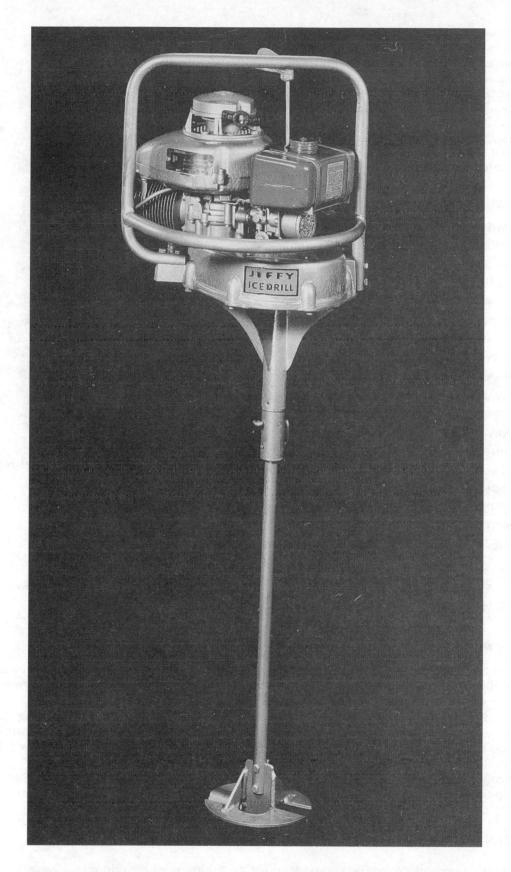

An old Jiffy power auger. Note the absence of the flighting along the auger shaft.(Feldmann)

thickness. Strikemaster even offers a tele-scopic extension.

Both companies, as well as a number of catalog retailers, also sell blade protectors, replacement blades and replacement parts.

Storage cradles, such as Jiffy's Wall-it are also a good investment. They install in minutes, keep your unit organized, utilize no floor space, and protect your investment from damage during the off-season.

Power auger safety:

*Study your operator's manual thoroughly before using the machine.

*Review all safety precautions carefully and never take unnecessary chances.

*Wear ice creepers when operating your power auger.

*Never wear loose clothing while operating a power auger.

*Always keep all clothes and your body clear of the rotating auger.

*Don't transport or carry a power auger with its motor running.

*Never leave the power auger unattended while the engine is running.

A demonstration of a Jiffy model 30 power auger (Feldmann)

*Never try to adjust or repair your drill while the engine is running.

*Avoid contact with the muffler or other hot components.

*Never allow a child to operate a power ice auger.

*Check the blade guard for cracks or broken straps. Replace the guard if broken.

*Always keep the blade guard on the auger when transporting the machine.

Auger noise

Most anglers try to make as little noise as possible when cutting a fishing hole so they don't spook their quarry. Some anglers prefer chisels, some hand augers, some power augers. But which is quietest? Believe it or not, augers are.

A study conducted by Jiffy showed that, because ice acts as an insulator, the whirring blades of a drill are almost inaudible underwater. However, the pounding of a chisel is transmitted through the ice to the water, where sound does travel well. Fish several yards away will hear and feel the vibrations sent out by the chisel.

Of course, the constant drone of an auger can turn fish off, especially in the case of unaggressive, spooky, or shallow water fish, but it also may arouse their interest and attract them.

Skimmers

A rather inexpensive, but necessary, item for ice fishing is an ice skimmer. Consisting of a perforated metal or plastic cup attached to a short or long handle, a skimmer resembles a kitchen strainer. The skimmer is used to clear ice chips from a hole after it's been drilled. Skimmers come in various diameters for obvious reasons—just try scooping a four-inch hole with a six-inch skimmer! The shopper has a wide choice.

*Lakco and Jiffy offer metal skimmers. Metal tends to be more durable than cheaper, lighter plastic, and I've found riveted metal construction, such as on the Lakco and Jiffy models, to be superior to welding. In cold weather, a weld eventually may break. Jiffy's Chipper-Dipper features a skimmer on one end and an ice chipper on the other.

*Strikemaster offers an interesting hybrid: a flexible plastic cup riveted to a lightweight aluminum handle.

*HT also uses a combination concept in its durable 3:1 skimmer. The unit comes with a pliable cup for ease in squeezing off ice buildup, an ice chipper on the cup end for opening skimmed holes, and a ruler stamped in the aluminum handle, which is riveted to the plastic cup.

*Two of the more interesting skimmers on the market are the Skim 'n' Gaff, a combination skimmer and gaff, and Tackle Tamer's "Flipper-Dipper," a skimmer whose cup collapses when plunged into the hole, then opens when pulled upward. This design enables removal of most ice chips in one lift.

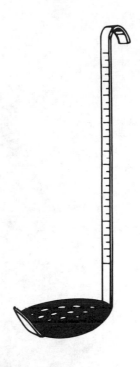

Keeping your holes open

Once set up and fishing, you'll be faced with the challenge of keeping each hole clear of ice and slush. If you're "on fish" and not moving much, drill a second hole beside the actual fishing

A skimmer

hole, chip out a channel between the two holes with a chisel, and place a coffee can full of hot charcoal briquettes into the false hole. Warm water will circulate into the fishing hole to prevent ice up. You can also use the charcoal bucket to warm your hands, as well as melt ice from line guides, auger blades and scoop. After dark, the glowing coals can provide enough light for unhooking fish and baiting.

Water spitters are another way to keep holes open. A spitter can is constructed using a coffee can and length of copper tubing. Bend the copper tubing into a coil, place the coil inside the coffee can, drill a hole for the intake at the base, and seal with solder.

Next, form a spout at the top, add sand to the bottom of the can, pile charcoal into the coil and place it in a shallow hole drilled next to the hole you're fishing. Finally, chip a small channel between the two holes, and with the spout positioned over your open hole, light the charcoal. As the can and copper tubing heats, the water around the can will heat slightly and spill into the adjacent hole. The tubing will draw in cold water, warm it, and "spit" it back into your fishing hole, keeping it from freezing in your absence.

Commercially made items are also available:

*HT offers the Thermal Hole Cover, a flexible three-fourths inch foam pad that works with any tip-up, and the Ice Guard, a plastic cover that adapts to any tip up, including wind-tip-ups.

*Northeast Products offers the Ice Hole Insulator, similar in design to HT's hole cover.

*Other interesting inventions, including the Hole Heater, can be placed in the hole or on the hole cover (with the line run through) to eliminate line freeze-up.

Permanent Ice Houses

Shelter from the cold can help you concentrate on fishing, rather than on staying warm. Portable models are less expensive, easier to move, and usually are better systems for effective fishing, but I still have a fondness for permanent "ice shacks" (as we called them years back, when they were little more than glorified privies). Some of today's elaborate "shacks," however, boast all the amenities of home, including two stories, carpet, woodstoves, tables, beds, generators, refrigerators, televisions, satellite dishes, and, like the old privy, portable toilets. I'll therefore refer to them as fish houses, although you'll sometimes hear fish shanty, fish shack, and fish hut (in Canada).

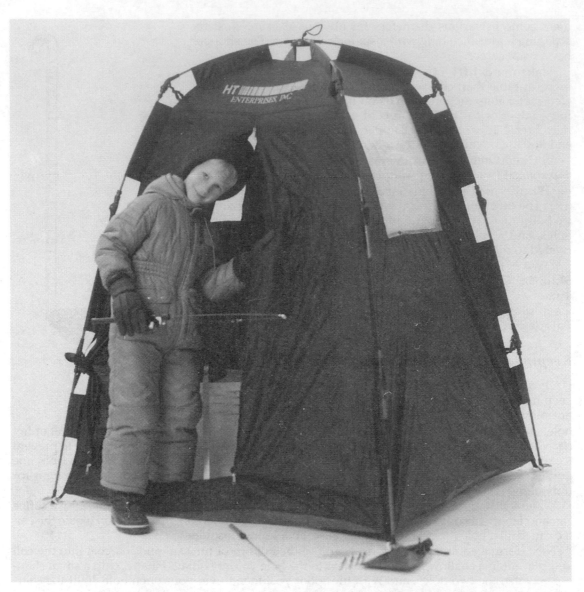

HT's Polar shelter (above), with shelter anchor (right), used to prevent the wind from carrying the shelter across the ice.

Ice houses can be rented, but if you wish to build your own, design it carefully. Be sure the design fits in your truck or trailer, unless you intend to trailer it. Be sure the unit has adequate space, organized hole setup, enough windows, and proper ventilation, which is required by law to prevent carbon monoxide poisoning.

Some states have strict codes for ice houses, so check your state's laws before building. These laws may affect windows, roof design, trailer design, lights, removal times and labeling.

When setting up your unit, slip wood blocks between the frame and ice, or the unit will melt the ice, settle into the pack and freeze down. Move the unit every ten to fifteen days, especially during warm periods or late in the season. Remember to take the blocks after each move rather than littering the lake.

Portable Shelters

In today's mobile strategies of ice fishing, permanent shelters play little if any role. Don't get me wrong. If set over a productive spot, and if you want to play cards, watch football, or cook while you fish, a permanent fish house is ideal. However, a comfortable, portable shanty is a clear choice for mobile ice anglers who desire shelter from the wind and cold.

Advantages

What are the advantages? First, today's lightweight, portable enclosures eliminate any excuse for not ice fishing, no matter what the temperature. Second, a portable shelter allows you to neatly organize, transport and store your gear. Third, a portable shelter stored in your home rather than left on the ice won't fall victim to vandals, arsonists or thieves. There are other advantages as well. Most states don't require a permit for a portable fishing shelter (although some states do). A portable doesn't require special attention to prevent freeze-down, and doesn't have to be towed off the lake before the ice weakens.

Most importantly, however, a portable enables you to move, to follow moving schools of fish without sacrificing the warmth and comfort of a shelter. A permanent fish house, on the other hand, stifles mobility. The comfort of a warm shelter is hard to leave, making it easy to feel lazy and just "sit it out." If you're not positioned over fish, the day turns into a card game.

Example of a large portable ice shelter (USL)

Evaluating features

Choosing a portable unit today isn't easy. Ten years ago only a dozen models were available, but now you must choose from more than 100. When looking for a portable ice shelter, consider the following questions:

    *How much room will be needed for people, equipment and gear?
    *Are the holes positioned to suit your fishing style?
    *Does the unit show quality materials and workmanship?
    *Does the manufacturer provide a warranty?
    *How compactly does it fold up and what is its weight?

Frabill ice shuttle/windbreak shelter

*Is it easy to transport, carry or tow?

*Are ice anchors included?

*Will you be able to fish effectively inside it with your preferred equipment and methods?

*Is there adequate room to set the hook using your preferred rod length?

*Are the lighting and number of windows satisfactory?

*Are the windows shaded?

*How many doors are available?

*If you plan to use a heater, does the shelter have adequate ventilation?

*Is it easy to set up?

*Is the unit self-contained, or does it have loose parts that may get lost?

Popular choices

*In case you want mobility without compromising comfort, some semi-portables are available. **Brainerd Outdoor Sports** makes a 4x8-foot trailered aluminum fish house. **Northern Lites** offers a similar unit that almost looks like a camper with holes in the floor.

*The **USL** Clam Sleeper (8' x 8' x 7'6") is the largest, truly portable shelter I've seen—larger than most permanent shacks. The Sleeper comes complete with a flat plastic floor and six holes. Smaller Clam models also are available. Another USL model, the Fish Trap, is termed a "Bass Boat on Ice". Its high-walled, waterproof base keeps slush out and equipment in, and its molded runners make towing easy.

*The **Otter Sled** with shelter "lean-to" works similarly to the Fish Trap, but features no seat, carpet or rod racks.

*The **Lodge**, from Michigan, is a two-man shelter based on the same principle as the above unit.

*Distributed by **BLI**, another similar design is Erv's Best Tip-Up Sled. This portable features a convertible-like top that can be set up as a windbreak or as a completely enclosed shelter. The unit is compact, fitting easily in the trunk of most cars.

***FOF**'s popular Pop 'N' Fish is a unit that snaps together firmly and easily. FOF also makes a variety of other easy to use portable shelters.

***Frabill** offers several portable models. The popular Ice Shuttle's enclosed sled base sports a padded seat, and comes with poles and a nylon windbreak for convenient, roomy storage and wind protection. The well-equipped Hideout Deluxe is unquestionably one of the easiest and fastest two man shelters I've used. It requires only seconds to raise or break down. The Hideout provides plenty of room to stand. Frabill's Speed Shak, featuring the same self-contained, quick setup design, is twice as large as the Hideout. The Ice Explorer is a highly compact model.

***Shappell** offers units with a folding polyethylene base with no center ridge, a quiet, carpeted floor, and other features. The unit folds in half to create a fully enclosed sled with bucket carriers molded into the base.

***HT Enterprises** offers a tripod design windbreak, as well as a highly portable shelter that folds into a small pack that can be slung over the shoulder. It weighs fewer than 6.5 pounds! This one-man unit sets up in less than a minute.

***Superior Products** offers a popular line of Trophy Portable Shelters, available in both 5' x 7' and 7' x 8' models.

A variety of other portable shelters and windbreaks are available from **Viking Roth Enterprises**, **Warner Shelter System**, **Bluff Country Coverings**, **Innovative Outdoor Products**, **InsTent**, **J-Moe Manufacturing**, **C&S Innovations**, **Senco**, **Mankato Tent and Awning**, and **Canvas Craft**, among others. Each, of course, offers a unique combination of features and design. The hard part is making up your mind about which one to buy!

Heaters

Small shelters are quite easy to warm with just a simple white gas lantern, but today's portable heaters are effective. There are several that I recommend.

***Mr. Heater**'s portable radiant propane heaters come in several models. Some even double as cookers and portable stoves.

*Coleman offers compact Focus 5 propane heaters, available with or without electronic ignition. These can be adjusted to provide either diffused or focused heat. The larger Focus-15 heaters mount on a 20-pound propane cylinder.

*Uncle Josh has two models suitable for shelters. The wood-stove can handle up to 14-inch firewood. The propane model pumps out 14,000 BTUs.

*Strikemaster has a series of propane heaters ranging from 12,000 BTU to 30,000 BTU. Two models have thermostatic controls. Accessories include heat shields and carbon monoxide detectors.

Tip-Ups

With a hole drilled and skimmed, and a comfortable shelter in place, you're ready for a tip-up or two. These will be discussed in more detail in a later chapter, but for now, understand that tip-ups are just elaborate "set lines."

The usual tip-up consists of a plastic or wooden frame that supports a submerged spool. The spool is attached to a shaft that extends to

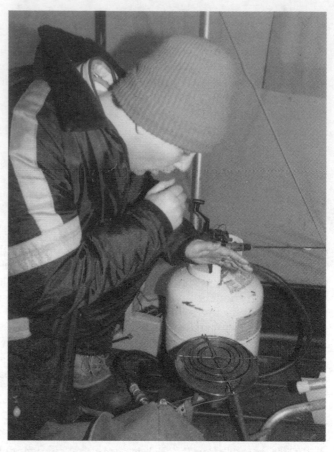

A portable propane heater is a necessity in conquering winter's extremes.

release a spring-loaded flag. When a fish strikes, the spool turns and thus spins the shaft, which trips the flag to signal a strike. The angler then must grasp the line and manually set the hook, and pull the fish to the surface.

Important features

A wide variety of tip-ups are offered today. The main features to look for are:

*A spool that rests underwater to prevent the line from freezing.

*A lubricated tube so the shaft running from the spool to the trip mechanism doesn't freeze.

*A smooth, well-machined mechanism that smoothly trips the flag when a fish pulls line from the spool.

*A spool that turns freely.

*Parts that appear durable and well-made.

*A unit that sets up and folds down easily.

Wood tip-ups

Most common wooden stick tip-ups (usually imported) don't impress me. I do recommend a number of domestic brands.

*If price is a factor, some inexpensive American-made wooden stick tip-ups, produced with good materials and design, are available from companies such as **U.S. Line**, **K & E Tackle** and **Lakco**.

*HT's Fisherman Tip-Up, though quite similar to the above, is made of almost indestructible plastic that won't absorb water and freeze into the ice as easily as wood, and won't splinter apart if it does freeze down. It has a grease-filled tube, smooth trip mechanism, and an extra high flag for improved visibility. A larger, upscale model made of deluxe hardwood is called the Frontier, which features a higher profile and flag for better visibility in deep snow. A

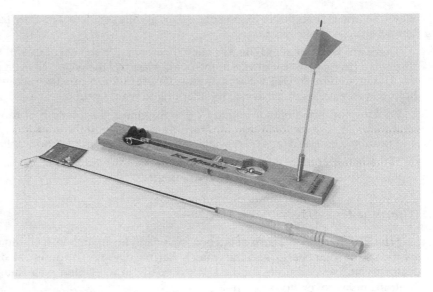

HT's Icemaster tip-up

popular model in the eastern part of the United States is the Heritage.

*As for low-profile tip-ups, the **Moosehead** and **Thompson** units are popular on the East Coast. These feature a wide, stable base so even the largest fish can't slide the unit.

*The **Arctic Fisherman** tip-up was first in modern freeze-proof design. The original model, still produced, features an enclosed tube and a shaft mechanism sealed with lubricant to keep out ice.

*Similar in function is **Fremont**'s Shur-tip or **HT**'s Icemaster. The latter has several unique features, and is guaranteed against freeze-up.

*One of my favorites is **HT**'s Polar tip-up. It's exceptionally smooth and reliable, and grows smoother with age. Fully guaranteed against freeze-up, it's made of almost indestructible ABS plastic. HT's heavier Polar II will easily straddle any 10"-12" hole. Its large heavy-duty wood frame is excellent when fishing larger holes for trophy pike or lake trout.

Wind tip-ups

The wind tip-up uses wind to jig bait. The line passes through a plate that catches the wind, causing the bait to bob up and down. Several good models are on the market.

HT's Windlass tip-up

***HT**'s Windlass has a fully adjustable drag and jigging control that allows you to preset the amount of drag and jigging action for any combination of wind speed and bait size. As many other HT tip-ups, it is made of plastic.

*The **Mr. Tip-Up** appears similar to the Windlass, but is made of hardwood instead of plastic. This tip-up leaves enough free room so you can fight and land a fish with the unit still in position. It has a built-in lighting system, and an optional beeping signal.

*K & E's Wind Waver and **Fishing Specialties**' Wind Jigger are also excellent products.

Wind tip-ups have one major drawback: the spools are above the water, so line is susceptible to freezing. To avoid this problem, I usually fish wind tip-ups when the temperature is above freezing.

There are ways to avoid this situation, however. On the **Mr. Tip-Up**, for instance, the line runs through a freeze resistant device at the point it reaches the water, so even if the hole freezes slightly the line moves freely. **HT**'s Thermal Hole Cover, a foam pad that prevents ice from forming in a hole, comes with a similar device for adapting to wind tip-up use.

Looking for a homemade solution? Simply glue a short length of three-fourths inch PVC tube inside a block of wood or styrofoam. Feed the line through the tube, then place the unit in the water and pour in a couple drops of vegetable oil in the tube. Presto! A non-polluting antifreeze device.

*To further combat ice, try **Blakemore**'s Reel Magic, a silicone-based spray lubricant that repels ice buildup on reels and monofilament.

Thermal tip-ups

*The **Rinehart** Igloo Thermal is a hole cover and tip-up in one. It eliminates snow and ice buildup by the use of solar energy and the water's thermal energy. The design also offers a wealth of unique features, and several units can be stacked neatly in a 5-gallon pail. Rinehart's Solar Tip-up has a built-in hole cover to stop hole freeze-up and block light. Its protected reel shroud prevents line tangles during storage.

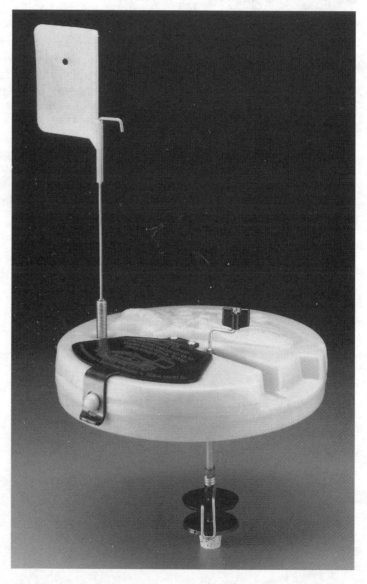

*HT**'s Polar Therm tip-up resembles the Igloo, but is filled with a special material that captures the solar heat while trapping the water's thermal energy, virtually eliminating hole freeze-up. The Polar Therm features a multiple setting trip shaft that is guaranteed against freeze-up.

*Other interesting thermal designs include **Productive Alternative**'s Thermal Tip-up—a box type non-freeze unit, and the **Ice Pro Tip-up**.

Other tip-up designs

Ingenuity seems to know no bounds in tip-up designs. Several interesting products are available.

*Worth Company**'s Pop-Up is a magnetically tripped underwater unit.

*Fishing Specialties** makes the Walleye Special Tip-Ups, a unique smooth-tripping unit designed with walleyes in mind.

*HT**'s Ultralite Balance tip-up is actually a tip-down that dips when a fish bites and releases line without offering any resistance to the fish.

*Moldex**'s Tip-N-Jig combines tip-up and jigging style presentations by anchoring to the ice a base that holds a special jig rod

Rinehart's Igloo tip-up (Rinehart Industries)

combination. When a fish strikes and trips the flag, the rod tilts forward. The fish then can be reeled in and fought on the jig rod.

*The **Lite Strike** is a spring-loaded device that holds an ice rod. When a fish strikes, the rod is released and the spring sets the hook.

*The **Shurkatch** reflects a similar concept as the Lite Strike.

Other designs, such as umbrella and tip-down units, are available also. But whichever model you choose, tip-ups let you cover more water than you could with a standard minnow and float. (Most states and provinces allow each person at least two lines for ice fishing). A group of anglers can easily scatter tip-ups over a large area. Spool each one with line, tie on a leader and hook, tip it with a minnow lowered to the desired depth, and wait for the fish. Simple as that.

Jigging

Tip-ups are especially fun to use when combined with a jigging presentation. You can go for simple or elaborate when choosing a jig stick, pole, or rod—and yes, there are differences (which will be covered in detail in the chapter on jigging).

Until recently, anglers often fashioned ice rods from broken tips of summer rods by gluing them into simple wood handles. Not any more. The explosion of inexpensive ice fishing rods makes purchasing a jigstick with a linewinder or plastic ice reel too easy for most anglers to bother with homemade.

A Jiggle stick

Jiggle sticks

Most panfish anglers use short fiberglass sticks called jiggle sticks. Usually two or three feet in length, most jiggle sticks come with line wound around a linewinder. A slender two-foot dowel with screw eyes for guides and screws or wood pegs for wrapping line will serve the purpose. In fact, such models are available from **Lakco** and **Northern Specialties**.

Many commercially made jiggle sticks are available with smooth metal or plastic linewinders, and in many cases, such as those made by **HT Enterprises**, they're fully rigged and too economical to justify taking the time to make one.

Jig poles

Similar to jiggle sticks, jig poles are available fully rigged with line wrapped on small, specialized ice reels. Many of these ice reels, such as those from **Schooley's**, **Northern Specialties**,

A Jig pole

Lakco, and **HT Enterprises**, feature a depthmarker. When a fish is caught, the depthmarker is plugged into the reel, and line is then reeled up over the top of the peg. To reset the bait at the same depth, simply unwind the line until the peg is exposed.

Jig pole designs vary in length from short for shanty fishing, to long for leverage and control. Materials include fiberglass, solid graphite and hollow graphite.

Anglers fishing shallow water or small panfish often use linewinder style rods and a small bobber. However, those fishing deeper water or large fish prefer jig poles rigged with spring bobbers and plastic ice reels. Spring bobbers signal even the faintest of bites, and allow depth adjustment at any time without resetting a float. **HT Enterprises**, **Lakco**, **Northern Specialties**, **K & E** and **Schooley** produce such models.

For most panfishing, these fiberglass rods and plastic ice reel combos will work just fine. If you wish to make your own combo, rig the reel with four-pound test line and a small ice lure and you'll be ready to fish.

Ice rods/ice rod combos

Many companies now have gone beyond traditional basics, offering more than is really needed, but dedicated ice anglers can't get enough. Today's lightweight, ultra-sensitive fiberglass, graphite composite and graphite ice rods are fun to use and come in a variety of styles. Each model can make ice fishing a far more enjoyable experience; and more successful as well.

Normark, for instance, offers Panfisher I and II, ultralight, light and heavy action ice rod combos with ice reels designed for various fishing purposes. Their popular Thrumming-Rod is an interesting version of a basic jig pole with ice reel. It features a line counter for measuring how much line is out, and enables bait jigging with a switch near the reel or by squeezing the reel handle.

Bad Dog Lures has a full line of premium ice rods with maple handles. The wood offers sensitivity superior to that of traditional foam, corkalon or cork, because it's more dense.

Custom Jigs and Spins offers a line of similar designs.

A large variety is also available from companies such as **Loomis**, **Berkley**, **Fishing Specialties**, **Eagle Claw**, **Jig-A-Whopper**, **Shakespeare**, **South Bend**, **Zebco**, **Silstar**, **Johnson/Mitchell**, and **HT Enterprises** (which offers over 200 different ice rod designs).

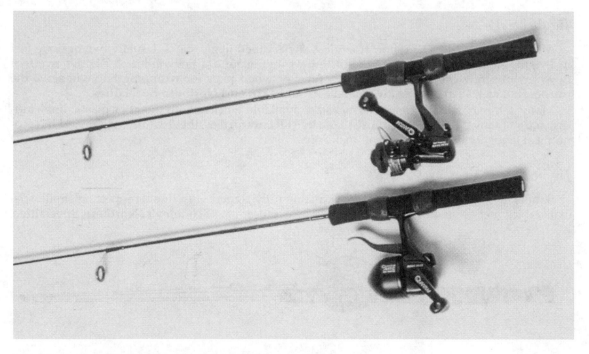

Micro ice rods (Zebco Corporation)

Use electrical tape to attach a reel to a rod. Tape is warmer to the touch and holds better than metal, plastic or graphite seat rings.

Choosing the proper weight rod

Ultralight rods are great fun for panfish. But for fussier fish and lighter presentations, micro spincast or spinning-combinations are better bets. Many modern ice anglers fish panfish with microlight lines, some testing only one-half to three-fourths pound. Due to decreased algae and reduced mixing caused by winds, water below the ice is generally clearer than during the open water season. Microlight lines thus help avoid spooking fish—though these lines do break more easily.

Excellent micro, ultralight, light, and micro spincast and spinning combos and reels are available from **Zebco/Quantum**, **HT Enterprises**, **Silstar**, **South Bend**, **Shakespeare**, **Shimano**, **Daiwa**, and **Fenwick**, as well as others. Choose a model with a smooth, free-flowing drag, smooth-turning ball bearing, brass pinion gears, positive line pickup device, firm bail spring, and free-turning bail roller.

To further minimize the line breakage problem with lighter lines, combine your favorite reel model with the use of a fast action jig rod. These fast-tipped rods absorb the shock of a hookset rather than transferring the hit directly to the light line. A good drag offsets the angler's mistakes, reducing the chance of line breakage.

For heavier applications such as larger crappies, ciscos, bass and walleyes, a variety of light, medium-light, medium and medium-heavy action ice rods are available. Trophy pike and lakers call for stiff, heavy action rods. To properly balance these outfits, use larger reels and heavier lines.

Attaching the reel

On any rod, regardless of action, use black electrical tape to attach the reel. Tape is warmer to the touch and holds better than metal, plastic or graphite seat rings. Reel seats are also good, but too heavy for a smaller, lighter ultralight rod to balance well.

Line

When choosing a line for ice fishing line, as for most any fishing situation, look for thin diameter, low visibility to fish, low memory, and strong knot strength. Also be sure the line matches and balances your chosen equipment.

Tip-ups, for example, demand heavy, braided dacron tip-up or ice line. Micro rods demand micro lines, while stiffer heavy action rods for pike and trout demand heavier mono. More on this later. Just remember that the right line makes a difference.

Bobbers/Floats

During winter fish often bite very lightly. To enhance the detection of subtle winter panfish bites, you need small thumbnail sized floats, or better yet, a spring bobber.

Spring bobbers

A spring bobber is a sensitive wire attached to the rod tip with either a clip, tape, winding thread, or shrink tube. The line runs through the rod tip, out to an eye on the end of the wire, then down to the lure. The slightest tap from an interested fish causes the wire to twitch, enabling an angler to hook even the fussiest fish. The advantage? Line depth can be adjusted effortlessly because no bobber adjustment is necessary. Sensitivity also can be adjusted by simply retracting or sliding out the wire. There'll be no buildup of ice resistance on the float, and fish can be reeled up instead of being pulled hand-over-hand, which is important in deep water.

Conventional bobbers

For shallow fishing, modern sponge floats such as those made by HT Enterprises, K & E or Dickey Tackle are good bets because they can be squeezed to remove ice (that can make a bobber overly buoyant and thus less sensitive). HT even offers one model that is pegged with a chemi-light glow stick for night fishing.

Hint: Try pegging a float on the bottom instead of the top. Bobbers pegged at the top accumulate ice faster, increasing resistance and eventually tipping the bobber on its side.

Balsa floats

Modern balsa floats are my preference. These can be set until they're neutrally buoyant, thus offering no resistance to a fussy fish. Excellent models are available from **HT**, **Lindy-Little Joe/**

Lighted Sponge Floats by HT Enterprises add some light to those evenings when they just won't quit biting.

Thill Tackle, and **Class Tackle**. Ultralight split shot of precisely calibrated weights are affixed to the line below the float at varying intervals, thus suspending the float at just above neutral buoyancy.

Ice Lures

Ice lures, like summer lures, feature a multitude of designs, actions, sizes, weights, styles and colors to match a variety of conditions. Many of these lures will be covered in another chapter, so for now, we'll just skim the basics.

Knowledgeable panfish anglers rarely fish with hooks or lures over a size 6. The most popular panfish sizes are 8, 10, 12, and even 14. These small lures effectively imitate various food items and minnow species that panfish prey upon during winter.

A variety of Teardrop ice lures and ice jigs

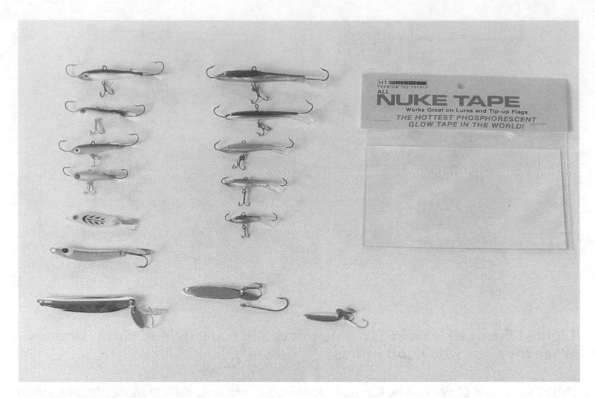

Flash lures, Jigging Minnows

One type, the teardrop, is tipped with a small maggot, minnow or worm for increased attraction. A popular technique is to gently move the lure up and down at various depths, trying to imitate the forage on which panfish feed. The panfish love it.

Lures designed for trophy fish cover a spectrum of styles. These include:

*"Flash lures" and other spoon type baits such as the popular **Swedish Pimple**.

*Swimming minnow lures, which swim in a circle when jigged up and down. A good example is **Normark**'s Jigging Rapala.

*Blade baits, slim metal lures that vibrate with a tight wiggle when lifted. **Reef Runner**'s Cicada is an example.

*Various plastics, leadhead jigs, ice flies, rattle baits and more.

Lures will be covered in detail later.

Lure tipping

Tipping the hook with a touch of live bait adds natural texture, scent and flavor to an ice lure. Good baits for panfish include corn borers, grubs, meal worms, angleworms, wigglers, bloodworms, mousies, freshwater shrimp, goldenrod gall grubs and salmon eggs, lightly tipped on a small hook.

Berkley Power Baits (Berkley)

For larger panfish and gamefish, or rigs set up below a tip-up, try hooking a minnow under and slightly to the rear on the dorsal fin, with the hook barb angled toward the tail. However, don't put the hook through the spinal cord. This kills the bait.

Packaged baits include:

*Uncle Josh** offers small pork rind "flecks" for tipping jigs.

*Berkley** Power Baits are an interesting addition to the ice angler's arsenal. They're specially formulated to stay soft and disperse scent and flavor ingredients in cold water.

*Wisconsin Pharmacal's** Ultimate Baits and **Johnson's** Crappie-Candy are similar to Power Baits in design and purpose.

*HT Enterprises** also offers excellent ice fishing baits.

Buckets

Buckets are an ice fishing tradition. Normally, a five-, or better yet a six- or seven-gallon plastic pail becomes the ice angler's tackle box, holding auger sharpeners, lake maps, tip-ups, jig sticks, poles, rods, reels, line, lures, bait, gaff hooks and lunch. Some anglers have fashioned seats to fit the top, or belts that fit over the outside to hold rods, tip-ups, tackle and other gear. Larger pails are normally taller than the five-gallon size, and thus are more comfortable for sitting.

Commercial versions of these buckets are also available.

*Frabill's** Sit and Fish was one of the first bucket innovations. The combination bucket features an eight-quart foam liner and an organizer tray. The padded Strato Seat transforms a five-gallon pail into a comfortable stool, and its kidney shape allows fish to be dropped into the pail without removing the lid. The Jumbo Sport Tote is a combination six-gallon bucket.

*Shapell's** Limey Louie is a five-gallon bucket with seat, storage and a large lower compartment. The Yellow Belly is a six-gallon model.

*Rinehart's** Quarter Bucket System is perhaps one of the nicer pail adapters I've seen. The insert unit fits any five- or six-gallon plastic pail, and is brimming with features.

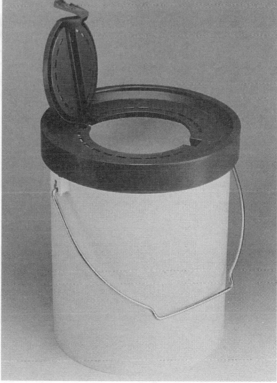

Plano's 722 insulated minnow bucket (Plano)

Rinehart Pail, (above) Rinehart Pail Pal, insert (right) (Rinehart)

*Tool belts for buckets include the **Frabill** Pail Pak and **Rinehart** Pail Saddle. Other such products come under the names of Bucket Buddy and Pail Pal.

In the eastern part of the United States, pack baskets are popular for transporting gear. The idea hasn't caught on in most other parts of the country.

Seats

In addition to pail seats, a variety of folding stools are available for ice fishing. One well-adapted unit, **HT**'s Sit Pack, is lightweight, offers numerous pockets and a detachable rod case. It folds to an extremely compact size.

Minnow buckets and minnow scoops

When fishing with minnows, a thick-walled Styrofoam minnow bucket will keep the water from freezing quickly. **Frabill** and **Plano** make excellent products. Plano's 722, a styrofoam lined, high impact plastic bucket is one of the best I've seen.

Don't forget the minnow net, because dipping fingers into icy water on a winter day is anything but smart. Mesh scoops quickly become caked with ice in cold weather, but a molded plastic minnow scoop works well, as does a wire net because the coiled wire allows ice to be pushed off easily. **HT** makes a floating minnow net with a foam handle that stays above the surface of the water.

To prevent freeze-up, a battery-powered minnow aerator such as the Min-O-Mizer is highly recommended. Other models are available from **HT Enterprises**, **Walker** and others.

Gaffs

Larger gamefish, such as pike and trout, that are intended to be kept should be landed with a gaff. These come in a variety of styles and lengths, ranging from 6 to 40 inches, sporting single or treble hooks on the handle end. A longer handle is best when standing. If you're sitting with a short rod close to the hole, a shorter model will suffice. Some models even float.

Most important, however, is hook design. Larger, single-hook models work well for larger species. Treble-hook models are fine for smaller fish, but often only one or two tines of a gaff enter the fish, leaving an exposed tine to snag the ice. This may enable the fish to escape. Worse yet, the open tine might catch you.

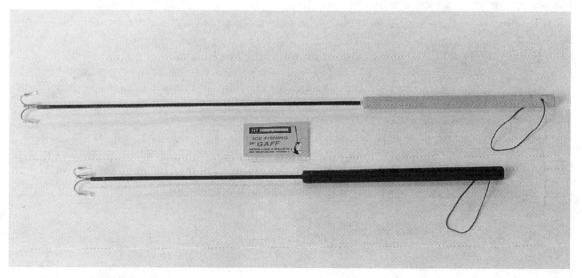

Gaff hooks (HT Enterprises)

Dipsy Depthfinders

The dipsy depthfinder is an old standby of ice anglers. This device is clipped to the hook and lowered to the bottom. This allows you to suspend the lure a specific distance above bottom. By experimenting with different depths you can gather information that will increase your success.

The dipsy depthfinder

Tip-Up Accessories

Line keepers

Line keepers prevent line unraveling from spinning reels or tip-up spools. The plastic "C"-shaped clamps snap over the spool and secure the line. Good products include **Tite-Lok**'s LineKeepers, and **HT**'s LineHolders.

HT's LineHolders

Spare tip-up flags

If you spend much time fishing in windy areas, tip-up flags may tear loose. **HT** is one company that offers spares—in a choice of colors!

Spare tip-up reel spools

Like interchangeable summer spools, spare tip-up spools can be loaded with various line types and tests, different leaders, even different hooks, rigs, and lure sizes. **HT** offers three sizes.

Reflective tapes

In the light of a lantern or flashlight across the ice, glow or prism tape will shine back a message that the flag has been tripped. Simple to apply, such tapes are available from **HT** and **Witchcraft Tape**.

Tip-up lights

In areas where anglers night fish for walleyes, eelpout, or other twilight and night-active species tip-up lights are especially popular.

***HT** offers the Micro Light, as well as the extremely small and light (and reliable) Omni Strike Lite.

*The **Mr. Tip-Up** Headlight features an exceptionally bright light.

*Chemi-lite sticks, also from **HT**, often are taped or rubber banded to the flag or flag wire as makeshift tip-up lights. They last about twelve hours.

Tip-up bells

These are rod bells that clamp to the flag wire of a tip-up, and ring when the flag pops up. If windy, they'll continue to ring in the breeze. This handy accessory is available from **HT**.

Linemarkers

To make re-setting a unit at the correct depth easy, some sort of linemarker is helpful. I've seen people use matchsticks, buttons, knots and a variety of other items for this purpose, but I strongly recommend **HT**'s linemarkers. Unlike homemade methods, they clip on and off easily.

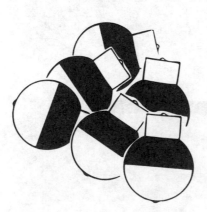

HT's tip-up linemarkers

Other Accessories

Rod accessories

Rod holders and stands keep rods handy and out of the slush, water and ice. The **Triangle Tool** model is a handy device to organize ice rods for transport. **HT**'s Wire Rod Holder is also unique, as the unit securely holds a rod, then tilts the rod tip toward the hole when a fish bites.

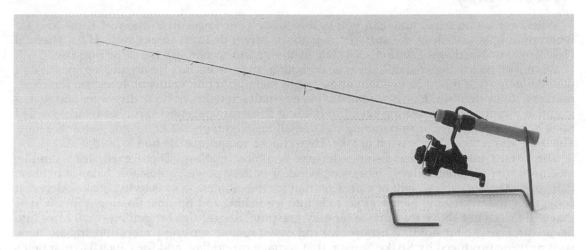

HT's Wire Rod Holder

Rattle wheels

Some anglers enjoy using rattle wheels or rattle reels. These are spools filled with line that mount on a shanty wall or pail. They visibly and audibly indicate when a fish has struck.

HOW TO USE
- Place jig eye through hole of Eyebuster point facing down. Squeeze with the thumb and forefinger, applying even pressure.
- Release pressure, jig eye is clean and ready to use.

TO CUT LINE
- Place line into Eyebuster at slight angle. Snip down with quick, even pressure.
- Hole supplied for lanyard attachment.

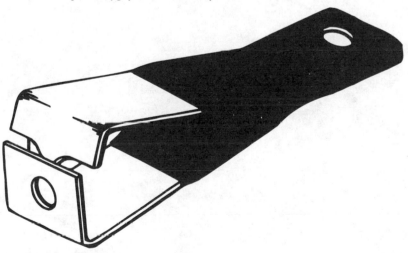

Merten's Eyebuster (Mertens Tackle)

The Eyebuster

A unique device I've used frequently is the **Mertens Tackle** Eyebuster, a simple concept that was long overdue. It's a simple tool for poking paint out of plugged jig eye line ties.

Hook sharpeners

A hook sharpener is a must for ice fishing, but I've found only one that works well on smaller ice hooks: **Marine Line**'s Shur-Sharp. Other hook hones are available that, if used carefully, will sharpen larger ice fishing hooks.

Miscellany

Whenever a flag trips, how can you best insulate your knees from the wet snow and ice when pulling your fish to the surface? A piece of carpet or foam works well. **HT**'s Thermal Hole Cover or **Northeast Product**'s Ice Hole Insulator will accomplish the same purpose.

Of course, no ice angler should ever be without a small tackle box for organizing the myriad of small items that might be needed. These might include: hooks; splitshot; lures; leaders; line-markers; dipsy depthfinders; a needlenose pliers; small screwdriver; hook disgorger and hemo-stat; fish mouth openers; plastic bags (for holding fish); camera; snacks; rubber bands; snelled hook holder (for storing tip-up and jig rigs); small flashlight; pocket knife; and extra reel lube. The list goes on. You decide what to take. Then choose an appropriate box to hold it all.

The list of interesting ice fishing devices is almost endless. There exist, for example: machines that automatically jig bait using wind or battery power; adjustable balance bobbers that counterbalance the weight of a presentation for the ultimate in sensitivity; Strike-Alert that converts standard fishing gear and jig rods into ice fishing rod tip-ups; floating minnow nets that will float a net above the surface for easy grasping; hanger rigs for getting small lures into deep water; packs for holding tip-ups; ice rod cases; remote sensing pagers and transmitters, such as those produced by **Strike Sensor**, that signal a tip-up flag; and the Cinch Tie that helps tie various knots easily. Clearly, ice anglers are some of the world's most ingenious inventors.

Chapter 3

The Modern System
Of Ice Fishing

*T*o someone who has never ice fished or who lives in a warm climate, scrambling about in several layers of clothing amid sub-freezing temperatures to catch a fish through a hole in the ice may not seem like fun. But there's a reason why avid ice anglers enjoy their sport: they catch a lot of fish, including some of the largest trophies in many northern regions.

However, all the ice fishing tackle in the world is useless if not used skillfully. Just as with open-water fishing, you have to know where the fish are and what they are biting. And you have to go with your equipment well organized.

The most important lesson I've learned during many years of ice fishing is that *fish act differently in winter*. They bite lightly. They feed less. And in the cases of several species, they roam a great deal, usually within predictable areas. A key to successful ice fishing, obviously, is to locate such productive areas.

Unfortunately many ice anglers spend too much time fishing where the fish aren't, or fishing when the fish simply won't bite. However, fish must feed, and they do bite throughout the winter—sometimes aggressively. Knowing when these aggressive bites occur will result in good catches.

The System

Most good ice anglers will agree that the more holes they try, the better their chances of catching fish. That's not a new idea. Yet I still see anglers drill one hole and remain there all day, whether they're catching fish or not.

I've seen the opposite, also, like "run and gun" anglers who zip about the lake drilling holes every 10 minutes with no apparent strategy. Neither approach is productive, although the latter offers a better chance for stumbling upon a hotspot.

The secret? *Don't fish harder, fish smarter*. Many factors affect where active winter fish will be found, but by following these basic guidelines, you can systematically search for concentrations of fish and measure their levels of activity, and thus put more fish on the ice.

1. Improve your odds dramatically by drilling holes quickly within the confines of what I call a high percentage area.
2. Learn where fish prefer to be. During winter, fish relate to many of the same areas they do during the open water season, although the lake environment under the ice is somewhat different from that of the open water season.
3. Learn the winter behavior and habits of your target species, so you will have clues about when, where and how to fish them.
4. Understand the characteristics of the winter lake environment.
5. Use modern "tools" such as lake maps and advanced electronics.

These principles will help you understand the fish so you can choose the best locations and presentations. So you will catch fish.

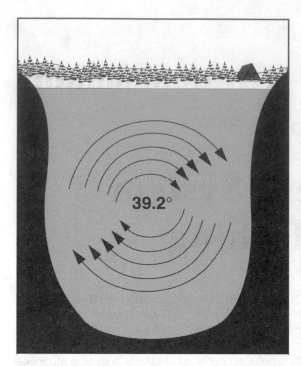

Spring Turnover

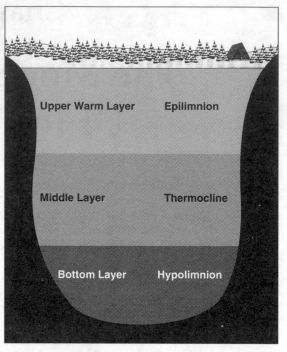

Summer stratification

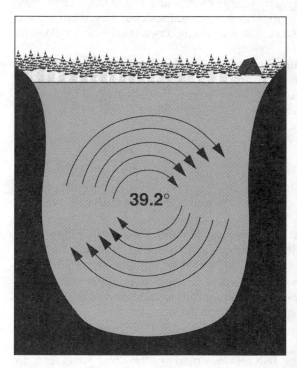

Fall turnover

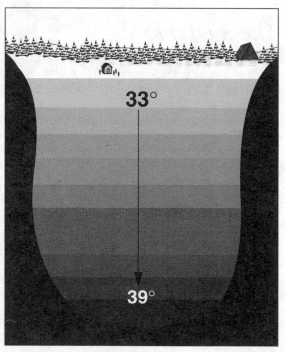

Winter stratification

Beneath the Surface: How Seasons Change the Lake Environment

Aquatic biologists and scientists call it limnology, the study of lakes and inland waters. This science involves three aspects: the physical, chemical and biological features of a lake. One of the most fascinating aspects of limnology is the study of lake stratification, or the layers of water temperatures. Such readings taken in spring, summer, fall and winter reveal some interesting changes.

During early spring, shortly after ice-out, the longer hours of sunlight warm the shallows and surface water. As the season progresses, the sun gradually warms the water further beneath the surface. Shallow lakes warm more quickly than deeper lakes, because more of their water volume is exposed to the sun's warmth. Wind, if present, helps mix the warm water into the depths, speeding up the warming process. Of course, this process begins with melted ice. This water, lying near the surface, is slightly above 32 degrees Fahrenheit. As the water temperature reaches 39.2 degrees, the water reaches its maximum density, or heaviest weight. This water mixes easily. Any wind then acts as a giant mixer that stirs the water, causing the entire lake to reach a temperature of 39.2 degrees. This process is called spring turnover.

As the surface water continues warming, water molecules above 39.2 degrees are lighter than those at 39.2 degrees, so they float on top of the colder water. Wind action no longer can easily mix these light and heavy molecules. As the surface warms and increases this weight difference, summer stratification sets in, forming three distinct layers of water, with the warmest at the surface and the coldest at the bottom.

The upper layer is almost uniformly warm, thanks to the hot sun and warm air. The cold bottom layer is almost uniformly cold, usually around 39 degrees. The middle layer, however, has a broad variety of temperatures, changing about one degree centigrade per meter of descent. Throughout the summer months this middle layer spreads continually deeper.

In the fall this fascinating process reverses. Shorter days, less direct sunlight and colder air temperatures reduce the temperature of the surface water until it becomes colder than the water below. The surface water thus becomes heavier, and begins to sink dissolving the summer stratification layers. This continues until the surface water has cooled to 39.2 degrees, its heaviest state. At this point, the surface layer and middle layers dissolve and descend into the lower layer. With the aid of fall winds the lake again mixes to a uniform temperature of 39.2 degrees.

How Lake Changes Affect Fish

We're ice anglers, not limnologists, so what does all this have to do with ice fishing? Let's look at the lake as the winter ice-up approaches.

When the surface water cools below 39.2 degrees (the heaviest state of water), it becomes lighter and rests on the 39.2 degree water below. When the surface reaches 32 degrees, it begins freezing, at which point the water molecules expand by approximately 10 percent and thus float on the yet-liquid water below. If the air temperatures remain cold enough, three or four inches of safe walking ice may form in a matter of just two or three days. As the ice thickens, this freezing rate slows.

The frozen lake's surface is, of course, 32 degrees. The water beneath is progressively warmer. The warmest water is 39.2 degrees, meaning it is also the heaviest, and therefore lies at the bottom.

Does this mean the fish will go deep, toward the warmest water? Maybe. Using this assumption, many anglers fish within a few inches of bottom almost all the time, and catch fish, though not consistently.

Fish need cover, food, and oxygen. Vegetation, just as an example, provides all those needs by offering secure cover, by harboring food for baitfish, which in turn provide a food source for larger gamefish, and by generating oxygen through photosynthesis.

In some lakes with healthy vegetation, fishing the weeds near bottom is the key to catching winter fish. However, photosynthesis requires sunlight, and there is a depth beyond which suf-

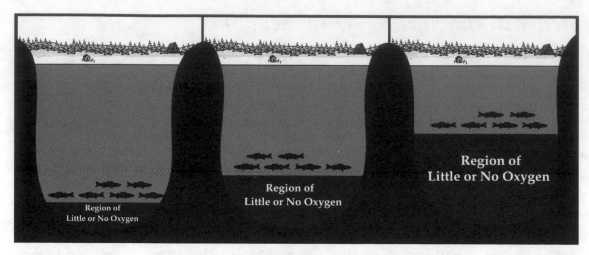

Oxygen shortage, which occurs on some smaller, shallow lakes, forces fish up from the bottom.

ficient sunlight cannot penetrate. (This depth depends on water clarity, which varies with each lake and each season.) Lack of sunlight means little vegetation, which provides little oxygen. Few fish will live there.

During the winter, low oxygen levels in small, shallow ponds and lakes sometimes force fish up from the bottom. These fish tend to be stressed and inactive. If the oxygen level drops to a dangerous level, "winterkill" occurs.

During first ice, when thin ice and snow cover allow sunlight penetration, plant life, deep and shallow water oxygen, and forage are fairly abundant. But during mid-winter, ice thickens, snow cover increases and light penetration decreases, so plant life and oxygen in the shallows and depths may be reduced. Without mixing, deep water oxygen may be depleted.

Water just beneath the ice, however, holds oxygen. Therefore, as the winter wears on, fish leave the oxygen-poor shallows and depths, and begin to concentrate in the mid-depth layer of the main lake basin. This change is most noticeable during late ice, when the fish must seek a compromise of suitable temperature and oxygen conditions.

Despite the concentration of the fish populations, fishing these patterns will not guarantee large catches. Why? These concentrated fish are stressed. Although the oxygen levels may be adequate, this layer doesn't necessarily provide the ideal temperature or cover for that species. They don't feed as aggressively, and you'll often have to present with special techniques to catch stressed fish consistently. These situations are most obvious on small, shallow, weedy lakes.

Just before ice-out, the conditions change again. First, new cracks and openings in the ice allow the relatively warm, heavier-than-ice meltwater to enter the environment below. This oxygenated water draws fish. Second, as snow and ice melt, sunlight penetrates more. This is especially prominent near shallow bays where many species are staging to spawn. The added

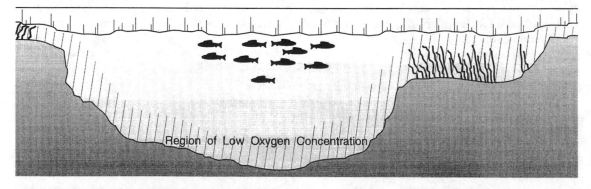

Oxygen deficient zone

sunlight and warming water cause plankton to rebound, drawing baitfish and panfish (eventually larger gamefish) into shallow water again.

These, then, are the keys to choosing the right depth for catching winter fish:

1. Cover.
2. Adequate food.
3. Preferred water temperature.
4. Preferred oxygen levels.

Where to Find Winter Fish: Structure

Rarely is a lake bed bowl-shaped with its deepest spot in the center, contrary to what a beginning angler might imagine. Instead, a lake hides a landscape much like what we view each day, with dips, rises, holes and hills with varying degrees of slope. Such bottom differentiation is called structure, a term often associated with open water fishing, but, until recently, virtually ignored by ice anglers.

For locating winter fish, few factors are more important than structure. These lake bottom irregularities that offer the best combinations of oxygen, water temperature, shelter, cover and food, are just as important in winter as in summer. So begin by locating classic structural features. Primary hotspots include: points; reefs; rock piles; shoals; bars; bays; drop-offs; weedbeds and their edges and turns; mud and gravel flats; stump fields; sunken wood; and deep water around permanent docks.

The areas that draw fish in summer also draw fish in winter, often for the same reasons. But remember, such features must coincide with the zone of warmest water, adequate oxygen and best cover, plus provide food.

As a general rule, the larger the structural feature, the greater its potential for attracting fish, because larger features usually attract and hold a greater percentage of the overall food chain. These features could include:

*Deep edges.

*Openings in weeds, on or near productive flats or structures.

*Areas with submerged timber.

*Deep water itself, if there's a shortage of shallow water structural elements or a great deal of noise (e.g., anglers or snowmobiles) spooking fish from shallow water structure.

*Shallow current areas and inlets, and narrow necked-down areas where water transfers between lakes. Here the current apparently replenishes supplies of oxygen and perhaps food, and thus attracts fish. (Be cautious of the ice conditions in these areas.)

Microstructure/Secondary Cover

"Microstructure," as I call it, is extremely important for successful ice fishing. Microstructure is a combination of two or more favorable structures occurring in one spot, such as a point off a point, or a bar off a sunken island. Add one of these to secondary cover, such as weed growth or broken rock, and you've increased your chance of catching fish dramatically.

Microstructures with biological diversity provide better cover and security; they also attract food. Locations at which two distinct habitats meet or overlap also are prime hotspots. Examples include: an area between two prominent structures, such as a so-called "saddle" between sunken islands and points; a transition from hard to soft bottom, or from one weed type to another; or even better, a combination of the above.

Structural variety is the key. Not every piece of structure holds fish during the winter. Bars, points and humps are good, but those with green weeds or medium-size broken rocks are most likely to hold prey items and thus attract the most gamefish during winter. Concentrate your fishing efforts on these areas.

Here is a general rule of thumb: Shoreline structure typically holds the most fish early and late in the season, and mid-lake structure tends to concentrate fish during mid-winter—practically a mirror image of summer. However, every lake is different. Once you've found structure in a depth range that provides suitable temperature and oxygen, you must find the spots along these high-percentage structural features that will deliver your target species during the times you fish.

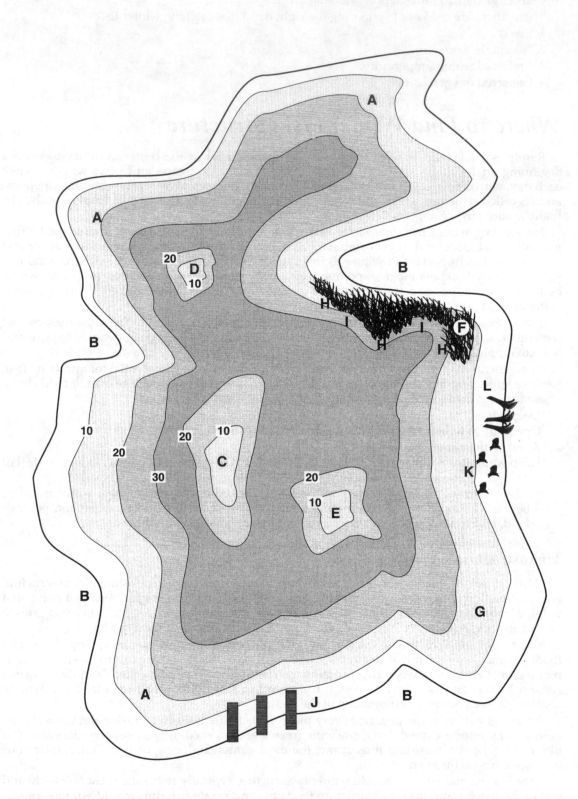

A basic lake map

Deep Water

Some fish may not relate to obvious structure. They simply prefer deep water, or deep water structures that many anglers assume too difficult to pinpoint. However, with a modern power drill, a hydrographic lake map, and electronics, the effort can pay off handsomely.

Large concentrations of active, deep water schooling species such as perch, walleyes, white bass, and cisco often go untouched, yet are catchable. These deep water fish tend to school heavily and feed aggressively in deep water. Protected by depth, they remain active in the same locations despite barometric changes, storms, cold fronts, and even heavy activity on the ice.

During a recent winter, after a dramatic weather change, I located a long shoreline point that dropped gradually before steeply breaking into 35 feet of water. Much of the surrounding water was over 30 feet deep, but this point, bottoming out at 15 feet, extended into the middle of the deep flat. On the deep edge, I discovered secondary cover, some of which was in line with a well-defined weed line at 17 feet.

After catching nothing above 15 feet, I moved to deeper water and began marking fish in 17 to 19 feet. I drilled over twenty holes along that edge, and within an hour had iced five walleyes over five pounds, with another dozen under three pounds.

Brush and a well-defined weed line off a primary deep structural feature was giving the walleyes quality cover and an easy source of forage in an ideal deep water pattern. So despite the poor weather conditions, I came home with a limit. I never saw another angler within 400 yards of my hotspot, and I never saw another walleye caught all day.

The Lake Map Advantage

Two items are especially helpful when seeking productive structures: a hydrographic map and an electronic unit. A hydrographic map shows important lake features, such as structure, depth, bottom content and cover, while the electronic unit will help you pinpoint these features once on the ice. A simple map can spare hours of roaming about a cold lake in search of a good fishing spot.

A lake map is a one-dimensional map of a lake and its surroundings. Most lake maps indicate game and forage species and their relative abundance, lake management efforts, creel census, and other pertinent fisheries data. It also may provide fishing tips from local experts (much of which is based on DNR studies). Most importantly, such a map provides a diagram of the lake bottom.

Two types of lake maps are available. The first, for man-made lakes, are called topographic quad maps. Because they usually are compiled from surveys of the land prior to impoundment, they tend to be quite accurate. Most show precise depths and bottom features, including underwater riverbeds, valleys, hills, fencelines, culverts, bridges, roads and their surrounding ditches, and even submerged buildings. All of these are potential fish-attracting structures.

Maps of natural lakes, or hydrographic maps, are contour maps assembled by sounding a lake with electronics, recording those spot depths, then linking the resulting depth points in a connect-the-dot fashion to outline depth contours. These maps identify various lake features, including rises known as sunken islands [A, p.74], and their structural opposites, deep holes [B]. Similarly, they show bays [C], and their opposites, points. [D] Any of these structures may hold fish.

While all maps provide information, some are more helpful than others. For example, contour spacing is more important than many anglers realize. To be especially helpful, a good lake map should include accurate, marked depth contours in 5- or 10-foot (or smaller) intervals. For a shallow lake with a maximum depth of 20 feet and an average depth of 3, 20-foot depth contours would be useless, because no drop-offs or structures would appear. In this case, a two- or three-contour spread would be appropriate.

Contour lines can disclose a great deal. Those coming close together indicate a steeper slope or drop-off than lines farther apart. Irregular contours mean potential fish-attracting features, including holes, sunken islands, and points. Just be mindful that a contour map of a natural lake seldom shows every detail, simply because bottom features are often missed when maps are created. Therefore, when charting with your own electronics, add details that are missing from the map.

As mentioned in the equipment chapter, quality lake maps not only include accurate, marked structures and depth contours, but also identify shoreline features and access sites,

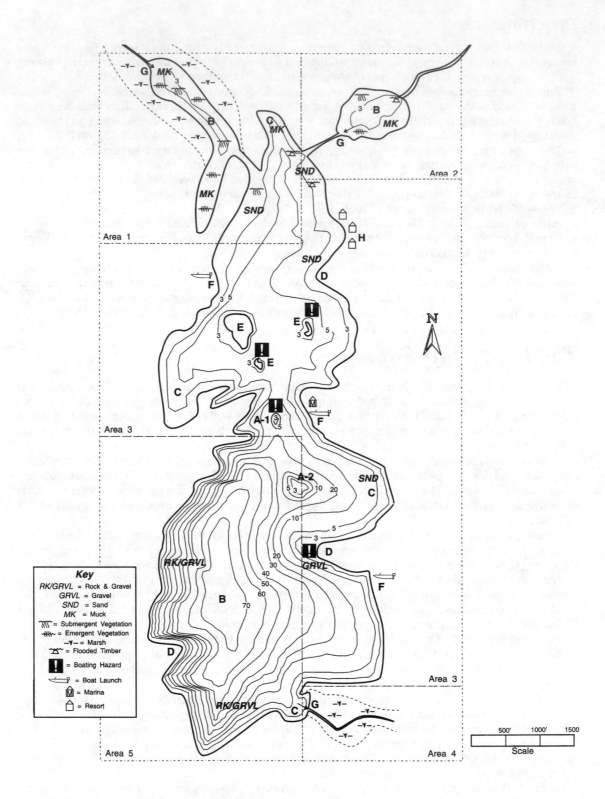

Lake map reference

Reviewing a lake map at the bait shop

inlets and outlets, prominent bottom content, vegetation, flooded timber and brush, boating hazards, boat launches, and marinas and resorts, as well as maximum depth and normal water clarity.

Although map analysis is valuable, expert information probably can be just as helpful. Show your map to a bait shop operator or local angler while purchasing supplies. Often, they'll be willing to help you find productive fishing areas. As they talk, have them mark exactly where any hotspots are. Ask them what techniques and types, sizes, styles and colors of lures and baits have been working well in each marked location—then write this information on the map.

Once you have acquired this valuable information, save it for future reference. A well-organized file of such documents will pay off in the future.

Using a Lake Map for Ice Fishing Success

Because not all anglers will reveal their hotspots, you must learn to read and interpret a lake map for yourself. Let's begin at the north end of our sample hydrographic map on p.74.

In Area 1 a creek mouth flows through a shallow, adjacent, dark-bottom marsh with exposed and submerged vegetation. The shallows where the creek enters the lake show wide contour spacing and vegetation, meaning the stream spreads out in a shallow fashion. At first ice, this should offer cover, thus attracting plankton, baitfish, and a variety of gamefish. During late ice, "warm" water runoff and a newly developing forage base will also draw fish.

In midwinter, however, most fish will abandon this area and migrate to the adjacent, main drop-off. They may hold temporarily along the submerged weed line before moving into the deeper southern basin.

On the east side of the lake, in Area 2, notice an outlet spilling into a pond. Pool B and Bay C could be good first-ice hotspots. In front of this sandy channel are numerous stumps, some flooded timber and a beaver lodge. This is excellent first-ice cover. Unless spring-fed, however, such shallows seldom hold midwinter fish.

Wide contour lines in Area 3 indicate that the water around this area is relatively shallow, and markings reveal relatively hard bottom contents. Such an area would provide sufficient cover and forage during first ice, and could hold fish periodically throughout the winter.

Bay C, Point D and the food shelves surrounding the islands would likely be good at late ice, especially if broken rock or vegetation is available to hold forage and provide cover. The sunken island (A-1) at the head of the channel between the two basins may be an early winter staging area for fish migrating toward the deeper southern basin. In fact, if suitable cover, oxygen and forage are present, this rise could hold fish throughout the winter.

The wide-swinging contours along the southeastern shore in Area 3 reveal a long, rocky, shallow shoreline point. During first ice, this area could attract a variety of species. The saddle between sunken island A-2 and point D also would be a good first ice area, and the deep, southwest side of point D should be good all winter for a number of species.

In Area 4, although the shallow bay adjoining the marshy area on the southeast corner might be worth fishing early in the season for a variety of species, the marshy shallows fed by a feeder creek and surrounded by shallow water in the northwest corner (Area 1) may be a better early season hotspot. That area receives maximum exposure to sunlight and will grow better vegetation, thus drawing forage and creating more cover and oxygen.

Area 5 shows sunken island A-2 in the midlake area, likely a late winter hotspot. A high southwestern bank and close contours also indicate deeper water along the southern and western shores. These will be good midwinter hotspots for a variety of species, because the area offers a lengthy food shelf along the shoreline, yet quick access to deep water. The entire deeper, more structurally diverse southern basin probably would be well-suited to good mid- and late-season fishing, with any prominent weed lines being especially productive. The shoreline point in the southwest corner also should be an excellent midwinter holding place for a number of species, as would the deep, irregular contour points and turns along the west shore.

Go for the Food

A successful ice angler systematically searches for actively feeding concentrations of fish. Finding structure usually is quite simple, but finding the key microstructure at the right depth that features desirable cover isn't always easy.

There is one rather obvious, yet often overlooked, variable that provides the key to success: the presence of forage. Food must always be present in order for fish to actively feed. Concentrate on microstructure holding the primary forage of the species you're seeking, and you'll rarely strike out!

How can you do all of this effectively without wasting your entire fishing day searching for the right location? Electronics!

Introduction to Electronics

Proper use of electronics and lake maps during the open water season can save hours of random cold-weather structure searching. The use of electronics on ice will be discussed in a later chapter, so let's just cover the basics, beginning with Loran.

Loran is actually an electronic compass. To use this technology, locate potential winter hotspots on your lake map, find the actual spots with sonar, then enter those "waypoints" on a Loran unit.

Do this on open water, as close to ice-up as possible. Fish usually don't change location between late fall and first ice, so any fish you find just prior to ice-up should be around when the ice forms.

To store the location in a Loran unit's memory, simply push the appropriate buttons to assign the spot a number or waypoint. (You also may obtain coordinates from a well-marked map and enter them on the unit.) Once the ice has formed, simply recall the desired waypoint. The unit will show in which direction and how far you must go to reach that location.

GPS units use satellites to electronically mark hotspots. (Eagle Electronics)

Watching electronics in the boat, prior to ice-up

If you want to be more high-tech, Global Positioning Systems (GPS) are another efficient method for marking hotspots electronically. The major difference? GPS uses satellites, while Loran uses land-based radio transmission towers.

After reaching the spot with the help of your Loran or GPS, pinpoint the structure's layout using your lake map and a sonar unit. Brush snow and slush from the ice, then squirt down some water. With the bottom of the sonar's transducer completely in the liquid, place your transducer level on the clear surface. You'll get a depth reading. Take several readings in the locale until the structure and primary fish-holding areas become obvious.

Obviously, by using a flasher or LCR (liquid crystal recorder) to read under the ice, you can zero in precisely on cover, microstructure, forage, and hopefully, active fish. Talk about exciting!

Patterning Winter Fish

If you properly employ maps and electronics, you'll realize that fish seldom follow the same location patterns from one body of water to another. A shallow lake, for example, may not present distinct structural elements like a deep lake might. However, it may feature distinct weedbed pockets or stump field edges that become prime structural locations. Even groups of the same species in one lake seldom follow the same location patterns.

This means numerous winter patterns can be operating at the same time. Frequently, however, one stands out, and it's best to search for clues that will reveal the most productive patterns. For example, if a large school of active fish appears on a gradually sloping shoreline point covered with cabbage weeds that stretch from deep to shallow water, you'll probably find fish in similar locations throughout the lake.

To accomplish this consistently, you must record as many important details as possible, including:

*Prevalent weather pattern.

*Predominant bottom content.

*Vegetation.

*Any well-defined "edge" in the form of a weed line, change in bottom content, depth, cover or other variable that may cause the fish to hold there.

*Specific forage.

*Depth of forage, and position of fish in relation to forage.

*Depth of the most active biters.

Every lake is different, so don't expect fish in any two given lakes do be doing the same thing at the same time. Every lake has its own combination of water clarity, bottom content, prominent vegetation type, nutrient concentration, oxygen content and so on. You may find similar lakes, but you'll never find two that are identical.

Lake Type

Before setting out, you need to decide which lake will be best for the fish you intend to catch. In other words, you need to determine lake type. Knowing if your target lake is large, small, deep, shallow, fertile, infertile, weedy, rocky, clear, stained or muddy, will greatly increase your odds for success.

Size

If your goal is a trophy, a large lake generally offers more trophy potential than a small one, because the large lake offers more water in which the fish can hide, feed and grow. Of course, with so much area to cover, hotspots can be more difficult to find.

Depth

Deep lakes usually offer more diversity of structure, more forage and fish species, and better oxygen concentrations. Hence, these lakes have a wider variety of potentially productive patterns than a shallow lake, simply because they offer a greater volume of water in which fish can hide, feed and grow. Deeper, more oxygenated water also may offer better fishing during mid-season. At this time shallower, fertile waters suffer oxygen depletion that stresses fish populations and influences productive patterns.

Fertility

While highly fertile waters are likely to sustain large populations of fish that are competitive for food and highly aggressive, the fish

Electronics provide accurate depths enabling you to pinpoint hotspots.

may be overpopulated or stunted. (This may be good if you're taking a child out for the first time, or just looking for action.)

Infertile, structurally diverse lakes, on the other hand, generally support smaller populations of fish. If the lake is not overfished, its fish can grow to immense trophy proportions. These fish often are difficult to locate and catch because of the sheer number of potentially productive patterns.

Water clarity

Water clarity has a major influence on specific patterns. Is the lake clear, stained or muddy? Some species, such as walleye and crappie, avoid direct sunlight, and feed more actively in dim light or dark colored water. Pike or cisco, however, prefer to feed during brighter conditions, which vary with water clarity, time of day, and ice thickness and snow cover.

On a bright day, a clear lake covered by little ice or snow likely would provide the best walleye and crappie bite at twilight or evening. However, during overcast conditions, or in clear water lakes covered with a thick ice and snow, they likely would feed throughout the midday period.

Winter Periods

Productive structures vary according to the times of winter. Good early and late winter spots consistently include shallow shoreline points, shallow submerged points, edges of flats near deep water, and shallow bays near deep water. Good midwinter spots include sharp shoreline breaks, deep extensions of submerged points, midlake humps, and deep holes close to the early season hotspots. If the oxygen supply is low, many species may vacate structure altogether and suspend over deep water where oxygen is available.

Although that is a general principle, remember that every lake is different. Walleyes in clear Lake A generally inhabit deeper water than those in Lake B, a nearby low-clarity lake. Nonetheless, I expect the walleyes to be relatively shallow at first ice, middepth at midwinter, then back in the shallows toward late ice.

"Shallow," however, is relative. Shallow in dark water Lake B might be five feet, but in clear Lake A, where light penetrates more deeply, shallow might mean 25 feet. In each individual lake, however, the concept that fish move shallow-deep-shallow throughout the season holds true.

In lakes with little structure, fish sometimes relate simply to weedbeds or submerged timber. Rather than fishing directly within such cover, try to find a deep edge or opening among the weeds.

A simple guideline: If a spot produces fish in summer, there's a good chance you'll find fish there in winter, too. Always do your homework before you get on the ice. Consider the lake type and how far the winter has progressed before deciding where and how to fish. Your persistence and effort will pay off.

Keeping Track

A good method for discerning patterns is to mark on your hydrographic map each productive spot as you find it. Then add key information, such as date, time, weather conditions, prevalent bottom content, forage base and cover. Over the months and years, these records will reveal patterns that lead to consistent catches that few other anglers could match.

Don't be afraid to experiment. The more things you try, the more you're apt to stumble upon a pattern.

There is, of course, a variety of influencing factors that affect primary winter location patterns. You can find the best looking locations on the lake, but if the influencing factors aren't in your favor for those locations, you won't be consistent. You'll likely catch fish, because you've recognized and assembled part of the puzzle, but without assembling the entire puzzle, your results won't be as impressive as those of the angler who does.

Take advantage of modern equipment and techniques by focusing your efforts on the best locations: those areas that concentrate numbers of active fish.

Just as every lake is different, so is every day, every hour, and every minute you fish. Conditions change, including barometric pressure, current weather conditions, light intensity, forage movements, structure, cover, and forage. In addition, the time of day your target species interact with other fish species and primary forage bases changes continually. If you don't understand and consider such factors, you won't be consistently successful.

Deciphering Winter Location Patterns

You've located several high-potential structural areas on a hydrographic map and narrowed your search to a select few "microstructures." Now you can narrow your search even further to locate tightly concentrated groups of actively feeding fish. You simply have to read nature's signs and interpret them correctly. You have to know what to look for.

Major clues for the lake you're fishing include its physical characteristics, the species you're seeking and their behavior, their primary forage and predator/prey relationships, the prevailing weather, the phase of the winter season, and the time of day. Adding these signs to all your other data constitutes a true ice fishing pattern.

For example, I've found that different species tend to hold in different areas. Some like to hold near rocks, others near wood or weeds. Often, various species will relate to different depths, bottom contents, or specific forage bases.

Compiling all this information is a lot of work, but it pays off.

Species

By learning to recognize the clues nature provides, you'll locate schools of actively feeding fish. Then, with the use of electronics and modern power drills to pinpoint them, it's not that difficult to fish several of these major structures in a short period of time.

The behavior of bluegills, for example, is partly due to their unique shape. They are commonly found among weeds and brush because their relatively flat, plate-shaped, compact body allows them to make quick moves through such cover to capture minnows and plankton.

Pike, as you might guess, are different. Unable to change direction readily, pike are largely "ambush" predators. They hold along the edges of, or pockets in, the weeds, and attack prey with short, quick bursts of speed.

As you can see, the species you're seeking often determines exactly where they will be positioned on the structure and in the cover. So don't make the mistake of randomly drilling holes. Increase your success level with some research before you go fishing. Read up on the species you're after; get a hydrographic map of the lake you're fishing; pinpoint structures; get some hints from local experts.

A walleye emerging from a hole

Then, using your knowledge and electronics, find the high-percentage areas. Be prepared to drill a lot of holes, and always drill the holes prior to what you consider to be prime time, because noise may put the active fish down.

Forage

Accurately deciphering a pattern demands an understanding of other related variables as well. Take crappies, for example. You not only need to know the crappies' preferred locations, you also need to know their prey's location habits.

The author displays a fine walleye caught by jigging.

A musky caught on a Polar tip up.

During first ice, zooplankton and minnows (common crappie food) usually are present in shallow bays or shallow flats. Therefore, I tend to focus early winter crappie fishing in areas near the crappies' usual springtime spawning locations. These include shallow shoreline points, shallow bays, and the edges of flats adjacent to deep water.

Two or three weeks after ice-up, however, weeds begin dying off. Therefore, oxygen is depleted, and exposed forage is quickly eaten. Surviving forage creatures then move toward fresh cover, such as the remaining weeds along any nearby drop-offs or structures. Baitfish follow, and so do the crappies. Neither plankton nor baitfish seldom move far from the protection of the weed line. As these weeds die off, crappies simply move onto deep water breaks, or suspend over deep water, feeding on wayward plankton and baitfish that have little or no cover. Therefore, weed lines and open water along breaks or structures next to productive first-ice areas are the best for midseason crappie fishing.

As you can see, it actually is more important to understand the crappies' favorite prey than to understand the crappies.

A nice bluegill shown by the author.

Pike such as this often follow prey into deep water.

There may, of course, be other complications. If a target lake features an abundance of forage, fishing still may be difficult, because the fish have plenty to eat. Thus, a lake low on available forage would be a better target, because the fish will react more aggressively toward food supplies.

Predator/Prey Relationships

The predator/prey relationship is basically an extension of the forage principle. Many of the ice fishing patterns relate to the location of the target species' preferred forage. This, obviously, varies with each lake. But many people don't realize that the preferred forage also can vary throughout the season.

For example, if lake trout depend on cisco or whitefish as their main forage, the trout probably will be found deep, because these cisco and whitefish often stay in deep water. Toward last ice, however, ciscos spawn, but their spawning activity occurs in shallow water. The lake trout must either follow, or switch to a different forage. This will force them to change either their behavior or location or both, which will result in different patterns. Anglers unaware of this change will lose track of the fish.

Fish size also affects the predator/prey relationship. Pike, for example, are ambush fish that often hold near edges of cover that adjoins open water. This is especially true of small to medium size pike. When pike are on these distinct weed lines, they're easily fishable. However, large pike, trophy pike especially, may follow roaming prey such as ciscos, known to suspend over open, deep water, far from any well-defined weed edges. By doing this, the larger pike don't have to compete with their smaller counterparts.

To make matters more interesting, various segments of a fish population may be in different patterns in different parts of the same lake at the same time. Shallow water perch, for example, might be feeding on insect larvae in shallow muck bottom areas, while deep water perch are feeding on small minnows in rock bottom humps at 35 feet.

Crappies often hold in areas similar to those preferred by bluegills.

Interspecies Competition

Other fish species also may affect whether or not fish stay with a certain structural feature. If two species are competing for the same combinations of structure, cover and forage, the more numerous, larger and aggressive of the two will likely win. The losing species will move to other structures and forms of cover.

While most species set up territories, the location preferences of fish often overlap. Bluegills often hold in areas similar to those preferred by crappies. Pike often hold in areas similar to those enjoyed by walleyes. The result? Competition!

Fish compete not only for the same locations, but also for the best microstructures and forage holding areas. Therefore, you might find bluegills in the shallowest, thickest cover, and crappies holding on the weed edge or suspending off it. Both may still be feeding on plankton, they've simply adapted to each other's presence.

You might also find larger individuals of both species holding in deeper zones and feeding on baitfish, letting smaller fish fight over small minnows and limited plankton in the shallows.

The same behavior occurs with pike and muskies, walleyes and pike, walleyes and sauger, crappies and largemouth bass, and a host of other fish species that prefer similar forage and locations. Of course, these patterns are quite complex and have been simplified here for illustrative purposes, but they're extremely important. In some extreme cases, one species may force another to move into an entirely unexpected pattern. An angler with the knowledge to find the right lake and the right location will capitalize on such a pattern.

Time of Day

If you fish winter walleyes, you've probably realized they tend to bite best during the low light periods of morning and evening. The same with crappies. I believe this is because tiny-eyed baitfish need time to adjust to the changing light conditions. Large-eyed gamefish such as walleyes and crappies can see better under such conditions and thus exploit the situation. At night, the baitfish have had time to adjust, so their predators lose some of their advantage.

Such "bites," however, are dependent on lake type. In clear water lakes with little ice and snow cover, the above ideal situation applies. In dark water lakes or those with thick ice and snow cover, the reduced light penetration causes walleyes or crappies to feed best during the day when they can see best. Twilight and evening may not allow enough light to allow productive feeding. This tends to slow fishing.

For consistent patterns and catches, fish clear lakes during overcast days, thick ice and heavy snow, and twilight or evening periods. Fish dark water lakes during bright days, low snow, or daylight hours.

Weather

As with open water fishing, these patterns can be influenced by weather. Good open water fishing generally occurs during periods of stable weather. Sudden weather changes, such as the onslaught of warm or cold fronts, produce different patterns.

Similarly, ice fishing after several days of mild, calm, stable weather, for example, is better than fishing the day after a major blizzard tailed by a severe cold front. This holds true for just about any species, on virtually any lake type.

Summary of influencing factors

The difference between a "good" ice angler and an "expert" is that an expert spends more time looking at maps, thinking about the predominant conditions, and drilling holes than actually fishing. But once he is in the right location, the action is fast and furious, and he often leaves the lake with more fish than the person who spends all day fishing in just one or two mediocre spots.

I've often tried dozens of holes in several key locations before encountering a school of active fish, and still come off the ice with a nice limit. Basically, I spend quality time fishing within the highest percentage areas! Understanding how physical, chemical and biological factors combine to affect productive winter patterns puts me ahead of 90 percent of ice anglers. By doing the same, you also will be way ahead of the game.

Presentation Patterns

Going this far will place you among the top 10 percent of the ice fishing crowd, but you can get even farther ahead by pinpointing the most productive presentation patterns.

At the close of a recent open water walleye tournament, I listened as the emcee quizzed winners about the patterns they followed for success. Everyone listened, and no one seemed surprised.

In contrast, at the conclusion of a recent ice fishing tournament, I noticed that "pattern" never was mentioned during the closing exercises, and no one seemed surprised by this, either. For some reason, anglers have accepted patterning for open water fishing, but haven't incorporated the concept into their ice fishing efforts. They're missing a lot of action.

Fish behave differently in winter. At times they may even settle into almost semi-dormant states. However, while winter patterns can be complex, they're based on two basic principles: the locations where fish will be most active, and the most suitable presentations needed to catch them (presentation patterns).

Choosing the right presentation isn't a random process. Because each species of fish is unique and responds differently under various conditions, experts must select their presentations carefully to best suit the targeted species. These choices are based on the angler's instincts and senses, the lake being fished, the prevailing weather, the depth being fished, the water clarity, and even the habits, size and color of the target species' main forage.

In dark water, for example, fish can't see well and instinctively rely on their senses of hearing and smell, and their ability to sense vibration as they seek food. Thus, aggressive jigging presentations with vibrating blade baits, as well as large profile lures and baits with rattles or fins, often attract fish and create consistent catches. The same for bright or phosphorescent colors, because they help the fish find the bait.

In clear water, however, oversized noisy lures and unnatural color schemes may spook fish. In such instances, quieter, realistically sized, naturally moving, naturally colored baits are most likely to catch fish, because clear water fish rely on their sense of sight to feed. Because they have ample time to examine your bait, you must make the fish believe they're looking at something real.

In either case, adding live bait is helpful. This adds natural scent, taste and texture to the lure in any environment, enhancing the appeal to the fish's senses.

For best results, locate schools, then determine their activity levels and primary prey. If applicable, begin fishing larger, more active lures such as wide-swinging and vibrating lures. Active fish will strike almost anything, and larger, fast-moving "action lures" are the quickest way to attract and catch active biters.

While using such lures, observe the fish's response on your electronics. If the fish spook or strike at the lure halfheartedly, switch to less active jigging lures and motions, or baits with more subtle actions, styles, sizes and colors. Keep trying till you know which ones draw the most strikes.

To prepare for such a situation, rig several rods and tip-ups with a variety of lures and rigs. Then, like a golfer who chooses a different club for each situation, you'll be able to change quickly to a presentation that best suits the situation and adjust that presentation to the conditions.

No two plankton, minnow, or insect species look and act exactly the same. Some are short and fat, some are long and skinny. Some just lie at the bottom, some swim slowly up and down, others dart horizontally, and others combine such movements. These motions may vary with lake type, time of day, and light intensity. So experiment with lure weights, sizes, colors, designs, and jigging actions. The extra effort often pays off.

Mobility: The Secret of Consistent Success

During the open water season, many anglers use a knowledgeable, mobile approach to catch fish consistently. Armed with a game plan, they launch their boats. Their detailed hydrographic maps and high-tech electronics are part of a systematic, mobile approach for locating primary structures, breaks, drop-offs and cover-laden areas.

They carefully narrow down the best of these productive areas, searching for structures that feature the combination of physical, chemical and biological factors that best suit the species they are seeking. They come ready to experiment with a variety of rods, reels, lines, lures and baits to find and pattern active fish.

The contrast in the winter fishing habits of the same people always baffles me. When handed an auger and ice rod, these anglers will tramp out from shore and fish among the crowd, thinking that a concentration of anglers means active fish are present, or worse yet, they will just walk out and randomly drill a hole, then proceed to sit in the same place, whether or not they catch anything.

Ice pros go directly to the fish instead of waiting for fish to come to them.

Why haven't these anglers adopted the same philosophy when a layer of ice covers the same water? Doesn't this system apply to winter fishing? It most certainly does.

Ice anglers who use a fully independent, high-tech, mobile fishing approach are enjoying tremendous levels of success. And these ice fishing veterans realize that true mobility means more than just moving. It means moving efficiently and effectively.

By using a well-planned, well-orchestrated fishing system, these ice pros go directly to the fish instead of waiting for fish to come to them.

With electronics, you can quickly determine the depth, and find primary structural features such as sunken islands, points, holes, or rock piles. You also can decipher the bottom content, secondary structure and cover, mark forage, watch where fish are coming through, and even monitor how they react to your presentations. Instead of just drilling a hole over an unknown area, you can begin patterning the fish simply by taking multiple electronics readings.

Say, for example, you've used your hydrographic map and electronics to pinpoint a long shoreline point with a distinct weed line along a bottom content change at 17 feet. Although it looks good, after several readings you still haven't marked any fish.

Whatever you do, don't give up. Instead, systematically search for special features along this structural element that might attract and hold active fish. Start by taking readings along the shallow, flat portion of the point, looking for vegetation, timber, holes, inside weed edges, springs, inlets or other fish-attracting structural features. Then move out along the drop-off in search of turns, points or indentations along the outside weed line, as well as around the deep flat at the base of the break. Then move out over the main lake flat, along the entire length of the structure, always exploring for the presence of available forage near schools of potentially active fish.

Once you locate potentially active fish, monitor them to see if they're moving, and be rigged, ready, and willing to move. You don't want to lose track of them, because they often lead directly to permanent staging and holding areas. Once you've found such locations, determine why the fish are there.

Various features might be attracting fish to these spots, such as: a turn or point on a prominent weed line near or on deep water springs; a change in vegetation or bottom type; a change in oxygen content; light penetration; a particular form of cover; a place holding a preferred forage base; or, more often than not, a combination of the above. Narrow down the pattern by being mobile, continually searching for the productive "spots on the spots."

Depending on the results of your efforts in such a spot, either fish similar structures in other areas of the lake, or repeat your efforts in entirely different areas on different structures as you keep trying to pattern the fish. Believe me, the system often works!

Drilling

Once you've pinpointed hot areas, and narrowed down the structural features that offer the best combination of cover and forage for the species you're seeking, you must search for fish—the most active fish possible.

This requires drilling many holes and fishing several depth ranges within each hole. Of course, these holes always should be drilled over primary structural features that hold potentially active fish. (For best results, try fishing above and below every marked fish, both gently and aggressively, with a variety of lures.)

Drilling over productive features is the best way to find active fish.

Even using this efficient approach, expect to find some quiet holes and "uncooperative" fish. This is why successful ice pros rarely stick with an unproductive hole for more than a half hour. In fact, many such anglers spend no more than 10 or 15 minutes at any one hole, often trying dozens of areas and depths before finding the precise hotspots that are holding and consistently producing active fish.

Still, many "modern" anglers simply are not willing to work this hard. They'll use a mobile approach while searching for fish, but once on the fish, they will drill a hole or two and sit all day trying to make the fish bite. Don't make this mistake.

After going through all the work of getting this far, it doesn't pay to get lazy. Instead, keep drilling holes and trying various baits. If the fish won't cooperate, mentally note the area for future reference in case you want to try it again later. But always keep moving in search of active fish. Remember, if the fish won't cooperate, move!

At the same time, don't expect unrealistic catches. You may locate a school and catch two or three active individuals, or if you're lucky, even a dozen or more from a single hole, then the action may stop. A fish or two might still come to look at your bait, and you might even catch one every half-hour or so if you sit long enough. If that's satisfactory, or better than other anglers' catches, stick it out.

Should you wish to move on, however, experiment thoroughly and move frequently from hole to hole. You'll tend to pick up a fish or two from each hole, thus catching your limit faster.

Versatility

Once you've found active fish, work your presentation with a variation of the mobile technique that I call "versatility." This is done by trying different size, shape and color lures and baits with a variety of retrieves in a variety of depths. It also requires working a number of dif-

Having a variety of rods rigged and ready increases your versatility.

Join the ice fishing revolution!

ferent holes to determine which baits will catch the most fish. Basically, you need to pattern the fish "presentationally" as well as "locationally."

This presentational patterning is best done by being rigged and ready to go. Have several tip-ups rigged with various set-ups, as well as jigging rods rigged with lures of different sizes, styles and colors. This way you'll be able to switch baits quickly and efficiently without having to retie.

I recommend having the following set-ups: a tip-up with a large minnow; a wind tip-up with a small jig and minnow; a rod rigged with a faster moving jigging or vibrating bait that will trigger the predatory instinct of highly active fish; a rod rigged with an "in-between" action lure, such as a flash lure, for instigating strikes from neutrally active fish; a rod with a less-active ultralight style lure for enticing finicky fish; and at least one ice rod rigged to fish live bait on a slip bobber, in case you must tempt strikes using live bait beneath a bobber. Having a variety of rods rigged and ready increases your versatility.

By planning and by being prepared to employ a truly mobile approach, you'll be systematically and effectively patterning active fish both locationally and presentationally. You therefore will very likely enjoy a dramatic rise in your winter fishing success.

Join the Revolution

The present ice fishing revolution is much like the historic open water fishing movements of the mid-1970s, and you can be a part of it! Just use the system.

Before setting foot on the ice:

*Talk with local experts.

*Consider lake management, creel census and fishing tips.

*Review a lake map.

*Analyze prominent structures and fish holding features.

*Keep in mind the primary and preferred forage of the species you're seeking.

*Consider the phase of winter.

*Observe current weather conditions.

*Adjust for time of day.

*Mark primary locations.

*Fish your primary spots thoroughly and efficiently.

*Use a mobile system to find active fish.

*Be versatile in trying various presentations.

With these strategies you'll soon see your catch rates and productivity increase significantly.

Why? Think about it. If walleye fishing in summer, do you anchor in one spot and vertically jig without moving, or do you back troll, cast, and drift across and around it? Most anglers cover plenty water to increase their chance of placing a lure in front of active fish.

Ice fishing is no different. Granted, this system may take time, but you'll soon find such a system easier and considerably more efficient than just sauntering out onto the ice blindly in search of fish. In the long run, the rewards for your efforts will be great.

Chapter 4

Electronics

We finish strapping our ice tackle securely to our sleds, then fire up our four wheelers, and with loaded sleds bouncing down the launch behind us, drive onto the frozen lake.

The piercing midwinter sun glares with intense brightness off the glittering snow-covered surface, and I respond by slipping on my polarized sunglasses to tone down the intensity.

Relieved, I reach back, flip on my GPS and enter the waypoint for a small sunken island located two miles off shore. My partner does the same, and guided by our units, we begin steering across the lake amid gusts of blowing snow swirling along the trail behind us, gradually spreading out in two different directions. I watch my partner's cloud of blowing snow disappear into the distance, then focus on my GPS.

The unit leads me directly to a spot I'd marked just before ice-up, where I stop, reach into my sled for my sonar, and referencing our marked lake maps, begin taking readings through the

Four wheelers are versatile machines for reaching those winter hotspots.

ice. I'm successful. In less than ten minutes, I've got the structure outlined, found the weedline and pinpointed fish.

Quickly I drill a hole, lower my lure, and watch with enthusiasm and fascination as my electronics reveal a marked fish rise, nip, and swallow my bait. After several fish, I radio my partner, who takes notice and immediately joins me, but after hooking several fish, the school disappears from our screens. Reacting quickly, I press a couple beeping buttons, and my "Sidefinder" unit switches from the narrow to the wide cone, revealing the wandering school moving to the side. I motion to my partner. He nods acknowledgment, and without wasting time, we begin drilling holes ten yards away in various directions to pinpoint the fish. Within a few minutes we are back onto the school, but the action doesn't last long. After two fish, the marks on my screen thin out, and the school disappears.

Again, we flip to the wide cone to relocate the school. The attempt succeeds. In fact, we're able to continue repeating this process successfully when the school eventually slows, sinks toward bottom, and becomes inactive. Thirty minutes of intensive searching fails to reveal any more active fish in the area, so we place everything back into the sleds and hop on our four wheelers, prepared to explore new waypoints.

Three hours later, on our sixth waypoint, I remove the hook from an eleven-inch perch that rounds out our limit, and while doing so, stop to consider how unlikely it would have been to catch any of these fish without electronics. After all, I was fishing in thirty-five feet of water, two feet off bottom before marking that initial suspended fish, so I had to make major presentation adjustments to catch it. Furthermore, throughout the entire day, we never marked a single fish within ten feet of bottom, and since the schools we found were continually moving in and out of the areas suspended mostly between ten and fifteen feet below the ice, it's unlikely we could have easily patterned these fish without electronics, even if we had moved often and meticulously worked various depth levels.

Without question, ice fishing strategies have quickly moved toward greater sophistication over the last several years. Thanks to an understanding of the species we were seeking and of the lake being fished, and to the knowledgeable use of hydrographic maps and modern electronics, we were able to quickly establish a key pattern, pinpoint a large school, and accumulate a limit within six hours. Best of all, I've found this systematic approach works for all species, throughout the winter, on virtually any lake type.

Some will laugh or shake their heads at this entire electronics discussion, jokingly calling it a miracle or wonder of modern science, and stick with their traditional approaches because they still work and are cheaper. So be it. Electronics are a new dimension capable of offering much to the ice angler, and those who don't follow will fall behind the times. If you don't want to keep up for now, that's fine, you'll eventually come around. No one drives a Model T Ford as a primary form of transportation anymore, despite that one would still work and may even be cheaper to operate than today's vehicles. There are simply better ways of getting around.

Like automobile technology, ice fishing has changed. Times were when most anglers walked onto the ice, cut a couple holes, plopped down on a pail and fished the same area all day. And they caught fish. Sometimes.

But today's ice fishing is different, and with an increasing number of people participating in the sport, innovative changes have occurred. Knowledge of winter fishing patterns and fish behavior has increased dramatically. This, combined with today's more comfortable, lightweight insulated clothing, reliable snowmobiles and ATVs, advanced ice tackle, and perhaps most importantly, sophisticated electronics, has made ice fishing a high-tech challenge.

Care to join the crowd of modern day ice pros? Read on! By using what I call "the right combination" of knowledge and electronics, you'll learn to catch more fish in a variety of lakes throughout a variety of situations. Here's how.

Fishing Structure...a Reminder

I think by now you realize the importance of fishing structure. Someone once said it's possible to find structure without fish, but not fish without structure, and in most cases, these words of fishing wisdom apply to winter fishing.

Consider the option of locating primary structural elements and features prior to fishing. As we've already established, primary winter spots include points, reefs, bars, shoals, rock piles, drop-offs, and such. Deep drop-offs, turns, openings, and edges in vegetation or weedlines on

Above: The author looking over the wide selection of electronic gear which can be found at most sporting goods retailers.

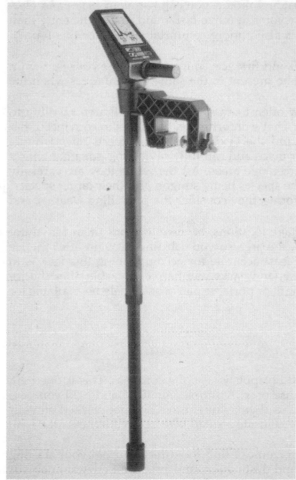

Left: The portable and versatile Fishin' Buddy II can be used pailside as well as boatside.

or near these productive structures and bottom configurations are especially good, as are similar areas with submerged timber or other forms of cover. Even deep water can be a form of cover if there's a shortage of shallow water structure or a lot of activity on the ice spooking fish out of the shallows.

This can be taken even further. Winter fish are often located in specific areas along the most productive looking structural features. Excellent illustrations of exceptionally high-percentage locations are 1) large, shallow bars supporting weed growth on inside turns near an inlet, 2) quick-breaking points containing a spring on a distinct weedline, 3) inside and outside turns on a wood-strewn primary breakline near a large food shelf, or 4) vegetated drop-offs on a creek channel.

Notice that in each of these examples, at least three favorable conditions are present in one general area. Remember, structural diversity is the key. Not just any piece of structure holds winter fish. Structureless, featureless flats may hold fish at times, but bars, points, and humps with distinctive breaks harboring green weeds or medium size broken rods are more likely to hold prey and therefore are more likely to concentrate active gamefish. By searching out such areas, then focusing your fishing efforts on or near them, you'll see an increase in your winter consistency.

This can be a difficult endeavor if you don't have the knowledge and right equipment for pinpointing such areas. However, with some background knowledge of your lake and the species being sought, along with the knowledge of how to use lake maps and electronics, finding such hotspots isn't as difficult as it may first seem.

Finding Hotspots

I've found the best way to find high percentage areas is by preparing for the ice fishing season before the lake freezes, using lake maps and electronics.

Why work so far ahead? Simple! With a boat and motor, you can use your maps and electronics to locate primary areas quickly, because you can move faster and more efficiently than is possible on the ice. The open-water season is also a more comfortable time for this type of research.

Also, fish seldom move far between late fall and first ice, so if you conduct your survey in late fall, any schools you mark will likely still be present in the same general areas when the lake initially freezes.

I mention this again because no matter how often I say it, most folks still aren't willing to work through this process to catch winter fish. That's unfortunate, because I'm convinced that the difference between a "good" ice angler and the "expert" is that experts spend hours researching their target waters, pondering over maps and carefully reviewing potential winter hotspots in order to consistently find high percentage areas. All the while they are carefully considering the lake they're planning to fish, the species being sought, and their target species' primary forage and their habits. Once the ice forms, they consider the prevailing weather and how far the season has progressed.

Once you've noted potentially high-percentage locations, be sure to mark them for future reference on your lake map and note or mark the area so you can find it again after the ice forms. The most economical option, although least accurate for accomplishing this feat, is to line up shoreline landmarks. Just be sure these landmarks will be recognizable after the ice forms. After all, leafy vegetation, a swimming raft, or portable pier won't likely be available for easy reference in January.

Compass

A more accurate method for finding marked hotspots is use of a compass. This is one item many anglers neglect, and get in trouble because of it. A simple, quality hand-held compass such as the popular Ranger Silva Compass, can lead you straight to a hotspot marked on your map or back to your exact location, even help you locate a small lake in a wilderness area with only a few minutes' work.

Once you've marked a hotspot on your map, you can find the direction from your starting point, draw a line between the starting point and destination, and prepare to determine your precise direction and route. Just be sure to factor in your magnetic declination when doing so. This is calculated by subtracting the declination of your location indicated on your map if west of the 0 degrees magnetic declination, adding if you're east of it. Then plot your route.

This is important because a matter of only a couple degrees between true north and magnetic north could send you a long way from your target destination. Much has been written about such calculations in hundreds of hiking, camping and survival books. I believe even the Boy Scout manual explains this effort, so I won't cover it here, but if you're interested in learning or refreshing your memory in regards to this means of navigation, it is an accurate, cost-effective means of locating and relocating winter hotspots. The practice can

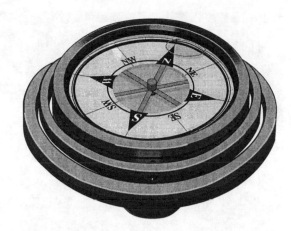

Using a compass is an accurate and helpful method of finding marked hotspots.

also help you find shore in an emergency, such as in a whiteout or the quick onset of darkness.

I realize this may sound funny in today's world of developed shorelines, electronics, and helpful crowds on the ice, but get out on Michigan's Saginaw Bay in the midst of a whiteout, and see if you don't appreciate that you stuck that little, lightweight compass and folded map into your shirt pocket. Ice anglers should always carry a compass and know how to use one in case of an emergency. Besides, a compass is helpful when used in combination with a Loran or GPS unit—today's modern electronavigation devices; electronic compasses if you will.

Introduction to Radionavigation

While compasses will do the job, to be more accurate and accomplish navigation more quickly, most serious, modern anglers mark such hotspots electronically. If you haven't tried this approach but are interested, prepare to enter the fascinating, incredible new dimension of radionavigation on ice.

Today's sophisticated radionavigation electronic equipment is so advanced and can tell you so much, many folks who don't understand their use refuse to believe the units can provide even some of the most basic information. But these electronics provide an incredible amount of accurate information. They won't catch fish for you, and they're not magic machines that provide the answers to everything, yet they do tell a lot. Don't let those who are naive regarding their use tell you differently.

High Tech Electronics: Loran and GPS Come of Age for Ice Fishing

It's no secret among veteran ice anglers that the same "classic" structural elements that hold fish in summer also draw fish in winter. The trick is finding these features when they're hidden beneath a thick layer of snow and ice.

Most often, hotspots are initially pinpointed using sonar during the open water season, then once there, are entered as waypoints on a portable Loran or hand-held GPS receiver, navigational devices that electronically record specific locations, allowing you to return to the same coordinates repeatedly. While not necessary, storing the waypoint number and a reference name indicating prominent structure, cover, and species and forage types present, along with other notes, will make an excellent future resource.

After the ice is safe, this process is simply reversed: you simply rig your Loran or GPS, recall your waypoint, and watch as the receiver provides a "map" indicating the direction and dis-

An angler with a handheld GPS

tance to the requested waypoint. Use your compass and unit's directions to help lead you there, and your journal will provide background information on the hotspot.

If fishing a new lake, you can bypass most of this process by obtaining a map of the lake with clearly marked lines of latitude and longitude. Pinpoint the area or structure you wish to reach, enter in the latitude and longitude coordinates, name the coordinates with a waypoint number and name, and you're ready. That planetary location will now be permanently affixed in the unit's electronic memory for you to recall at will.

With either method, once waypoints are saved you simply enter the "direct" command on your unit, and it will lead you to the indicated hotspot using a small liquid crystal display screen where a pointer indicates the direction and distance to your requested waypoint. Some units also provide your speed of travel, thus providing your estimated time of arrival.

Loran

Loran stands for LOng RAnge Navigation, a radionavigation system that became fully functional in the early 1980s. Loran-C receivers determine your global position using signals from chains of land-based radio transmission towers. A chain's coverage is determined by the power transmitted by each tower, distance between stations and the geometry of their locations. Loran-C receivers must be within the coverage area of a chain to function, because the receiver fixes your position in relation to these programmed station locations.

Thus, ice anglers can use Loran to return to productive spots, with two noted exceptions. In remote areas or locations between the functional distance of Loran chains, these systems are rendered unusable—something Loran users refer to as "fringe" or "dead areas". Also, many ice anglers don't recognize that if you find a potential spot in summer, store its coordinates in the Loran and return during summer, repeatability is good. If you try returning in winter, however, repeatability isn't always as accurate as one would expect.

Some theorize that differences in air density create slightly different readings, thereby reducing efficiency; however, there appears to be no sound explanation for these variations. Regardless, you will get close, and using navigation units will definitely save you time when trying to close in on your hotspot, especially on big water.

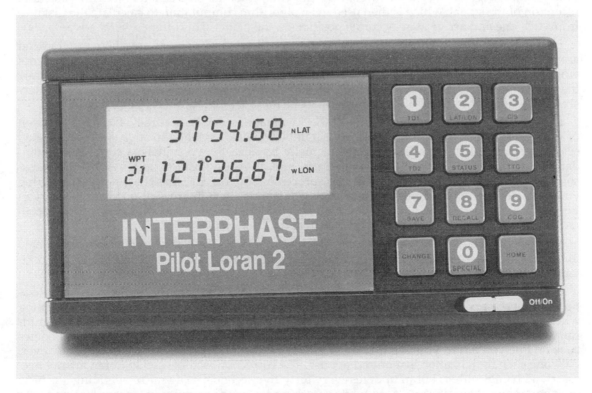

Loran unit (Interphase)

To set up a Loran for winter applications, attach an eight-foot whip antenna to your vehicle, snowmobile, shelter or sled, powering the unit with a 12-volt motorcycle or gel-cel battery, and recall the desired waypoint. Hand held models that operate on AA batteries are also available from Micrologic and Ray Jefferson. These are excellent units for ice fishing applications, and they're much more economical than hand-held GPS units.

Either way, the unit will tell you the steering direction and distance you must go, and the number or arrow on top of the screen will tell you whether or not you're on course. If the number or arrow appears on the left, steer left, if on the right, steer right, at the compass heading indicated. You'll eventually wind up at or near your hotspot, creating a valuable time savings, especially on big water, where you'll find Loran a tremendous asset.

Obviously this is a sure way to get on the right structure quickly and efficiently, and since the Loran's antenna doesn't require the constant power draw that a transducer requires, you'll waste much less battery "juice" searching for structure in cold weather.

However, Loran has its problems. Remember, Loran works off networks of land-based radio transmission towers. This causes two major problems: first, while the entire continental U.S. is covered by Loran chains, Loran chains don't exist globally, meaning their use is limited to areas where chains exist. And if you find a "dead area" between these chains, you won't receive a reading. Secondly, because these signals are transferred through the air, they're subject to interference and are often delayed slightly, so you must wait for an updated signal. With the introduction of GPS, Loran units may become history, but not as quickly as many may think. With millions of dollars invested in Loran chains, transmitters and units, it isn't likely this technology will simply disappear overnight.

Global positioning systems (GPS)

GPS systems use satellites rather than tower chains. When fully operational, these satellite based radionavigation systems will operate from a configuration of 24 satellites; 21 active satellites along with three spares, which will circle the earth in individual orbits arranged to keep a minimum of five satellites accessible from any location in the world.

Essentially, GPS receivers determine location by selecting at least three satellites offering the best positional geometry, then measuring the time interval between the transmission and reception of the signal, which is then used in an algorithm computation to calculate the distance from each one and arrive at an accurate position on the planet. This offers several advantages.

First, because GPS units are satellite based, regardless of where you are, there are no dead areas. You can use GPS all over the world, including remote regions, where Loran may not work due to the absence of Loran tower chains. GPS also has the capacity to be more accurate than Loran, reading out to thousandths of a minute in latitude and longitude (approximately six feet), while Loran reads out to hundredths of a minute (approximately sixty feet).

However, in reality, system errors steal the advantage from GPS accuracy. For the protection of our country, the military deliberately scrambles civilian signals through a process called selective availability. Thus, each satellite actually broadcasts two signals: a commercial Standard Positioning Service (SPS) for civilian use, and a Precise Positioning Service (PPS) exclusively for military access. If this "dithering" process is shut off, GPS has the potential of getting you darn close to your original location, but as it stands, even in areas of good reception, getting within 300 feet of your initial waypoint is considered good. Thus, in reality, overall accuracy is approximately the same for both Loran and GPS systems.

Several companies use a technique called Differential GPS (DGPS) to somewhat compensate for military interference to increase accuracy, but still, this signal is not as accurate as the military's PPS.

GPS also offers advantages in terms of initialization and fine-tuning. With Loran, initializations are necessary whenever you switch from one chain to another, which can be maddening when you're awaiting coordinates because there's a delay time in the signal, sometimes significant. You'll be traveling along and venture off course as the unit updates, and when it comes back on line you'll find yourself making significant direction adjustments. With GPS, however, only one such initialization is required per use. The correction factors used in Loran are not necessary with GPS, either. Loran updates every forty-five seconds, so if you're operating a vehicle or snowmobile at significant speed while searching for your waypoint, it's actually possible to overrun your intended location if you don't slow toward the end of your charted course. This

Accu-nav GPS unit (Eagle)

also accounts for the erratic paths often taken by those navigating with Loran. GPS updates, however, occur every second on multi-channel receivers, making navigation more efficient.

GPS isn't affected by weather, either. While GPS signals must travel further distances than Loran, these signals travel in a straight line with little interference. This is because they pass through space, as compared to lower frequency Loran signals, which pass through the atmosphere, and are interrupted by various geographical features and atmospheric conditions, leaving Loran readings the potential to break down during rough weather (which can brew up fast in winter).

Finally, rigging a GPS unit is easier. For example, GPS is less affected by other electronics, which means fewer interference problems, and it needs no cumbersome antenna. Yet while GPS offers better overall performance and accuracy, reacts faster to course and speed changes, is virtually unaffected by various forms of interference and is easier to set up, GPS costs more than Loran, which still offers proven radionavigation with reasonable accuracy at comparatively low cost. Over time, however, the price of this relatively new technology will come down; the process has started already. The choice is yours.

Radionavigation systems aren't being used by everyone, and many folks without receivers experience days where they find and catch just as many or more fish than those fully rigged with high-tech navigation systems. That's fishing. However, these electronic advances offer the satisfaction of planning strategic ice fishing approaches, adding new dimensions to the sport. So while such systems aren't necessary, they make the process more interesting and much easier.

Radionavigation equipment

Magellan and Lowrance/Eagle, industry leaders in navigational systems, offer several radionavigation systems that will suit the ice angler.

Some liquid crystal sonars (LCD) can have special modules installed, giving Loran or GPS capability along with standard LCD qualities. Split screen features allow you to see the sonar and plotter readouts simultaneously, creating excellent, compact units for ice fishing applications. "Event markers" on some units can even store the location of hotspots on the plotter electronically, which is more incognito than leaving an obvious stick or marking object on the ice for other anglers to find.

Several companies also offer pocket-sized, hand held models which are convenient for the truly mobile ice angler. More units each offering their own special features are available from companies such as Eagle, which manufactures a user-friendly model that features one handed operation, and the capability to enter numerous waypoints in a compact, lightweight design. Micrologic offers a unit that floats, and Garmin International and Raytheon Marine, among others, have similar products. With the growing popularity of these units, it is likely that many more will be developed. Watch carefully. This is technology that is revolutionizing ice fishing and will continue to do so. I can foresee maps and references appearing on the market that offer coordinates for primary hotspots, and information about each one. Without question, Loran and GPS will change ice fishing forever.

Using Sonar on the Ice

Once you've found the right area using your Loran or GPS, you'll want to pinpoint the structure's layout, high-percentage combinations of secondary cover, forage, and fish using sonar; namely, a flasher or LCR.

In fact, ask any ice pro to name their single most valuable piece of equipment, and most will say sonar. If anglers know how to interpret the appropriate signals, electronics enable them to decipher depth, bottom type, cover, forage, and fish. They can even estimate the fish's approximate size, and monitor the depth they're holding, their activity levels and their responses to specific presentations!

But do most ice anglers utilize these special tools? And of those that do, do they really know how to use these units to their maximum potential? I'd have to answer no to both questions. But before getting into the details, let's review the basics of how to use sonar on ice.

To start with, the unit must be transported. For ease in handling your electronics, I recommend converting a plastic tackle box into a storage compartment for your electronics. A friend of mine attached a swivel mount to the top of a tackle box, added a rod to the side to support

Example of a sonar-flasher (Zercom)

the transducer, and drilled holes through the back of the box to accommodate the transducer and power cords. There was plenty of spare room for the battery, unit, and a squirt bottle in the box, not only providing quick set up and storage, but a neat and secure way to transport the unit.

If you don't have time to build a box, don't worry, commercially available boxes such as Vexilar's P-160 or Winter Fishing Systems "IceBox" are perfectly suited for transporting electronics on the ice. Many portables are available in compact, hard plastic cases with nylon handles that convert into convenient shoulder straps—ideal for "pack in" style trips. Just keep in mind that portables operate on six volt lantern batteries, which do not hold up well in cold weather.

Some portable units are removable from these cases and can be rigged to a P-160 or Icebox and attached to a motorcycle or gel-cel battery for increased power and use in cold weather; in others, the divider separating the six volt lantern batteries can be removed to accommodate a twelve volt gel-cel battery. If not, go with the non-portable model.

Once set up, before going out on the ice, preset your unit to avoid problems. For example, for best reading clarity, your transducer, the sonar's signal sensing device, must be perpendicular to bottom (straight up and down). This provides the most accurate readout.

The transducer is basically a sending and receiving unit that sends electrical pulses through a megaphone-shaped cone to bottom. The transducer then times how long the signal takes to bounce off bottom and return, then translates these signals into depth readings. Anything inside this cone interrupting these signals is also marked.

If this cone moves so much as one degree from the level, depending on the depth you're fishing, your cone may shift a significant distance from center. This means the sonar pulses must travel farther to get a reading and the return pulses won't hit the unit square, generating inaccurate readings and making accurate interpretation of what's below more difficult, if not impossible.

To avoid such problems, set your unit on a counter or other level surface before fishing, adjust the transducer to perpendicular using a level, and when set perfectly perpendicular to the floor, affix a leveling bubble on top of the transducer with glue. Good units designed for ice fishing include such a bubble. If yours doesn't, check with your sporting goods dealer since he'll know where to get them. Just be sure you take the time to set your unit with a bubble since this will make re-adjustment on the ice much easier and more accurate.

Also be sure your unit is properly wired and ready to fish. Hook a fully charged battery up and double check that the unit is operative and ready to go. Believe me, you won't want to make adjustments or repairs in the field.

To use your unit on the ice, clear away surface snow or slush from the solid ice below, and squirt down some water. (I prefer heated saltwater because it doesn't freeze as easily.) Making sure the bottom of your transducer is completely immersed in the liquid, place your transducer level on the clean surface to establish a perpendicular "cone." Adjust the sensitivity until you see bottom clearly. This ensures a good readout when shooting your readings directly through the ice pack.

One note here: according to various sources, some "studies" have indicated that water and antifreeze mixtures can be used in place of saltwater with no harmful effects to the environment, but I find that hard to believe. I don't dump antifreeze or windshield washer fluid in my drinking water, nor my goldfish bowl for that matter, and I'm of the opinion it's not a good practice for the waters I fish and treasure, either.

Regardless, after spraying down a squirt of saltwater on solid ice and immersing the transducer in the liquid, you'll get a depth reading. Mark the depth next to each hole, and continue

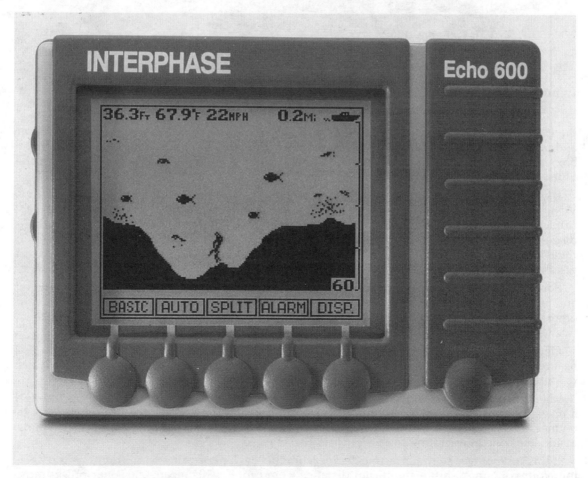

LCR (Interphase)

Tackle box electronics, open (above), closed (below)

Sonar: Valuable ice fishing equipment (Humminbird)

this process by taking multiple readings. If you don't, you'll be surprised how easy it is to get turned around while you're looking down at the unit and walking around, especially if it's dark or blowing snow prevents you from seeing the shoreline clearly.

However, by marking the depth and moving strategically, all while referencing your lake map, the bottom configuration, including structure, will be revealed. Once the structure is outlined, begin looking for unique features or irregular contours in association with each productive structural element. A finger on the edge of a submerged hump, a hook on a point, or a weed-edge near a drop-off would all be primary fish-holding areas, and can all be revealed by using electronics readings shot directly through the ice.

Of course, understand that several differences exist between using electronics during winter versus summer. For example, when shooting through the ice, your unit will disregard the presence of ice and tell you only how deep the water is. In other words, if the ice is two feet thick over ten feet of water and you shoot through it, the depth will read ten feet. But if you drill a hole in the same spot and re-check the depth by placing the transducer in the water-filled hole, the screen will read twelve feet.

The difference? Water now occupies the space where two feet of ice once was, and the depth-finder reads the water where it didn't read the ice previously. This may not seem important, but I've seen many anglers who mark the depth on certain structures in summer become needlessly confused or frustrated by such discrepancies after the ice forms. So remember to account for them by remembering that when shooting through the ice, the overall depth equals the depth reading plus the thickness of the ice. This is especially important when fishing shallow water, where such discrepancies are a more significant factor.

Understanding this, continue to take readings, referencing your map while doing so and you'll eventually locate various structures and their orientation by compiling depth readings. Once you've uncovered a good piece of structure, look for those unique features or irregular contours (microstructure) and secondary cover, weeds, rocks, wood, or bottom content changes, and fish them. If they aren't holding fish at the time, mark them as waypoints on your Loran or GPS so you can come back to them. Such areas will likely hold fish at some point during the winter.

Once you've found a potential area, drill lots of holes over these primary structures, and try them all, being sure to drill prior to what you consider to be "prime time" so the noise won't put active fish down.

Once you've settled on a suitable location and begin fishing, place your transducer in the hole you're fishing, and keeping the transducer level, set your unit so bottom, secondary cover and your lure are readily apparent.

Keep in mind there are distinct advantages to using electronics on the ice while you're fishing. For instance, you're always in a stationary position, so any movement on your screen is either forage, fish, your lure, or your bait. If you don't see any movement other than your lure, there are no fish within your transducer cone.

Such things are important to understand if you want to get the most out of electronics on the ice, but in order to make this all happen, you must understand how to properly set, operate, and interpret your unit.

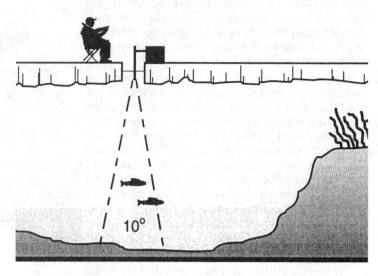

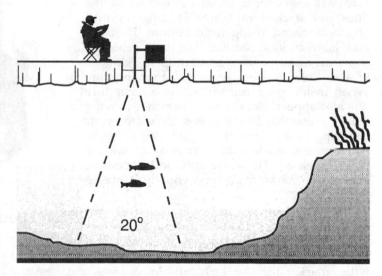

Cone angles

Setting/interpreting your unit

Unfortunately, I think many anglers have the impression they'll set their units on the ice, mark fish, lower their lure and quickly catch them, but this simply isn't true. In fact, you can mark fish and not catch them, as many frustrated ice anglers will attest. Furthermore, you can catch fish in places you haven't marked them, simply because the fish hold outside of your transducer cone until they suddenly appear and strike. However, your unit will definitely supply vital information, provided the transducer is level, your unit is set properly and you know how to interpret it.

There are many settings and features on today's units, which we'll get to later. For now, understand you'll need to set the power, sometimes called the "gain" or "sensitivity." This adjusts the strength of your signal and allows you to reduce interference. If the power is set too low, the bottom signal will be weak and fish won't show up. If set too high, multiple echoes and interference will result, making the screen hard to read. So be sure to monitor your unit and make the appropriate adjustments accordingly, and you should receive clear readings.

However, if interference persists even after this process is complete, you'll need to fine-tune your readings by adjusting the suppression. The higher you set the suppression, the less interference you'll get, but the harder it will become to mark fish. For best results, adjust the power high and keep the suppression set low, or if possible, turned off completely. Once these controls are set properly, you'll be able to decipher depth, structure, bottom content, vegetation, forage, your lure, and fish.

Bottom will simply appear as the depth at each reading, and by combining various depth readings, you'll be able to determine the placement and orientation of various structures. Furthermore, hard bottoms will register thick and dark and feature a "double echo" on a flasher, while soft, thin, dim readings are indicative of a soft bottom. The bottom figure at right, for example, shows a depth of ten feet, and a second echo at twenty, indicating a hard bottom condition. On an LCR, the bar graph for sensitivity will also read high in soft bottom areas, and low over hard bottoms.

If present, weeds and other secondary structures will also appear, usually as batches of fine lines and stacked markings forming columns attached to and rising from bottom. Plankton and baitfish look similar, but will generally show up as suspended scatterings or "clouds" of fine lines or dots separated from bottom. When inside your transducer cone, your lure will also appear, usually as a distinctive moving "blip" or line that moves as you lift or drop your rod tip. Notice on the figure how marks between the ten-foot bottom and the surface have appeared. These are fish, and hopefully, one of the marks represents your lure among them.

Accurate depth control will often make the difference between no fish and a limit, so before you begin fishing, measure how many inches of

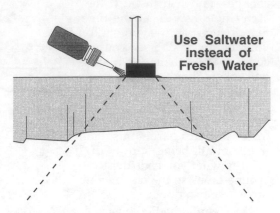

Use Saltwater instead of Fresh Water

Shooting readings through the ice

Electronics showing fish over a hard bottom on the flasher

line your reel picks up per revolution of the handle. Do this by marking the line at your rod tip with a marker, turning the handle 360 degrees, and measuring the distance between your mark and rod tip. Now you'll know precisely what distance every turn of your reel handle will move your lure, and this, combined with what your electronics show you, let you know precisely where your jig is in relation to bottom, or perhaps more importantly, where your lure is positioned in relation to fish.

Obviously, your lure or bait is most effective when placed near fish, and when you work a bait in conjunction with sonar, you can't help but increase your odds of being in the right place at the right time. It's simple. If you can see fish on your screen, you can lower your lure right to them, and seeing your lure in relation to bottom and where fish are coming through is vital to success.

For example, how would an angler fishing in thirty feet of water and not using electronics be able to consistently catch fish suspended fifteen feet down? I've had several instances where someone was fishing right next to me. I was catching fish right and left and they couldn't get a bite. The reason? Depth. They were fishing bottom, and the school was suspended. Without electronics, they were at a total disadvantage.

There's no excuse for not seeing fish, as they create obvious marks. If you're using an LCR that features a "Fish ID" style readout, fish will register as a conspicuous fish shape. Some units will even provide the precise depth the marked fish are holding. This feature can also be turned off if you prefer not to use it.

Otherwise, single, faint lines suspended off bottom and away from surface clutter are representative of suspended fish on the outside edge of your transducer cone, while thick, bright lines are fish suspended directly inside the cone. Fish on or near bottom will appear as thin lines barely separated from the bottom signal.

You can even estimate the size of the fish by the height of the signal. Remember, sonar measures the distance of an object from the transducer, thus large objects closer to the transducer will register smaller in length than objects of the same size located farther away. In addition, you're sitting stationary, which enhances this "lengthening" effect—another situation that demonstrates how thickness, not length, indicates size.

It may seem as though I'm dwelling on this point a long time, but that's simply because I've seen too many anglers mistakenly believe that long marks are large fish, when actually they're just marking fish holding high or stationary directly within the cone.

Also, by looking at the depth, bottom content, structure, secondary cover, and position of various numbers and sizes of fish, you can begin to pattern them. To a degree, you can also surmise the species being marked by noting their position. For example, perch and walleyes often hold near bottom, while crappies and trout tend to suspend. Consider all this while fishing.

Using an LCG with "Fish ID," fish will register as a conspicuous fish shape. Their depth will also be revealed. (Humminbird)

Obviously, electronics can do more than just read depth or help you find structure and fish. In fact, you'll actually be able to start piecing patterns together without drilling a single hole!

Cone angles

This brings us to cone angles, which determine the amount of water being covered by your electronics. Remember the megaphone analogy? Such cones come in various sizes, and you must understand what the advantages of various cone angles are in order to select the unit that's right for you, and to correctly interpret what it's telling you. I prefer units featuring narrow cone angles because their power is more concentrated within a smaller area, making it easier to determine the precise depth the fish are holding.

Although wider cone angles cover more area and allow you to cover more water and more fish, those located on the outside edge of the wider cone are so much further from the cone center that they may appear slightly deeper than they are really holding; hence, you won't know precisely where they're positioned.

This is why today's "three-way" or "Sidefinder" style electronics have so many beneficial ice fishing applications. These units actually feature three narrow-cone transducers. One points left, one right, and one straight down.

On most units, you can employ any one of the three, or all three in a composite picture to create a wider cone angle, thereby allowing the benefits of either a narrow or wide cone angle. Some of these units even provide a depth cursor that indicates the exact depth of suspended targets, which takes some of the confusion out of reading marks when operating wider cone angles.

Still, for most applications, it's best to utilize the center narrow cone to concentrate power, then take advantage of the wider cone under special circumstances, such as when fishing wandering schools. For example, if a school starts moving away from your current position, you can easily check the direction it's moving by simply enlarging your cone angle. Just relocate the

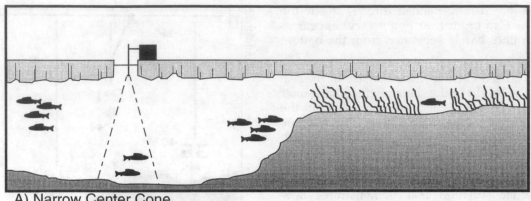

A) Narrow Center Cone

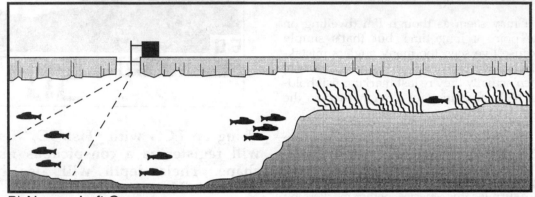

B) Narrow Left Cone

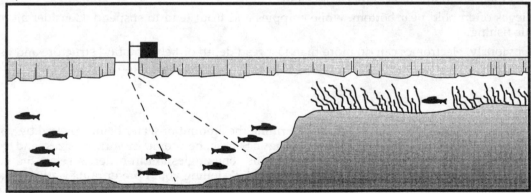

C) Narrow Right Cone

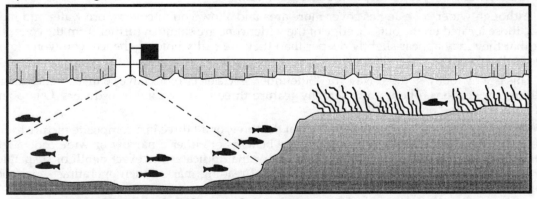

D) Combined Right, Left & Center Cone Angle
   create Wide Cone Angle

3-way transducer

school using the wide cone, move on top of them, then switch back to the narrow cone as you jig, repeating the process as necessary. You'll find the benefits of this strategy tremendous.

While not as practical, I should also mention that similar results can be attained using standard units simply by mounting your narrow cone transducer on a long, custom built, L-shaped transducer bar. When the school begins moving, simply loosen the bar, place it in the water and gradually turn it until you mark the roaming school. When the school appears, proceed to drill holes in that general direction to relocate the fish. When back on top of the fish, return the bar to the fixed vertical position.

Either way, remember to reset your sensitivity every time you move or switch cone angles, even periodically when fishing the same hole. You can only see things in the cone which appear at the precise gain and sensitivity setting you're currently at. Start by dropping your lure down halfway to bottom and turn your sensitivity all the way down. You won't see much.

Turn it up slightly, and bottom will show up. It's not that the bottom didn't exist previously, it just wouldn't show up at the setting for which you had your unit set. Now turn it up again, and your lure will appear. Again, it was there all the time, it just didn't read. Turn up the sensitivity more, and fish may appear. Again, you've turned up the amplification enough to show something that's been there the whole time, but didn't show up at your previous setting.

You must control such settings, and continually adjust them to best fit your situation. Obviously, one limitation of your electronics is knowing what they're telling you, and how to set them so they tell you what you want to know.

This is especially important when other anglers are fishing around you. Since their units are set at the same or near same frequency, your unit is shooting electronic pulses and waiting for the return, and in between is also receiving misdirected pulses from other units, causing interference. This is much like being in a room with several radios. Operate just one, and you can hear it distinctly. Turn a second on, locked onto a different station, and it's harder to focus. The more you add, the more difficult it becomes to sort. It is the same for an electronics unit.

To overcome the other units, you'll need to make yours the "loudest". This requires primarily three things: 1) the most powerful transducer; 2) the most powerful battery; and 3) a carefully adjusted gain and sensitivity. Together, these things add up to the greatest "volume."

If this all sounds confusing, start from this point. A wide cone angle is often suitable for use in less than forty feet of water because you can see more fish. Your resolution may not always be as great, but it's good for fish finding. A narrow cone angle simply focuses the same amount of energy into a smaller area, so you can see better in deep water or can read smaller objects. Once you've decided upon a cone angle, learn to use your unit and properly adjust it given a variety of conditions.

Read the manual. Practice. Use the unit and gain experience. The longer you use it, the more you'll become familiar and comfortable with it and learn to read what it's telling you. There's no substitute for knowledge and experience.

Monitoring fish activity levels beneath the ice

Watching a fish strike is always an interesting experience. It's fun to watch a fussy bluegill suck in a tiny jig, a trout dart out from under an undercut bank to hit a night crawler, a bass kiss a topwater plug, or a pike smash a spinner bait. Whose knees wouldn't shake as they witness a muskie crush their bucktail on a "figure eight" at boatside?

Without a doubt, most anglers enjoy watching fish strike, not only because it's exciting to see and adds to the fishing experience, but also because it's possible to judge the approximate activity level of the fish, based on how hard they strike and how often they hit.

Yet the above examples are all open water scenarios, and are only evident on the surface or in shallow or clear water where the fish are obvious to the naked eye. The question is, how can ice anglers enjoy the same type of experience and determine how the fish are striking if they aren't visible under the ice?

Electronics!

Obviously it's important to understand the use of electronics for finding high percentage locations and schools of fish. Knowing how you're positioned in relation to a school is of key importance. Yet to fully appreciate the applications of electronics for ice fishing, you must also understand that electronics are equally valuable in determining fish activity levels and monitoring presentation responses. When properly set, the units can accomplish this feat easily, you just need to know what to look for.

For instance, it's best to find clusters of fish as opposed to scattered ones because concentrated schools are more likely to be feeding, active fish. Schools of "squiggly" or "fluttering" marks near suspended forage are especially good indicators, as they designate groups of actively feeding fish moving in and out of your transducer cone, appearing and disappearing from your screen as they do so. If you run across this situation, drill a hole and quickly drop your lure to the school, then watch your electronics with an eagle eye to confirm they're active.

This can be determined by monitoring how the fish are positioned and how they react to your lure. Are they reacting slowly, spooking easily and short-striking, or aggressively chasing down your lure and completely swallowing the offering? Do they want the bait moved fast or slow?

Once such questions have been answered, you can adjust your specific lures and techniques according to the mood and activity level of the fish. For instance, if the fish spook easily, lighten up and work smaller and

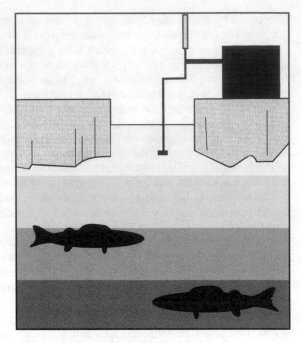

L-shaped transducer rod

slower baits more gingerly. If they're aggressive, work bigger, more aggressive flash or jigging lures, and work them hard.

Also experiment with lure style, action, and color. Do they show any preferences? If so, make adjustments in your presentation accordingly. Your extra efforts should pay off.

If the fish are producing firm, long marks, hugging bottom and won't react to various presentations, they're probably sedentary, non-active fish. Always try fishing them, but if they don't respond within ten minutes, don't get hung up trying to trigger these inactive fish. Instead, move on in search of an active school and consider coming back to try them again later.

The only way to consistently and efficiently find productive structures, mark active fish, accurately track their movements, and systematically monitor their activity levels (in other words, pattern the fish) is with electronics. Yet the use of electronics is dependent on a working knowledge of how to read hydrographic maps and interpret what your unit is telling you.

So next time you ice fish, don't make the mistake of randomly drilling holes. Instead, do your homework ahead of time. Read up on the species you're seeking and the lake you plan to fish, and carefully review a hydrographic map before you begin searching for primary structures, preferably during the fall when you can "run the lake" and mark high percentage locations and plot waypoints on a Loran or GPS unit most effectively.

Then choose a flasher or LCR that best suits your ice fishing needs, and more importantly, learn how to use its features to their fullest capacity.

Tips for keeping sonar warm and operative on ice

While this may all sound great, electronics can pose some problems in cold weather.

When it comes to sonar on ice, you've got two choices: flashers or liquid crystal units, which we'll call "LCGs" from this point on. Both offer advantages and disadvantages, but for now understand that both styles accomplish the same thing, and regardless of which unit you choose they must be kept warm in order to provide the best possible performance.

This is a major problem confronting today's modern ice angler, especially when using liquid crystal units, which tend to become "sluggish" in sub-freezing temperatures as the liquid filled crystals cool. First, be sure to always keep the unit warm until you're ready to use it. It's also a good idea not to switch sonar units on and off during use in cold weather since the heating and cooling of the internal electronics may form condensation and cause a short. Rather, turn the unit on when you begin fishing, then leave it on until you're ready to leave.

For best results, keep your unit and battery in a box like Winter Fishing System's Ice Box, and keep it fully charged until you reach the intended fishing destination. Then turn your unit and, if available, the light function on. Heat generated by the functioning unit and light will help keep the unit warm and operative during even the most extreme weather. A layer of insulation wrapped around the back and sides of the unit, which is easy to accomplish when set in the ice box, seems to help, too, especially with liquid crystal units. Some anglers also insert handwarmer-style packs into this insulation to provide additional heat.

Flashers vs. LCG'S: Debate on Ice

Most "modernized" ice anglers are now using some form of electronics, or while they may opt not to, at least they understand the advantages of using these high-tech navigation and sonar devices. For many, the choice of whether or not to actually invest in electronics depends upon a true understanding of their use, application, and cost, as well as on the amount of time the angler spends fishing, and how seriously he or she takes the sport.

Personally, I'd be lost without them. Without electronics, I can't easily find precise locations, depths, structures, bottom contents, secondary cover, forage, or fish. I don't know specifically what depth my bait is off bottom, and I can't efficiently monitor the fish's activity levels or responses to my presentation. Electronics are arguably one of the most critical tools a modern ice angler can use.

Setting aside the advantages of portable Loran and GPS navigation units for a moment, let's get into yet another debate: that of sonar, specifically, flashers versus liquid crystal units. Both have a following, and from personal experience, I can vouch that each group has valid points.

Until recently, I found it difficult to fully advocate the use of liquid crystal units for ice fishing applications. My first experience with an LCG on ice was in 1987, with a low-pixel portable unit. Besides being next to impossible to read in direct sunlight, the low pixel count made the squares that constitute a reading so large that even a bluntnose minnow looked like Moby Dick. Worst of all, the unit would function fifteen or twenty minutes, half hour tops, then the screen would begin forming black blotches that would start growing like a rash and slowly overcome the screen as the liquid crystals became sluggish, ruining several trips.

I soon reverted back to using my flasher. However, after spending the past couple winter seasons fishing with a knowledgeable ice angler who is a proponent of liquid crystal units and fishes them regularly on the ice, I'm ready to point out a few advantages involved with using liquid crystal units on ice.

Many of you will like the features of today's improved units. You'll now be able to read them, even in direct sunlight, thanks to features such as Lowrance's "Clearvision." With more pixels also, you'll get more detailed pictures than ever before, and more clear, accurate, and easily readable images. Lowrance's "gray scale" also enhances the ability to determine bottom topography and secondary cover, and helps separate fish from the bottom. Hoods are also available to shade bright sunlight from the screen for those without this feature.

Other added features on modern LCG's include side scanning for taking readings to the side as well as straight down, split screen features for viewing two different areas at once, modules capable of incorporating Loran or GPS functions onto the unit, and zoom screens for zooming in on specific depth sectors.

The zoom feature is especially helpful. Say you're fishing forty feet of water and locate a school of walleyes right on bottom. With the press of a button or two, you'll see the overall picture on the right hand side of the screen (zero to forty feet) and a "zoom" picture on the left. Programming the 30-40 foot depth range on the left screen, for example, will zoom you right down into the important area where the fish and your lure are located. Not only does this zoom you in, but it also focuses the entire pixel width into a small area of depth coverage, providing better resolution and hence, more detailed coverage.

Say you're in thirty feet of water, using a unit featuring 30 vertical pixels. Obviously, you have only one pixel per foot resolution. Zoom the entire screen into the 15 to 20 foot range, however, and you've got six pixels per foot resolution. Significant difference.

Eagle also makes several LCG units that can be used for ice fishing applications, mostly in portables. They also offer the "Ice Dapter," an extra long transducer bar attachment to help hold the transducer at the correct depth and angle for ice fishing usage. Some models also offer "Fish Trac," which provides the running depth of any fish moving in and out of your cone, and

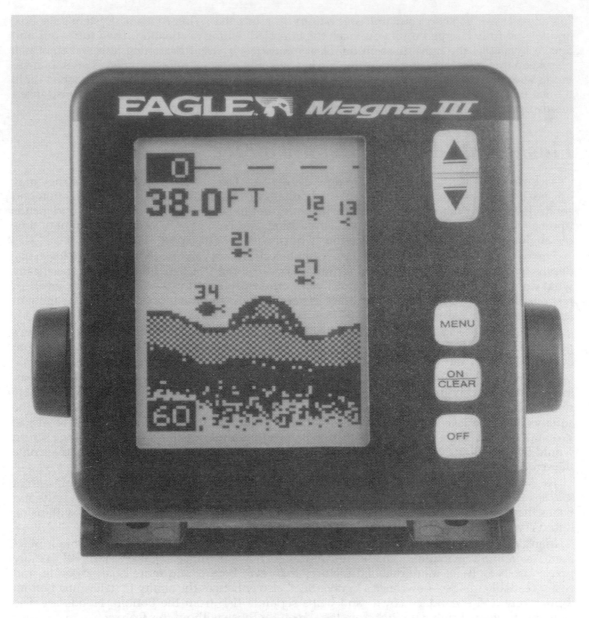

Above: Eagle Magna III LCG (Eagle)

Left: Portable LCG (Humminbird)

"Broadview," a three-way transducer system equipped with three 20-degree transducers for side viewing. Some also display remaining battery power. All Lowrance/Eagle units are filled with dry nitrogen to prevent corrosion, and sealed to prevent moisture or condensation damage.

A couple of models are also available from Humminbird, one of which can be quickly converted from a portable to a permanent mount in seconds and features Fish ID Plus—a feature that pinpoints fish in an individual beam and indicates their precise depth.

Among Bottom Line's LCD portable sonars is the Fishin' Buddy, a one piece, totally self-contained fish finder that clamps easily to a five gallon pail. The Fishin' Buddy is both a sidefinder and depthfinder so it lets you look sideways or straight down, using a nine-degree cone angle. A multi-view screen provides both side and down views at the same time.

The unit operates on three "C" cell batteries, which the manufacturer claims will operate it for up to twenty hours at zero degrees. The Fishin' Buddy flashes the precise distance to marked fish, offers superb resolution, has a backlit, high contrast display that provides bright, clear pictures in even the brightest conditions, and weighs only five pounds.

A number of other companies offer LCG technology in both portable and standard models, including Interphase, Impulse, Raytheon Marine Company, and Vexilar, among others.

Other portable depth reading sonar units with LCD display are also available, including the Ice Eyes hand-held sonar "gun" which can read depths up to ninety-nine feet through up to three feet of ice. Pull the trigger to activate the transducer, and the fifteen degree cone will read depth. The unit operates on two nine volt batteries and is waterproof. Vexilar's LPS-1, another hand-held unit that looks like a flashlight, is also available. Just point it down through the ice and shoot to read the depth. The unit weighs less than one pound. Just remember, most portable units are available in their own carry cases and operate on flashlight or six volt lantern batteries, which lack power, and depending on the model, die quickly in cold weather.

This can be changed, however. With my full scale Lowrance Ultra III portable, for example, I merely took a needlenose pliers, broke out the divider separating the two six-volt lantern battery compartments, stripped the wires, and with the addition of electrical clips, placed a 12-volt gel-cel wrapped with foam in place and hooked it up. It works well.

Otherwise, purchasing a non-portable model, mounting it to a Winter Fishing System's "Icebox" or Vexilar's P-160 holder complete with a more powerful power supply comes highly recommended, especially for full-day, extended trip diehards such as myself.

If you fish long and hard with a standard flasher or LCG unit, you'll want to tap the power of today's powerful, rechargeable, 10 or 12 amp 12-volt motorcycle or gel cel batteries. You'll have more than sufficient, sustained power to help keep liquid crystal units powered, warm, and operating in even the coldest weather all day long. Again, remember to keep your unit warm until you're on the lake, and once there, turn the unit on and leave it on. With an LCD, try turning the screen light on; leaving it on will also help generate heat, keeping the battery at maximum power and the liquid crystals fluid and functioning.

Again, if the fluid operating the crystals begins to freeze, it becomes sluggish, a black spot will appear, and will gradually grow larger. As you warm the unit, the black spot will gradually disappear. This can be avoided by keeping the unit warm. Many folks also don't realize that there are actually two types of liquid crystal fluids: consumer grade and industrial grade. Consumer grade doesn't have the freeze resistant capability of the industrial grade fluid, which while more expensive, is tested freeze resistant to minus forty degrees Fahrenheit. Vexilar uses such fluid in their LC-8.

Flashers, however, have no fluids to freeze and have one distinct advantage over liquid crystal graphs: they provide instantaneous readouts of the action below, whereas LCG's don't. When you work a bait below a flasher, you see the lure's response and movements simultaneously. There is not a moment's lapse like you'll receive with a liquid crystal. While some will try to claim signal send-out and return are virtually instantaneous, even the best liquid crystal units set on their fastest chart speed feature a minimum delay of about one-half second to one full second, because the signals must be processed and translated into a figure on the screen.

Yet technology is getting closer. The experts at Lowrance now offer a "Fast Trak" feature, which basically is a vertically oriented "flasher style" reading alongside the liquid crystal display screen. The readings here are almost instantaneous, just like a flasher—meaning this is closer to real time. If you lift your lure, it will move almost instantaneously on this display, similar to a flasher. This Lowrance unit is a sophisticated liquid crystal. With most units there is a brief, half second delay.

That's not long, but is enough to make a difference when you're trying to evaluate specific jig movements and immediate fish response to them. Drop a jig off a dock, and watch how fast a bluegill can inhale and expel your bait, and you'll see what I mean. Instant feedback lets you make split-second decisions about what to do to trigger and hook fish.

Some will argue, however, that a brief "history" can be advantageous, for it allows you to monitor what's happening "now" and a few seconds ago as well. For instance, should you look up just as a fish moves through quickly while using a flasher, the image would be gone. You'd never know it was there. On an LCG, the pixel furthest right is almost instantaneous, and the further left you go, the older the signal you're reading, so if you look up a split second after a fish goes through, you'll still see the mark briefly, providing a second chance to bring your bait to that level and work the fish.

Many will also argue that in most instances, instantaneous responses don't matter much in the first place. When jigging active gamefish, locating fish at a specific depth and knowing precisely where your bait is relative to the fish is enough to get action, and even with a momentary, delayed signal response, you still get this information.

Of course, electronics can indicate more than water depth, presence of fish, and depth of your lure. Electronics provide a picture of what's below, and the amount of detail revealed to you depends on how well you understand your unit's function and capabilities, how much experience you have using it, and consequently, your ability to correctly interpret its signals.

Almost anyone can learn to read depth on their unit; most learn to see their bait and fish. But after watching hundreds of anglers using sonars, I strongly suspect this is about all many folks really understand about interpreting signals on their units, which is unfortunate.

To seize the full potential of the electronics advantage, anglers must learn to evaluate structural oddities, bottom contents, secondary cover, forage, fish holding tight to bottom, suspended fish, lure action and fish response to various actions under a variety of conditions.

LCG's may hold an advantage here for beginners, because the unit produces a graphic given your current situation, making interpretation relatively easy. Once you get used to your unit's picture, you can become quite proficient in reading it. Bottom is marked clearly, and a depth reading tells the depth in digital readout. Your bait appears as a moving, suspended row of continuous dots running across the screen, as do fish. Some units even mark fish in color or fish shapes. Nothing too hard about this.

Flashers, while providing complete, instantaneous readouts, are subject to a great deal of interpretation. There's no automatic sensitivity adjustment; this must be done manually to find bottom, and to decipher depth, bottom content, and secondary structure. Your lure will appear as a simple "blip," as will fish, which will never show up as distinct fish shapes. Manual adjustments can also be made on LCG's. If your unit features automatic sensitivity, just turn it off and proceed to adjust the unit manually to find specific fish-holding locations. This will help you control the output; otherwise, you're dependent on the manufacturer's opinion of where the sensitivity should be set for the average fishing situation, and we as ice anglers are generally far from the average fishing situation.

This is where flashers have their advantages. Compare the flasher versus LCG debate to a photographer selecting a camera. A professional photographer, who fully understands his equipment and intentions, usually chooses a fully manual unit, so that given a specific instance, the correct lens, filter, amount of light, exposure and flash can be fine-tuned to create the desired results.

An amateur, however, often relies on automated cameras that automatically make such adjustments and corrections to attain a standard, which also results in a great deal of limitation in use.

It is likewise for a flasher versus an LCG. A flasher, correctly adjusted, provides purely instantaneous, raw data that isn't interpreted into a graphic. It's like a manual camera. Given a proper understanding of this raw data, you can make adjustments and interpret depth, bottom content, secondary cover, forage, and fish (the resulting picture) to fit the situation and purpose. It's adjustable.

Furthermore, as you lift or drop your lure, its movements are instantly signaled on the unit. If a fish moves in, up or down, fast or slow, the blip that represents it tells you exactly when and how. If a fish stops, so does the mark—instantly. You can instantaneously watch your lure's movements and the response of the fish, and immediately make the required adjustments to maximize your catch. Precision. With an LCG, you'll get a similar picture, but the lines and motions representing the lure, fish, and their movements would be delayed as it's interpreted for you; hence the "automated" limitation.

There are several such subtleties, many of them technical, in flasher use and interpretation that offer advantages over an LCG. However, suffice to say the ability to make precise interpretations comes mostly with knowledge and experience. Like a professional photographer with a manual camera, I've spent years studying my flasher, and can manually fine-tune the picture to produce the intended result.

A flasher provides raw data that isn't interpreted into a graphic. (Vexilar)

Fortunately, such precision isn't always necessary. Amateur photographers may be lost with a professional camera capable of offering superior pictures, but take satisfactory photos without the confusion using a fully or partly automatic 35mm camera. So unless they're fussy about their photography, the automatic is a better choice.

It is similar for electronics on ice. Presently, fewer precision things can be accomplished with an LCG compared to a flasher. But anglers who don't demand this type of precision and can learn to pinpoint structure and fish, then get their bait at the same level as active fish, will increase their winter catches tremendously. In this respect, properly used, today's LCR's may perform nearly as well as a flasher.

Like an amateur photographer who recognizes, understands and works within the limitations of a fully automatic camera, the resulting LCG pictures can turn out satisfactorily, and for many, the easier, less taxing method of accomplishing this end is more than sufficient.

Both work, and the choice is yours, although I must admit I like to use flashers on the ice. One of my favorite models is Vexilar's FL-8, which features a neon flasher bulb that pulls sensitivity levels in three colors. Signals in the center of the transducer cone appear in red, indicative of a strong signal. Orange, indicates an intermediate signal, and green, a weak signal.

This is much akin to watching a meteorologist showing the strength of a storm system, using color as a guide to intensity, with the darker colors indicating stronger intensity. The only difference is that while television stations can use virtually any color of the spectrum to show intensity, the neon LED bulb on the FL-8 flasher is limited to three colors, but still creates ease in interpretation.

Units without color readouts indicate signal strength by the width of the signal; thicker being stronger and thinner being weaker. This also shows on the FL-8's color readout, but the color creates an easier standard to go by, making interpretation of strong, intermediate, and weak signals easier, which makes it possible to monitor fish activity levels with ease.

Just don't abuse this setting. Too many anglers adjust their sensitivity so that their lures appear in red, which is overkill. What you want is to make your lure appear green or green with an orange fringe. By turning the sensitivity weak on the bait, any slight reduction of the signal shows. In other words, if a fish appears near the bait and steals the waxworm off your hook, the green line will thin or the orange fringe will disappear. This is more difficult to see if your sensitivity is set too high and the lure and bait appear thick and red.

More importantly, if properly set, when a fish enters your cone you'll see it in green, and as it approaches your bait, it will turn orange, and when right on it, red. This allows you to tell if a fish is approaching or moving away from your bait, and by watching how slow or fast, you can tell how active they are. To date, no flasher other than Vexilar's FL-8 offers this feature.

Another advantage of a flasher is that the flasher bulb reads out whatever signal the transducer is capable of sending out, which provides good resolution and display of what the transducer is reading. You can have a high powered transducer, but if an LCG screen isn't capable of projecting the full signal being received, you're at a disadvantage.

This is where the importance of pixels comes in on an LCG. The higher the number of pixels, the better the picture. Be sure to check out the number of vertical pixels, for they're more important than horizontal pixels. If your screen is a 30 dot vertical pixel unit and you're fishing thirty feet of water, each pixel, or dot, equals one foot. So it wouldn't do you any good to have a transducer with a receiver capable of reading resolution to a distance of two inches, even if the amplifiers could read it, because your screen can't show it.

Another disadvantage of LCG's for ice fishing application is the automatic sensitivity setting. Turn it off. This is set by the manufacturer's idea of the situation the average angler will be fishing, and being an ice angler, you're not an "average" angler. Be sure to use the manual sensitivity settings so you can customize your picture to the situation. Chart speed, gray scale, and screen darkness must also be manually set.

With a flasher, however, you always set your sensitivity manually. You can adjust the unit to read a tiny micro jig, even enough to show if the worm is stripped off the hook. Most manufacturers won't set the automatic sensitivity modes on LCGs this light, because the average operator wouldn't be able to see fish.

But remember, when you're trying to read a tiny ice lure, it's like trying to sense a stealth bomber on radar. The thin, knife-like edge, especially of a hook or vertical ice jig, is difficult for the pulse of an electronics unit to pick up. But set correctly, a good unit can and will show these fine targets. This is why ice experts use fully adjustable units.

Many also fish horizontal lures, which show up better because there's a wider surface area for the sonar to read. Thus, a Jigging Rapala is easier to see than a Swedish Pimple, because it's more horizontally oriented. When using vertically oriented lures, many of these same anglers will place a glass or plastic bead on the line above the lure to provide a larger surface area for better sonar reflectivity. One company has even developed a vertical, teardrop-style ice jig with a flat surface at the head for better electronics visibility.

Speaking of visibility, a sun hood of some sort placed over your unit will help you see your screen in bright sunlight. Skip Christman of Vexilar Electronics commented to me how folks would tease him about his "cannon," actually a three-foot length of stovepipe attached around his FL-8, which eliminated the sun's glare.

Another excellent flasher is Zercom's Clearwater Classic. The unit features an instantaneous liquid crystal flasher display, and a transducer orbital alignment device that features a twenty degree puck transducer and a precalibrated bubble level to assure the transducer is properly aligned.

Zercom's Clearwater Classic Ice System features a durable ABS box that holds a 7-amp gel pack battery capable of running the unit up to 140 hours. Even the battery charger is included. Clearwater claims the Classic, which reads like a flasher but utilizes LCD technology, is so sensitive that a micro ice jig can be seen in forty feet of water. The Clearwater Classic's cousin, the Clearwater Pro, features electroluminescent backlighting, battery charge indicator, and gray scale for bottom determination. It also reads well in sunlight, and is easy to operate.

The Clearwater series also features time variable gain to display fish equally on all depth ranges and always show true bottom. This makes secondary cover such as weeds easier to read, and offers the ability to easily mark and differentiate fish or other objects among them by adjusting the logarithmic sensitivity control. The Clearwater Series is also designed with super sharp gray scale display for easy recognition of bottom content; weeds and other structure; and fish holding tight to bottom. With Zercom's backlighting system, the display will show up even in bright sunlight, and even shows fish holding in thick weeds. Marks indicating your lure show up clearly whether you're just beneath the transducer or fishing just off bottom. Impressive.

Electronically, the Clearwater units feature fast cold weather response time, low battery current draw, super target separation, a whopping 1000 watts of power, and target separation of 2.5 inches for seeing fish, including those holding tight to bottom.

Humminbird has also reintroduced a flasher into their line. Humminbird's units are completely waterproof, are fully tilting and swiveling in their own portable case, and feature a quick disconnect mount from the portable case should you wish to mount them to a box capable of holding a motorcycle or gel cel battery. They also have an ultra bright LED and built-in sunshield.

Other flashers are available from Ray Jefferson and Fish Hawk Electronics. I would also suspect more enterprising manufacturers will jump back into this market soon.

Batteries

One recurring problem with using electronics on the ice, whether Loran, GPS, LCG or flasher, is battery power and life. Given harsh, cold conditions, batteries are much more prone to trouble.

Here are some tips for preventing such occurrences. First, with sonar, use 12-volt motorcycle or gel-cel type batteries. Lantern-type batteries, even alkaline models that offer great longevity in cold temperatures, don't have the power and "endurance" to handle operating electronics in cold weather for extended periods, unless you get the rechargeable models. Also they're difficult or impossible to recharge, making them expensive. Most portables can be converted to use with motorcycle or gel-cel batteries by breaking the tab dividing the battery case, and inserting the battery and packing foam around the battery to hold it securely.

Motorcycle batteries are a step up, but are bulky and heavy, and if tipped, will leak acid. Despite these disadvantages, a motorcycle battery features longer ampere hours, so, by buying a motorcycle battery, you'll somewhat sacrifice longevity and convenience for larger capacity.

My preference is gel-cel power pack-type batteries. They're relatively small and lightweight, generate excellent power, and are capable of operating a flasher type sonar unit for 16-24 hours of continuous use, and an LCR for 30-40 hours of continuous use.

The only thing to remember is that these units should be drained down prior to charging, lest they may develop "memory" and not hold a full charge over time. The cyclic use of a bat-

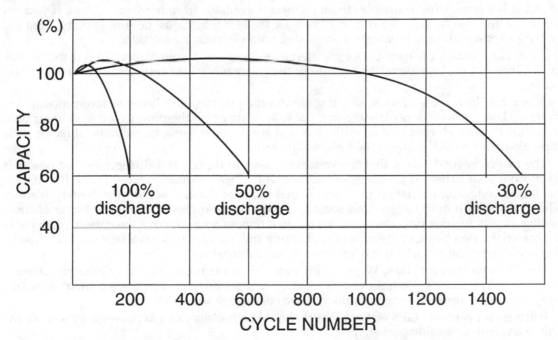

Cycle life is very dependent on the depth of discharge the battery experiences during each cycle.
The number of cycles varying with the depth of discharge are shown on the graph.

Battery charge chart (Union Battery)

tery is dependent on the depth of discharge that the battery experiences during each cycle, the number of cycles varying with the depth of discharge as shown in the graph.

For best results, run your batteries down as far as possible; leave the unit running on the way home if necessary. Charge them eight or nine hours overnight on a small, 12 volt, one or two amp trickle charger, and you'll be back in business. Never overcharge a gel-cel battery. With a one-amp charger, never leave the unit on more than twenty-four hours. With a two-amp charger, never leave it on more than eight hours. Try to purchase the larger amperage batteries, 7-10 amperes being good. The smaller four-amp units are satisfactory, but you'll get more time between charges with the higher amp units.

Again, be sure you don't overcharge your unit. Your charger should be no more than a 15-volt unit, or you may overcharge your battery. Vexilar makes a charger that automatically shuts off at 14.5 volts, eliminating the chance of overcharging.

Zercom Marine's Clearwater Classic Ice System, which they advertise as "no assembly, no hassles," is nice. It features a lightweight ABS box, seven-amp gel pack battery, transducer orbital alignment device, pre-calibrated bubble, and even the battery charger, all in one convenient system. It comes fully assembled and ready to fish.

Also remember a cold battery has one-third of its overall capacity lost just by cold temperature. This is why a larger, charged battery will provide you more power. In addition, you'll double the life of your battery by placing it on a regular charging schedule: once a month while in storage is highly recommended.

Also, gel-cel batteries feature a putty-like liquid inside, thus, like acid batteries, function better if stood up and not laid on their sides. These are also subject to freezing. Vexilar, however, makes a special battery with a thick electrolyte solution described as having the thickness of "peanut butter" by the manufacturer. This is pressed between the battery plates and doesn't flow, causing no problems on the ice or if tipped.

For easier use of standard gel-cel units, you can enlarge the holes in the battery tabs and insert 6/32 brass bolts into these tabs. Secure them by soldering or threading them to the tabs, or fitting the posts with a suitable clip or connector available from hardware stores. If you opt to use the brass bolts, three-fourths inch bolts are the best length, just be sure to paint them red or black to easily identify polarity when making your electrical connection.

Next, cut a chunk of foam packing material, and cut out a void that will hold the battery firmly, then cut the outside of the foam to fit the entire block into your locator's carrying case firmly.

A one-half inch piece of foam sheeting should then be cut, with holes to accommodate the batteries' bolt "posts" to insulate the top. For ease in attaching the power cord from your unit, either tip the power connections with electrical snaps, or if using brass bolts, alligator style clips, also color coded to match the batteries' polarity.

The theory beyond this is that the system is easier to rig up, and furthermore, as power is taken from your battery it produces a small amount of heat, normally insignificant. But in winter, the surrounding insulation performs a dual purpose. First, it keeps your battery warmer when you bring it onto the ice, and second, it traps the heat produced by this battery action, adding greatly to your time of use on the ice. Just remember to remove the battery from packing material when being charged, as the charging process also produces heat, and the insulation could potentially start a fire if left intact around the battery.

Finally, keep the unit clean. Wipe it with water or an alcohol dampened cloth only. Always charge it before storing. Periodic supplementary charges during storage are a smart idea; just carry this out according to the recommendations of the manufacturer.

Batteries for portable GPS or Loran units should be alkaline, and kept warm by storing the unit in a warm, accessible pocket.

Summary

Choose your electronics units carefully, then become intimately familiar with their use. Learn to properly use and set the unit, and in the case of sonar, to read depth, bottom content, structure, secondary structure, cover types, forage, and fish. Regardless of what your electronics are telling you, always try fishing any schools you mark, and experiment with various rods, lines, lure styles, sizes, colors, and jigging motions until you find the best combination.

I usually start by trying tiny ultralight presentations. I then gradually work up to large lures and presentations with more active jigging motions (or vice-versa, depending on the conditions and the species being sought) until I determine the fish's activity levels and the most efficient presentation for catching them.

However, if nothing happens after ten or fifteen minutes, move! It's always tempting to fish long and hard when a school is found, but finding fish doesn't mean you'll actually catch them, as many frustrated ice anglers will attest. So don't get caught up in this Catch-22. It completely defeats the purpose of this efficient ice fishing approach. Rather, fish wisely and efficiently, stay mobile, and whatever you do, always search for the most active fish.

Do this at several high percentage waypoints, and it's unlikely you'll strike out on each one, but rather, find active fish on some or even most of them. One waypoint may hold nothing, another nothing but inactive fish, while a third is bustling with activity. Find the active schools on each, stay with them as long as possible, and when they move or become inactive, move to the next waypoint. Such efficient processes lead to consistency. By doing so, you'll gain invaluable experience. Over time, you'll also learn to more consistently narrow down and pinpoint the "best of the best" in terms of the top fish-producing structures, saving valuable fishing time and becoming an increasingly more efficient ice angler because of it. Not only will you discover the correct combination of positive variables to reveal true daily patterns, but you'll also enhance your overall fishing experience and knowledge by learning how to better understand winter fish behavior and activity levels on various lakes.

Like a scientist collecting data and making solid conclusions to discover high technology breakthroughs based on the scientific method, you can collect solid information based on your findings. Consequently, you'll determine high-tech breakthroughs in winter fishing patterns and methods, further enhancing the value and fun of your ice fishing experiences.

You might think, this is getting to be high tech stuff! And you're right. But it works. So don't just randomly walk out onto the ice and sit in place without waiting for fish, or casually use your electronics without fully interpreting what they're telling you. After all, the correct use of

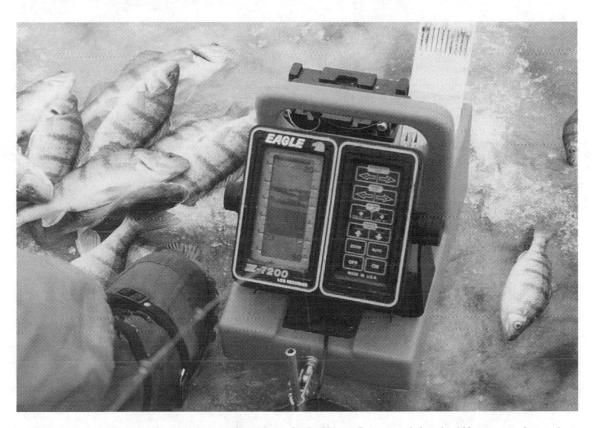

Using sonar to mark groups of active fish like these adds thrill to modern ice fishing methods.

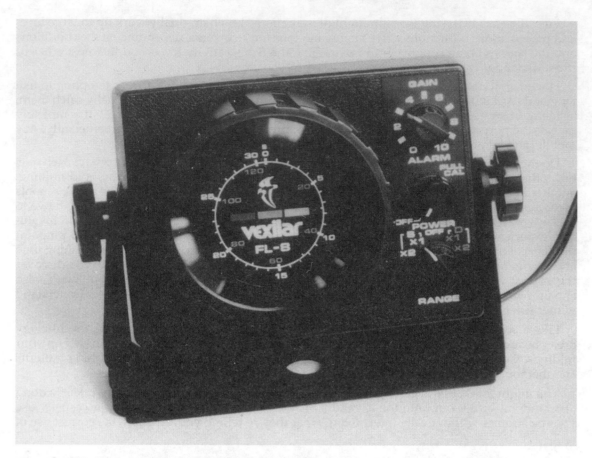

The Vexilar FL-8 high technology flasher

electronics enhances the fun and challenge of ice fishing. Through these high-percentage efforts, you'll undoubtedly become a better ice angler.

As further improvements and advances continue to develop, we'll likely be able to accomplish even more using electronics on the ice. By learning now, you'll be able to better keep up with new advances and developments later. After all, we will soon likely see more units designed particularly with ice fishing in mind, boasting features that cater to the serious ice angler, perhaps even having units with specially set ice fishing modes. I, for one, look forward to and welcome these new developments. You, now understanding their application and advantages, should too.

Chapter 5

Tip-Up Tips

As dawn breaks over the ice, it's time to fish. In the last five years this area has yielded me three northern pike over 35 inches, as well as numerous fish in the four to six pound range. Something is going to happen today. I can feel it as surely as the cold stinging my fingertips. My hands almost twitch with anticipation as I set my first tip-up.

After setting my other lines, I join my partners at the shack. I step in, pour some heated milk in a cup, and stir in the cocoa. The rich smell of hot chocolate steams from the mug, blending with the savory tang of bacon frying in the pan beside one of Bill's "world's best" ham and cheese omelets. We begin talking and dishing out the usual verbal abuse concerning the taste of Bill's one-of-a-kind omelets. Then it happens.

Through the frosted window, Bill sees a distant orange flag pop up. "Tip-up!" he barks between bites. The plate of eggs drops to the table, the door flips open, and I dash out like a greyhound at starting time.

After a brief struggle the fish emerges from the water, and Bill shouts in the distance, "He's got it!" I remove the hook from the fish's jaw, hold him up, and motion to my partners.

They approach at a run, blurting two words almost simultaneously: "Nice fish!"

Tip-up fishing has that effect on countless ice anglers. Why? Primarily, because tip-ups are effective ice fishing tools that a group of anglers can scatter over larger areas to help locate active fish. (Most states and provinces allow at least two lines per person.)

Secondly, most quality tip-ups feature underwater reels, so even if the hole freezes over, the flag will signal a bite. This is a nice feature if you need to do something important, such as play cards with friends, jig in other areas, or enjoy a cup of hot chocolate.

How a Tip-Up Works

A tip-up is an elaborate set line. It features a freeze-resistant spool mounted on a plastic or wood frame that supports a flag. When a fish hits, a release mechanism trips the flag and alerts the angler of a strike. The angler then must set the hook and hand-line the fish to the surface.

The first tip-ups probably were just spools of line set on the ice, with the line loosely looped around the tip of a flexible stick, and dropped into the hole with a baited hook. A fish would pull the stick down as it struck the bait and took line from the spool. These eventually became commercialized products. Unfortunately, many "cheapie" tip-ups of the past didn't function smoothly, causing fish to feel resistance and drop the bait.

Such practice has given way to new ideas and technology. Today's quality tip-up consists of a sturdy plastic or wood frame that rests on the ice, straddling or covering a hole. This frame supports a vertical crossbar on the so-called stick tip-ups, or a tube that shrouds a shaft protected by freeze-resistant lubricant, on deluxe models. The vertical crossbar or shaft has a spool on the lower end, attached to a release mechanism on the top. The end with the spool lies in the hole, underwater, so the line won't freeze up.

When a fish strikes, it takes out line and makes the spool turn, activating the release mechanism that trips a spring-loaded flag on the frame to alert the angler. It's a bit like a complex mouse trap with a much more appealing prey.

Although many interesting tip-up designs have been introduced through the years, tip-ups can be categorized into four general groups: fixed position or stationary tip-ups, thermal tip-ups, automatic hook-set units, and wind tip-ups.

Fixed position tip-ups

Fixed position tip-ups are designed to present bait without moving. These vary from a tripod model that stands almost five feet high and can set the hook, to lightweight, compact freeze-proof models that can be stacked (six or more) in a five gallon bucket, to designs with built-in hole covers and solar heat panels to prevent holes from freezing over.

Stick style tip-ups

The first major development in tip-ups, and probably the most popular through the years, has been what I call the stick tip-up. Its simple frame and crossbar design features a horizontal stick that straddles the hole and supports a second vertical arm tipped with a spool. A wire trip mechanism, leading from the spool to a trip, is attached on one side of the vertical arm. A flag on the opposite side is attached to a thin strip of steel on the first side. The "flag steel" is extended up, then bent around to the trip mechanism. When the spool turns and trips the wire, the flag pops up.

Such tip-ups vary greatly in quality and price. Cheap import models tend to be small, lack a greased tube, and don't trip smoothly. Good domestic traditional models include **K & E Tackle**'s Bear Creek Tip-Up, **U.S. Line**'s Forty-Up, and **Lakco** brand tip-ups.

Newer designs that use this basic concept reveal dramatic improvements. **HT Enterprises'** Fisherman Tip-Ups, for example, are made of high-impact plastic instead of wood, reducing frame freeze-up into the ice, and virtually eliminating breakage. (I've seen such a unit survive even the impact of a carelessly driven snowmobile.) These units feature three sizes of plastic spools that don't reflect light and spook fish, and can be purchased with optional drag features.

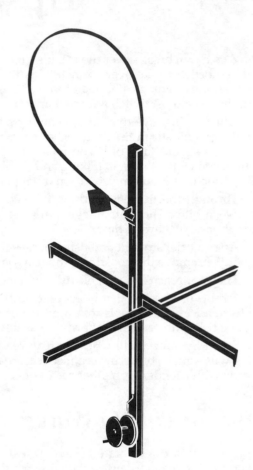

A stick tip-up

The **Thompson** and **Moosehead** tip-ups, popular in the eastern part of the United States, obviously were designed by anglers frustrated with cheaper stick style tip-ups that didn't hold up to big fish or toppled in stiff winds. The wide-bottom design of the solid hardwood frames on these units is stable.

Recognizing the advantage of a sturdy, high profile tip-up, **Heritage Tackle Company** introduced the Heritage Tip-Up, a hardwood framed, high-profile tip-up with an extra high flag and smooth trip mechanism. It is a beautiful unit. **HT**'s Frontier Tip-Up is similar in design, but also features a tension drag system, a high flag for added visibility, and a trip mechanism that virtually eliminates wind trips. Unlike any other stick tip-up I'm familiar with, the unit is also guaranteed against freeze-up.

The **Worth** Pop-Up employs a unique magnetic mechanism. A magnet on its underwater spool locks onto a second magnet attached to the bottom of a vertical shaft that is enclosed by

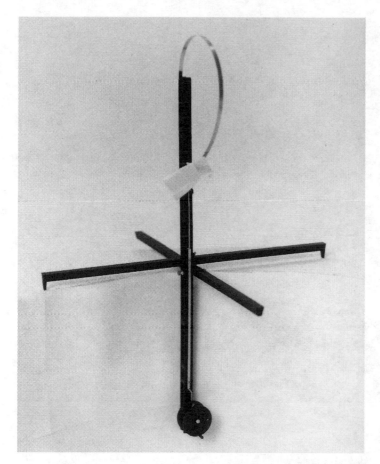

HT's Fisherman tip-up

HT's Frontier tip-up

Choosing a tip-up

the tube assembly. This hidden shaft has a flag on the end opposite the magnets, and is held out of sight by the magnets.

When a fish strikes, the turning spool separates the magnets, allowing the spring-loaded shaft to pop up and reveal the flag. Freeze-proof and offering little resistance to the fish, it's an excellent concept.

Stationary freeze-proof tip-ups

One of the greatest improvements in tip-ups has been freeze-resistant releases. These carefully machined mechanisms use sealed main shafts packed with freeze-resistant lubricants. They trip smoothly and with little resistance, virtually eliminating lost fish.

The pioneer of this concept is **Arctic Fisherman Company** of Beaver Dam, Wisconsin. Its Beaver Dam tip-up offers super-smooth trips that make fishing

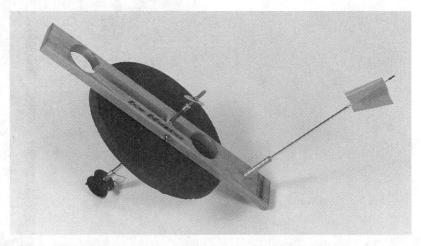

HT's Icemaster tip-up, shown with attached thermal hole cover that helps prevent hole freeze-up

a pleasure. Competitors include **Fremont**'s Shur-Tip, the **Predator**, and **HT**'s Icemaster.

HT also offers wood frame tip-ups called Polar II and Polar II Husky. The Polar II is the smoothest unit I've ever fished.

Thermal tip-ups

The so-called "thermal" model tip-ups obviously were designed by anglers tired of ice and blowing snow closing up their holes. (Blowing snow mixes rapidly with water and acts as a sponge, soaking up water and eventually covering the entire tip-up.) If an angler has to chop away ice after a fish strikes, the fish is likely to be spooked beforehand. This design solves the problem by surrounding the tip-up shaft with insulating protection that hampers freezing.

The first such unit I knew of was **Productive Alternative**'s Thermal Tip-Up. The Thermal Tip-Up features a simple wooden box that surrounds a hole. When loaded with a couple of

A Polar tip-up (HT Enterprises)

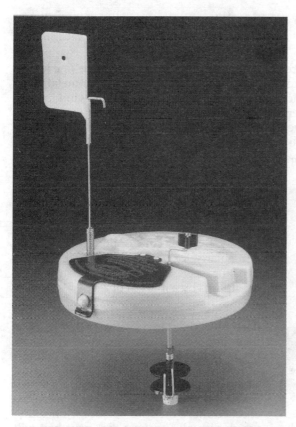

An Igloo tip-up (Rinehart Industries)

activated heat packs or a small candle, the heat chamber allows hours of ice-free fishing. The Thermal Tip-up has an adjustable trip mechanism that can be set to accommodate large baitfish, or even the lightest of strikes.

More recently, the **Rinehart** Igloo Thermal Tip-Up entered the market. This design creates a shelter for ice holes, blocking the cold from above and capturing the thermal energy of the water from below. Before 32-degree water can freeze, it must release 80 units (BTU) of heat into the air. The Igloo Tip-Up stops this heat transfer and prevents freeze-up. The design also keeps blowing snow from building up in the hole.

The Igloo's design also blocks light from entering the hole. Bright light entering an uncovered hole is not natural, and therefore may spook fish.

Rinehart's Solar Tip-up features flexible flaps, called "solar panels" that lie on each side of the frame to seal in the water's thermal energy and to absorb sunlight. The unit can cover a 10-inch hole.

HT's Polar Therm, equipped with HT's smooth trip mechanism, includes a plastic "Ice Guard" hole cover. The cover inhibits both freeze-up and sunlight.

Automatic hook-set tip-ups

All the tip-ups listed above require the angler to set the hook manually. Some anglers, however, prefer units that set the hook for them.

One of the earliest automatic hook-set tip-ups was introduced by **North Lake Sports**. The Hook-Set, a tripod, stands almost five feet tall. Its spring-loaded trip mechanism not only signals a take by a fish, but also automatically sets the hook when a fish strikes.

Another model is the Lite Strike, essentially a spring-loaded rod holder with adjustable settings. The trip is set against the rod so that when a fish strikes and bounces the rod tip, the spring trip releases, snapping the rod upward and setting the hook with preset force. This device does require a slightly longer than normal ice rod with some tip action to absorb the shock of the hook-set and provide a little give if the fish makes a hard run.

The main drawback of such designs is the loss of ability to control the hook-set on light biting fish. The force of an automatic hook-set would likely pull the bait away from a wary fish and spook it, as well as any others nearby.

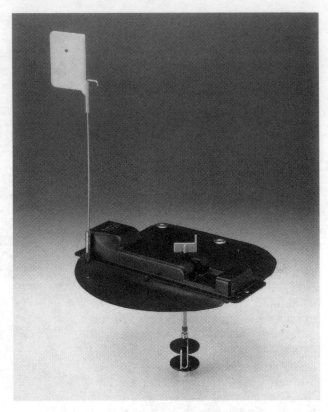

A Solar tip-up (Rinehart Industries)

Wind tip-ups

Wind tip-ups use the wind to jig the bait or lure automatically. On most models, the line leaves an above-ice spool mounted on a mobile, rocking arm. The line runs through a plastic or metal wind fan mounted at the end of this arm, and down into the hole. On the end opposite the wind fan is a spring-loaded tension device that allows the angler to control the amount of jigging action, depending on the weight of the lure and the velocity of the wind.

A tip-up must achieve four things: present bait, interest the fish, provoke a strike, and signal a strike. Wind tip-ups simply enhance the "provoking" factor, especially when water is dirty or deep (so fish can't easily see a stationary bait), or when aggressive fish prefer a more active presentation.

Movement is not always essential, but usually some jigging option is important, particularly for walleyes and pike. In fact, I've often seen wind tip-ups outfish stationary tip-ups by a margin of 2:1.

Moving bait attracts predators, and the flash of a frightened baitfish often triggers them into hitting. The presentation offered by a wind tip-up imitates this natural action. Note, however, that the jigging action produced by a wind tip-up tires minnows quickly. This means bait must be checked more often to be sure it's healthy, which virtually ensures that your bait will be lively. And since fresh, lively bait is

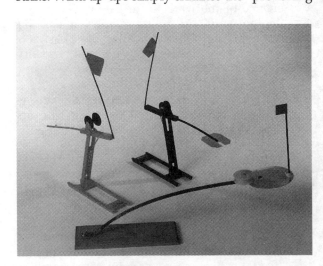

Various wind tip-ups

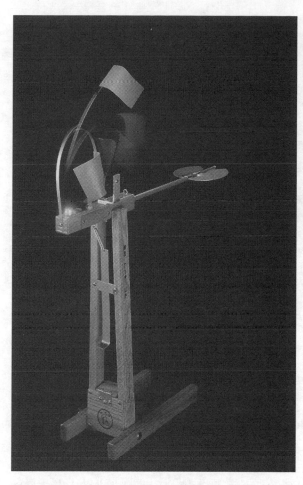

Left: Mr. Tip-Up (Mr. Tip-Up)

Below: Anatomy of a Windlass (HT Enterprises)

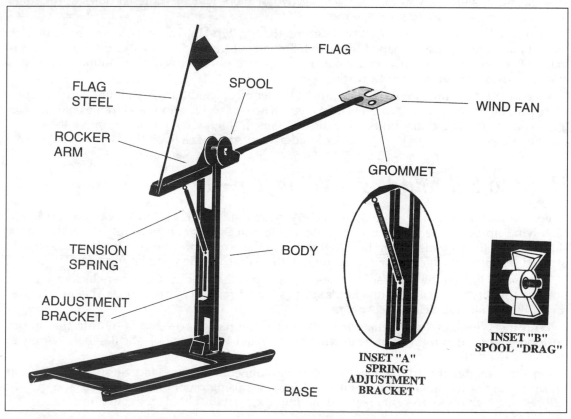

FLAG

FLAG STEEL

SPOOL

WIND FAN

ROCKER ARM

GROMMET

TENSION SPRING

BODY

ADJUSTMENT BRACKET

INSET "A"
SPRING ADJUSTMENT BRACKET

INSET "B"
SPOOL "DRAG"

BASE

The author approaches a tripped Windlass flag with anticipation.

another key to consistent success, this will produce more fish.

Wind tip-ups enable you to effectively jig two or more widely scattered holes at the same time. Try doing that with a single jig rod!

Two excellent models are **HT**'s Windlass and the **Mr. Tip-Up**. The Windlass is made of high impact plastic and has a V-shaped frame to help prevent freeze-down, while the Mr. Tip-Up is made of wood. Both are fully adjustable, allowing control of their jigging motion. The plates and springs are coated to prevent rusting.

When is the best time to use wind tip-ups? Under most conditions, I've found wind tip-ups more productive than standard units. However, when excessive wind or extreme cold is a factor, freeze-proof or thermal units are your best bets. In high winds, bait can move too much. And in extreme cold, wind tip-ups' lack of underwater spools is a liability.

How to Set and Rig a Wind Tip-Up

For the sake of example, we'll rig up **HT**'s Windlass and **K & E**'s Wind Waver. First, position each wind tip-up so the wind blows parallel to the arm and from behind the blade, then pack slush around the base of the unit to hold it firmly in the proper position. On the Windlass, gusts of wind will blow the blade downward, jigging the bait when the wind lets up.

Now wrap line on the spool so it comes off the top of the spool in a counter-clockwise direction. Use quality tip-up lines with brands such as **Gudebrod**, **HT**, **Cortland**, or **Mason**, or a premium fly line such as **Scientific Anglers**.

With the Windlass, loosen the wingnuts, adjust the rocker arm and body into the proper position, and tighten the wingnuts down. On the Wind Waver, the plastic flag base simply is twisted into position.

On either model, thread the line through the grommet in the wind fan, tie an HT or Bait Rig tip-up rig to the terminal end (or make your own rig using monofilament leader and quality ball-bearing swivels to prevent line twist) and tip the rig with a hook or jigging lure.

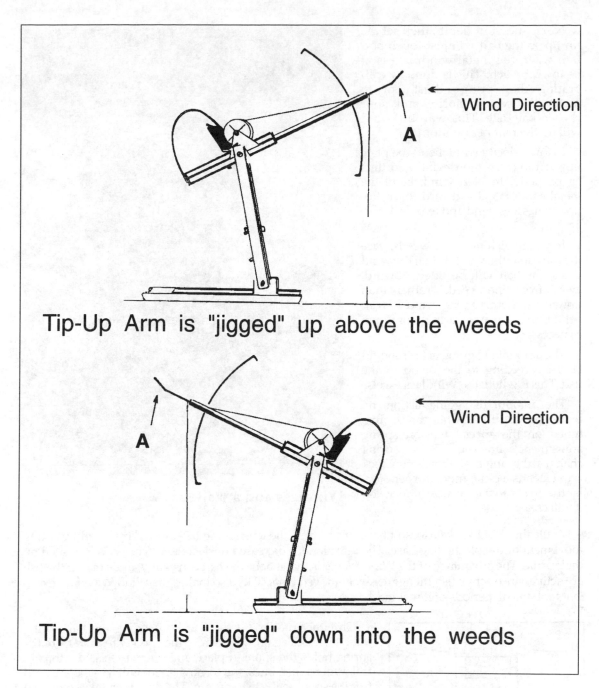

Tip-Up Arm is "jigged" up above the weeds

Tip-Up Arm is "jigged" down into the weeds

Above: Windlass settings

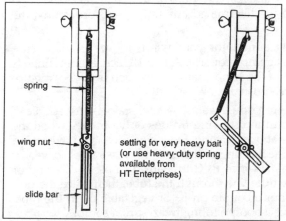

spring

wing nut

setting for very heavy bait
(or use heavy-duty spring
available from
HT Enterprises)

slide bar

Left: Windlass adjustment spring

Next, find your depth, then set the tip-up so the bait will just touch bottom when the metal windplate is at its lowest reach. This is done by calibrating the spring adjustment to match the wind velocity and your chosen bait size. This way the wind will jig the bait near bottom.

In low velocity wind, bend the plate upward to catch more wind and thus jig properly. In high wind, bend the metal windplate downward so the tip-up catches less wind and avoids "over-jig."

If you're fishing over weeds, face the plate into the wind. When the wind gusts, the bait will be lifted upward, away from the weeds, rather than down into them. On the Wind Waver, bend the steel waving arm up or down as necessary.

The amount of jigging action should be set according to the mood of the fish. This is where the Windlass excels.

The amount of jigging action, no matter how stiff the wind, can be fine-tuned on the special tension spring adjustment bracket. This spring changes the angle at which the rock arm extends, so the more perpendicular the arm is to the ice, the more action it will create.

Windlass and a walleye

While the Wind Waver doesn't have this feature, the tension can be adjusted by a slight twisting movement of the plastic flag base. The direction for increased or decreased tension is indicated on the paddle. The advantage of the Wind Waver is that it bobs the bait constantly, indicating if the fish are active, since active fish hit aggressively-moved baits. This also makes the Wind Waver an excellent tool during periods of low wind.

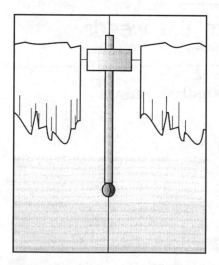

Windlass freeze-proofing device

On either model, set the flag by bending the flag spring until it presses against the rear of the spool. Pressure from the spring holds the spool in place and offers precise depth control. When a fish bites, the turning spool will trip the flag and free the spool so the fish can run. The drag then takes over and maintains the predetermined amount of tension against the spool.

Once in place, monitor your wind tip-ups to make sure they continue jigging properly. A 6 to 18 inch jigging range is generally best. If the wind changes direction or speed, the tip-ups must be readjusted.

Because a wind tip-up's above-water spool is susceptible to freezing, it's best to use wind tip-ups only on days when the temperature is above freezing. However, diehards have found ways to fight the freezing problem. Simply use a hole cover, or glue a piece of 3/4-inch PVC tube inside a block of wood or styrofoam, feed the line through the tube, then place the unit in the hole. Pour a couple drops of vegetable oil in the tube, and you'll have a non-polluting freeze-proof setup.

It is important to keep line and leaders as untangled and kink-free as possible to assure yourself of the best chance at success.

If night fishing, it is a good idea to check your lines and baits before darkness sets in.

After catching a fish, run the wet tip-up line through your fingers to strip the water and ice before wrapping the line back on the spool. This will help prevent the line from freezing up.

How to Set and Rig a Fixed Position Tip-up

To demonstrate the useful features of high-tech tip-ups, we will use the Polar, Polar II, Icemaster and Polar Therm tip-ups as examples. These feature multiple setting trips that have four possible settings: heavy-heavy, heavy-light, light-heavy, and light-light.

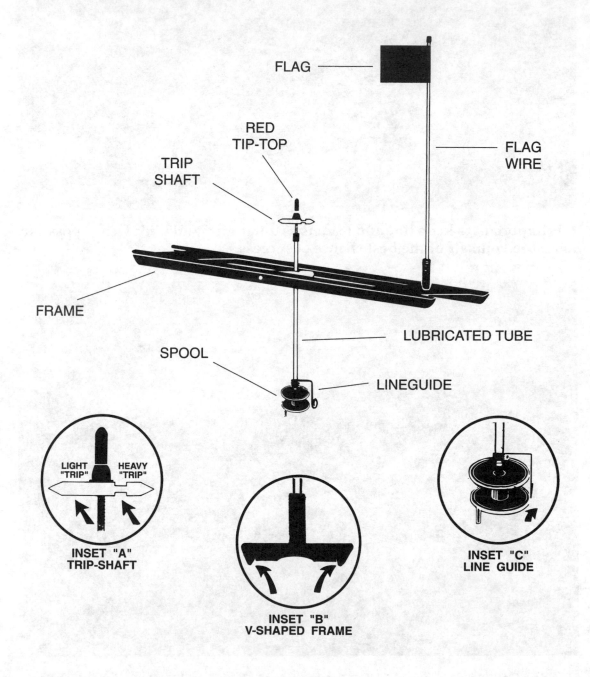

Anatomy of a Polar (HT Enterprises)

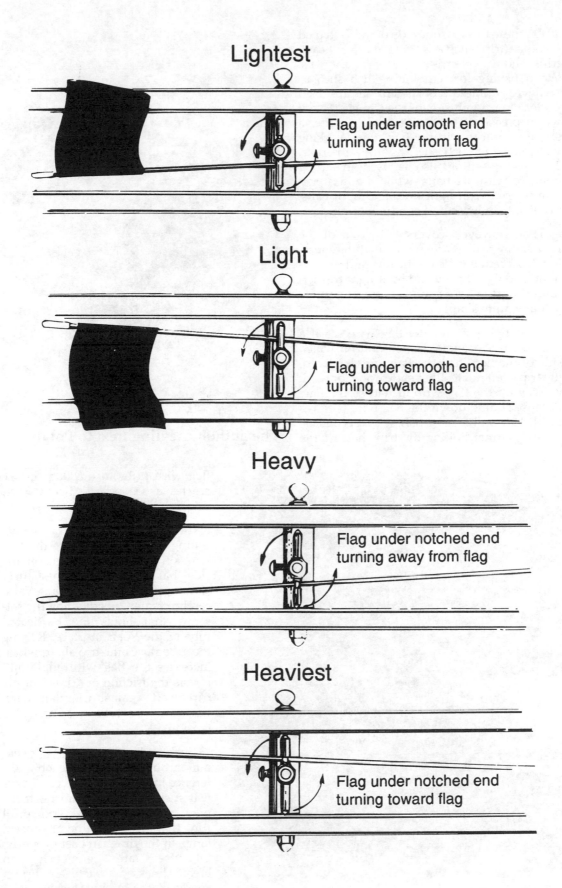

Lightest

Flag under smooth end turning away from flag

Light

Flag under smooth end turning toward flag

Heavy

Flag under notched end turning away from flag

Heaviest

Flag under notched end turning toward flag

Polar trip settings (HT Enterprises)

On these tip-ups, one side of the T-shaped spindle (trip shaft) is notched for heavy trips, and the other is smooth for light trips. When fishing for light biting fish such as walleyes, crappies, or perch, set the arm under the smooth side of the trip shaft, so it will trip easily. The grooved side requires a stronger pull to trip the flag, thus working well on larger fish such as northern pike. The heavy setting also is used in strong wind or with big baits, while the light setting is used with light lines and light baits, preferably in low-wind conditions.

That, however, covers only two of the four settings. The tricky part is differentiating between the heavy-heavy and heavy-light, and light-heavy and light-light trip settings. But don't get confused, the concept is actually quite simple.

Polar tip-ups have the flag wire set at a predetermined angle. Depending on which side of the trip shaft the flag wire is placed, the trip shaft must either slide down or work its way up the flag wire to release the flag. Because sliding down the flag wire requires much less pull from a fish, it's a secondary "light" setting. Pulling the trip shaft up the

The author kneeling next to Polar

flag wire prior to the flag release creates a secondary "heavy" setting.

To arrive at the "heavy-heavy" setting, for instance, place the flag wire on the notched end, on the side that requires the trip shaft to slide up the flag wire. "Drag" also can be created by adjusting the set-screw that holds the lubricated tube of the Polar in place. Raising the tube raises the trip shaft, which increases the flag wire angle and boosts the friction or "drag" of the trip shaft against the flag wire. Lowering the tube decreases this tension.

Such adjustments may seem minor, but they can make a big difference in ice fishing success. Large fish such as muskie and northern pike may make quick, powerful runs that can break line or cause a tangle if the drag isn't set properly. Likewise, large gamefish can break lines or backlash tip-up spools if the proper tension isn't maintained.

Aggressive northern are an excellent catch.

Waiting for the fish to make a run is a key to setting the hook.

On the flip side, less tension on the spool is critical when fishing for light biting or spooky fish, such as walleye, crappie, or perch. If these finicky species feel the resistance of a heavy drag, they may drop the bait. In either case, taking the time to set the drag properly will make for more consistent ice angling.

When I fish with large minnows and need even greater drag effect, I adjust the setscrew that holds the lubricated tube of the Polar in place. By loosening the setscrew and raising the tube (and hence the tripshaft) the flag wire angle is increased. This increases the friction of the trip shaft against the flag wire, minimizing false trips.

Line

Ice anglers constantly debate which type of line is best for tip-ups. Traditionalists use only braided "tip-up" line, which generally is made of dacron, a strong material that is easy to handle with cold hands. Admittedly,

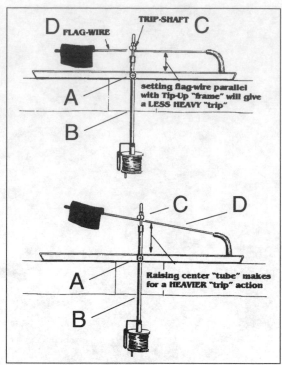

Polar drag settings

braided dacron lines function reasonably well, but they aren't up to snuff for the modern ice angler. For consistent success I've found low-diameter, teflon coated braided dacron to be a superior line for backing, because it resists freezing much better than standard braided dacron.

Vinyl-plastic coated line also prevents freeze-up, but tends to develop significant memory and coil, which you don't want. A light biting fish may straighten the coils when biting and never trip the flag. The fish can drop the bait without you ever knowing it was there.

Some anglers also use squidding lines, or even sinking tip fly lines, for spooling their tip-ups, and swear by them. Fly lines do work well on tip-ups, as they flow smoothly and evenly from the spool and are easy to handle.

In any case, tip your favorite line with a monofilament leader attached to the main line with a small #14 barrel swivel. This can double your catches on most days.

Tip-Up Rigging

All tip-up units feature similar rigging methods. My favorite terminal rigs are simple. Start by properly spooling with good line.

HT's tip-up line

When nice northern such as these begin biting, it may be necessary to switch from monofilament leaders to wire in order to hold up to their aggressive attack.

There is a difference in the quality of line, so always use a premium grade. Here's a summary of recommended line brands and types:

*HT's Tip-up line features a vinyl coating to prevent freeze-up.

*Gudebrod offers a similar freeze resistant product.

*Mason produces braided dacron line.

*Cortland Tip-Up is an excellent line.

*Tackle Marketing's Tip-Up ice line is also available in hi-visibility yellow.

*Premium fly line or squidding line.

While tip-up lines easily may last several years without showing signs of wear, I recommend changing tip-up lines at least every other year; annually when fished often. Tip-up line can rot and weaken, causing problems on the ice.

Next, attach a monofilament leader on the end of the tip-up line, using a ball-bearing barrel swivel such as a **Sampo** or **Berkley** Cross-lock.

For toothy fish such as pike, a thin, strong homemade wire leader built from quality wire (from **Sevenstrand**, **American Fishing Wire**, or **Malin**), or a good commercial design (from **Bait Rigs**, **Tackle Marketing** or **HT**) can be advantageous.

I often use pre-tied tip-up rigs specifically designed for pike, walleyes, crappies, perch, trout and others. These are available from **HT** and **Bait Rigs**. Using such rigs avoids the problem of tying multiple knots with cold fingers.

You can, of course, pre-tie your own tip-up rigs. Again, be sure to use premium lines such as **Berkley** Trilene, **DuPont** Stren, or **Bagley** Silver Thread. Cheap monofilament becomes stiff and brittle in sub-freezing temperatures. Set these rigs and place them in a spring-loaded snelled hook holder for easy access later.

I like to keep rigs with a variety of monofilament and wire leader lengths, hook sizes, and attractors, then replace them as needed in the warmth of home. Dacron tip-up line, however, is easy to handle in cold weather.

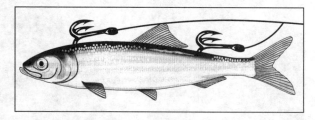

Minnow with hooks

What's the best leader length? This varies, but here's a good rule of thumb: *the clearer the water, the longer the leader.* And more importantly, rig with the lightest leader you can get away with. I've found a clear correlation between the number of hits and line classification.

If the fish are biting sluggishly, use a "stinger hook." Just tie a five to six inch length of mono to your terminal hook and then tie a second hook to the opposite end of the mono. Stick one tine of the first hook through the minnow's lips, and secure the second hook just below the dorsal fin. This enables four tines to be exposed to the fish rather than two, increasing the likelihood of a solid hook-set. Place the stinger hook with the points angled toward the tail of the bait. To make sure the rig is legal, rig a small spinner in front of the rig, effectively making it a "lure."

As for minnows, in most waters and for most species, one to five inch minnows work best, with 3-1/2-inch baits being the best all-around size. However, in deep, dark or dirty water, at night, or at first ice, larger baits tend to get better action.

When fishing dark water or aggressive fish, or when using a wind tip-up, try splicing a June bug-style spinner, a small Swedish Pimple, or a Mepps Syclops into the rig about 12 inches above the minnow. When jigged, the additional flash created by such a lure helps attract big fish.

A jigging lure such as **Bay de Noc**'s Swedish Pimple, **Northland**'s Fire Eye Jig, **HT**'s Bohemian Rocker or #6 Daphnia Jig, or the **Mepps** Syclops can be used as a substitute for a plain hook. However, tipping such a jig with a minnow seems to produce the best results, because the minnow adds natural scent, taste and texture to the presentation.

The author caught this walleye with a jig on a Polar II tip-up.

Use only small, sharp hooks when fishing live minnows. If using trebles, slip just one tine into the minnow. This increases hooking percentages greatly, because two tines are left free to stick the target fish. When placing a hook into a minnow, whether you are fishing below a stationary or wind tip-up, always hook the bait so it rests horizontally.

Position the hook just beneath the dorsal, with the point facing the bait's tail. Because baitfish can't swim backwards, gamefish usually strike baitfish head first. This will provide the optimum hooking potential.

Outstanding hooks for tip-up fishing include the extremely sharp **Partridge** VB, and models from **Mustad, VMC,** and **Eagle Claw. Tru-Turn** has excellent single hooks, and the **Excaliber** has a unique treble design that turns in the direction of the hook-set.

Whether you use a hook or a lure, always keep the hook sharp. Carefully sharpen a hook with a quality hook sharpener such as **Marine Lines**' Shur-Sharp.

Tip-Up Terminal Tackle

As a rule, avoid heavy leaders and big hooks. They're unsuitable for tip-up fishing because they spook fish even more than heavy line, and they don't hook well.

Tip the terminal rig with a small #8 to #14 hook, which will rig you up for catching crappies and perch of trophy proportions. (In many cases, no one else is fishing them!)

Small trebles increase hook-setting percentages with larger gamefish as well. For toothy fish such as the northern and walleye, a small #8 or #10 hook tends to catch between the teeth and

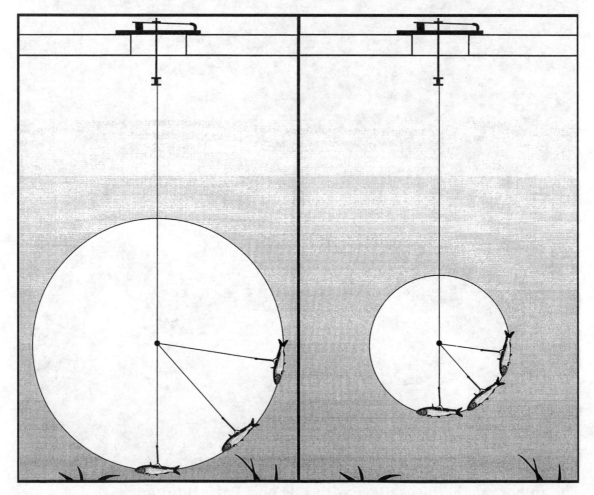

Anchoring a minnow

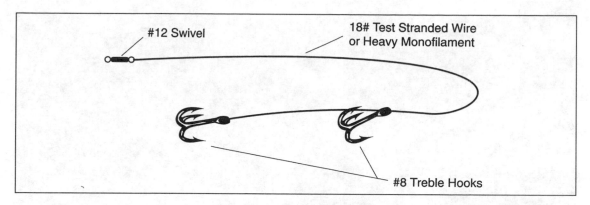

Quick Strike rig

slip into a fish's lip or jaw. A larger hook doesn't accomplish this feat easily, and won't allow you to catch a broad range of fish sizes as a small one would.

Don't think larger gamefish don't eat small to medium-size minnows. In fact, a two- or three-inch minnow is a highly versatile bait.

Another trick increasing in popularity is the "quick strike rig," which is basically a short length of monofilament tied to a treble hook, with an additional treble rigged on the opposite end of the mono. Usually I place split shot 6-12 inches up the leader to weight the rig down, especially if I'm fishing with dead bait such as smelt. This quick strike rig makes hook-setting faster, because it has twice the hook-setting potential. Add a few green and orange beads, yarn, or fish attractant to the presentation, and you may see even better catches.

As for splitshot, use enough to help your minnow get down and stay down at your chosen depth. In addition, attach sinkers far enough from the bait so they don't interfere with the desired swimming motion. A minnow weighted with a small splitshot, lure, or jig can swim around in a large circle, while a minnow "anchored" with a larger, heavier shot or lure covers less territory. Vary weight according to the activity level of the fish.

Strategic Tip-Up Placement

Structure, cover, and food are just as important to fish in winter as in summer. Therefore, high percentage tip-up spots include classic structural features, deep weed lines and openings in the weeds. Even deep water can be a form of cover if there's a shortage of shallow water structure, a great deal of noise from anglers or snowmobiles, or if the presence of deep water forage such as ciscos draw gamefish deep.

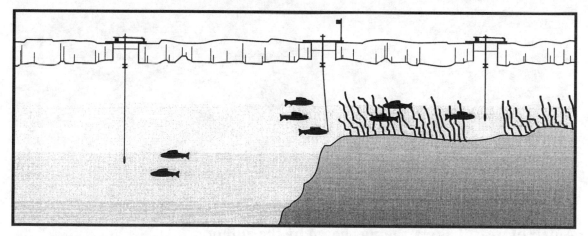

Strategic tip-up placement

A pair of nice "Lakers" being shown by the author.

By considering such factors when planning your tip-up placement, you'll cover productive water instead of randomly setting units over "aquatic deserts" with no fish.

Effective scouting for winter fish requires time. Reviewing hydrographic maps prior to getting on the ice is essential to success. Before selecting a hotspot, consider the lake type, the fish species being sought, the phase of winter, and the primary forage of your target species.

Once the preliminary study is done, search for hotspots with the aid of electronics. If you've done your homework prior to ice-up, GPS will put you close to primary areas, and sonar will help you pinpoint the structure, microstructure, and the presence of fish. If you find fish, be sure to drill many holes in your chosen area.

For example, if fishing a point with an adjacent reef nearby, drill enough holes to adequately cover the top of the point and reef, as well as surrounding drop-offs and the saddle between the reef and point. Scatter tip-ups strategically across several depth ranges in primary, high-percentage spots, leaving a few extra holes for moving tip-ups or for jigging.

I often use electronics to locate high percentage spots, drill holes over them and areas in between, then "leap frog" my tip-ups in search of fish, while jigging in the interim.

In areas allowing only two or three lines, fish with several people to cover water. Where five, six, or more lines are permitted, you can do a good job covering water with a small group or even alone.

Landing Fish

Once set up, monitor your units and wait for a strike. If a flag trips, approach the unit slowly to avoid spooking the fish. (Thinner ice carries running noise quite well.) If the trip shaft is spinning, wait until it slows, then grasp the line. Rather than setting a hook immediately, allow the fish time to pick up the bait. Once you feel the weight of the fish, set the hook with a sharp snap of your wrist and carefully pull the fish up.

Let the fish run a few feet before you set the hook. Getting a solid hook-set into the bony jaw of a walleye or northern pike is much easier if done at a wide angle, as opposed to a vertical hook-set when the fish is located directly below you.

No matter what tip-up or terminal tackle you are using, don't hurry a fish after it's hooked. Instead, play it out until it tires. This is especially important during the final moments of a fight by the hole, where most tip-up fish are lost.

Apply excessive pressure on the fish and your line during the last stage of the battle, and you'll experience the empty, sinking feeling that comes after the loud snap of breaking mono. Your last recollection will be the sight of a broken piece of line slipping down the hole as the fish darts away.

To avoid such misfortune, carefully case the fish's head into the hole as if leading its head into a landing net. A fish can't swim backwards, so if you get its head into a landing net, the fish will swim right into it. The same principle applies to ice fishing. Once the fish's head is in the hole, the fish can only swim up the hole, toward you. All you have to do is land it, provided the fish is no larger than the diameter of the hole.

For landing large gamefish, have a gaff hook handy if you plan to keep them. Simply stick the hook under a gill flap, and slide the fish onto the ice. Never attempt to lift a large fish out of the hole by the line, and never use a gaff on fish you intend to release. In such cases, grasp the fish carefully behind the head, remove the hook, shoot your photo and release the creature.

Tip-Up Lights and Other Accessories

Most tip-up accessories are designed to enhance a particular quality of a tip-up, to best adapt the unit for a certain situation. As mentioned in an earlier chapter, most tip-up lights are sold in regions where twilight and evening walleye fishing are popular. Good models include the **Rite Lite**, **Mr. Tip-Up** Headlight, and **HT**'s Micro Lite and Omni Strike Lite.

When fishing with light flag steel tip-ups or wind tip-ups, try using a small, lightweight chemi-lite. To activate such a light, just snap or bend the plastic and shake. The resulting chemical reaction emits a bright phosphorescent glow for 10-12 hours.

For best results, attach a chemi-lite to the tip of your flag steel or stick. If you're a long way from your sets, try placing the chemi-lite by the horizontal bend in the flag steel, and slide a short length of one-half inch PVC tubing over the chemi-lite to cover it. When a fish strikes, the tube will slide

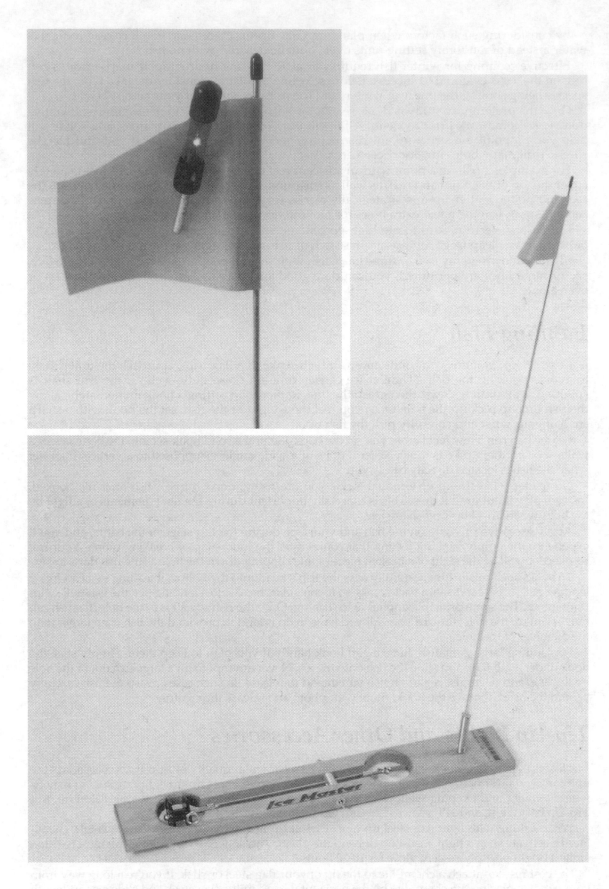

Top Left: "Omni Strike" tip-up light   Above: Telescopic flag wire

down the flag steel or stick, exposing the light and indicating a strike.

For the do-it-yourselfer, parts are available to customize or build tip-ups. HT offers a full line of spare spools, replacement flags in various colors, flag steel of various lengths and thickness, and a variety of other components.

When "low profile" tip-ups such as the Beaver Dam, Polar, or Solar are set at a distance or in deep snow, a tripped flag may be hard to see. The answer? HT's telescopic flag wire. Simply extend the telescopic flag wire to the desired height, and set your unit.

Several companies offer a simple bell or double bell set-up that clips to the flag wire of the tip-up. The bells ring when a flag trips, and continue to ring as wind vibrates the flag wire.

HT's lineholder, which clips around the spool and secures the line from unraveling when not in use, is useful. This not only enhances organization, but enhances safety by making hooks less likely to come loose.

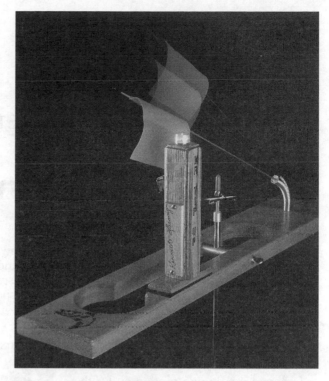

Mr. Tip-Up headlight (Mr. Tip-Up)

Homemade linemarkers, such as matches, monofilament knots, and buttons have been used for long a time. However, plastic clip-on linemarkers for tip-ups, such as those made by HT Enterprises, are much easier and more efficient.

Lubricant

Even the best sealed tube tip-ups eventually will leak lubricant. This happens more often when tip-ups are improperly stored in high temperature areas during the off-season, especially if they are stored vertically. Always store sealed tube tip-ups horizontally in a cool place.

Repacking the lubricant is a simple process with tip-ups such as HT's Polar. Turn off the tip, acorn nut and trip shaft located on top of the shaft, grasp the reel, and slide out the shaft. In the case of the Polar, replace the lubricant with **HT**'s Blu-Lube. When finished, reassemble the mechanism and wipe off any excess lubricant.

If stored properly, most units should go ten or more years without repacking. However, if lubricant leaks out, it is replaced by air. In cold temperatures, condensation builds up in the sealed tube, and it eventually freezes. This results in a sticky inoperable tip-up, and you'll need to relube.

Summary

There's more to tip-up fishing than meets the eye. But learn how to set your tip-up in just the right place, with just the right rig and bait, at just the right time, and you'll be catching fish.

Presentation options for tip-ups are endless. We're in the midst of an ice fishing revolution, and new presentation techniques for stationary, thermal, and wind tip-ups are appearing continually. Put them to work and you'll see an increase in the number of fish you ice.

Chapter 6

Jigging

I lower my jigging spoon toward the depths below, jiggling it gently. As it descends I watch it on my electronics screen. I stop its fall about six inches from bottom and begin working the bait. Soon a fish appears, approaches the bait, pauses momentarily, then swims off. I experiment with some alternative jigging motions. No response. Changing sizes, colors, and actions seems to make no difference.

I switch to a lighter action rod and lighter line. After tipping a horizontal Marmooska jig with a slice of plastic, I try again. Another fish appears, looks the bait over, nips at the lure, then swims off.

I change my jigging motion and a third fish appears. Without missing a beat, the fish strikes. In an hour, after amassing a respectable pile of jumbo perch, I leave the lake happy. Others, still fishing the lake's traditional jigging spoons, are faring poorly.

Jigging is regarded by many as the most effective approach for catching winter fish. Of course, a great deal of knowledge and skill is required to properly understand and use the tools of winter jigging. You will get the most benefit from ice rods and jigging methods by understanding what items are available and how they work. By learning to modify standard jigging methods into new, creative techniques, your ice angling can go beyond the ordinary.

There is no single, more effective method of ice fishing than modern jigging. The ability to move from hole to hole, and easily fish any depth from just under the ice to bottom with total control of your presentation, is a versatility luxury you can't surpass.

Jigging is especially popular with winter walleye anglers.

If you're still practicing the same old typical live bait, slip-bobber and minnow, or basic, traditional jigging tactics every time you ice fish, it's time you learned how to really jig. By combining both traditional and modern jigging techniques, you'll be able to apply the most effective approaches at just the right times, and maximize your catch.

Of all ice fishing methods, jigging demands the most skill. You must choose your location accurately and drill holes strategically. You must know how to use electronics to find and pattern fish, then monitor their depth, movements, activity levels, and reactions to a variety of baits and presentations. You must understand how various lures and baits demand different lines, reels, rods, and jigging methodologies. Sometimes even the most advanced angler can become confused.

Choosing the Right Rod

Why so many models? It's like golf clubs. One club simply won't do it all, because each club has a unique purpose. Likewise, no single ice rod will do it all.

I tried for much of my life to find an all-around jig rod that would handle most ice fishing situations. I finally gave up. No single rod will work in deep or shallow water, with light or heavy line, with large or tiny jigs, in various lakes, at various times, under various conditions, for any species of fish. It's impossible.

Ice rod designs have changed dramatically over the years. Today's are lighter, stronger, more sensitive, and easier to use. They're available in a wider range of styles, lengths, compositions, and handle designs than ever before.

Choosing a rod at the store

Each modern ice rod is designed to be used with a specific setup, such as micro lures and light lines, ultralight lures and lines, jigging flash lures, deep water lake trout jigging, and even "quick strike" and live bait rigging. It's no wonder a beginning angler strides confidently into his favorite bait shop, only to find the selection of ice rods overwhelming.

Proper ice rod selection requires more than just knowing how the rod will be used. It also requires knowledge of rod characteristics, including:

*Blank design
*Length
*Composition
*Action
*Power

Various reel sizes and combinations for jig poles

Crappie are considered a delicacy by most when it comes to panfish.

These aspects must then be paired with:
*Handle design
*Style
*Material
*Guides and guide placement
*Tips
*Your budget

The basics

First consider the obvious. An ice rod is designed to furnish several things:
*Leverage and flex for working a bait or lure
*Sensitivity for feeling a strike
*Strength for setting the hook
*Resistance for fighting, tiring, and icing fish

Your challenge is finding the rods that best suit your needs. To make selection easier, some ice rod manufacturers now label each rod with the correct line ratings and lure weights. Nonetheless, every angler has an individual "feel" he expects from an ice rod, so the labels aren't the final solution. Fortunately, each manufacturer offers slightly different designs, actions, and prices. This means greater selection, and a complicated process of choosing the right rod.

Ice rod features

The best way to choose the proper ice rod is by the process of elimination. Start with the basics, narrowing your choices to models labeled for your anticipated needs, then look at specific features.

First examine the rod blank (See B, page 150). Note length, composition, sensitivity, action, power and weight.

Length: Short rods may be advisable for small children or for fishing in tight quarters. However, for most applications, a two to four foot rod with a stripper guide (see C, page 150), and five or six smaller guides (see D, page 150) properly spaced and graduated in size to the tip (see E, page 150), is a standard quality rod.

A long, whippy rod is more forgiving, because a hooked fish often darts straight up. This can mean slack line and a lost fish. A longer rod, thankfully, allows you to pick up more slack when the rod is lifted.

On the other hand, a short, stiff rod allows more slack line each time you work a lure, giving looser, more natural jigging action. And just try using a rod longer than 24 inches inside most portable ice shacks!

Blank composition: While ice rods have been made from a variety of materials, most are now made of solid or hollow (tubular) fiberglass, spun fiberglass impregnated with plastic, or graphite. Fiberglass rods are popular because they're durable.

Many anglers prefer graphite, a stiffer, lighter material that transmits strikes better than fiberglass. However, graphite rods are costly and easily damaged. Today's higher grade fiberglass blanks are nearing the sensitivity of graphite at less cost, so many graphite fans are taking a second look at fiberglass and fiberglass composite designs.

Sensitivity: An important aspect of rod sensitivity is tip flexibility, or action. Varying from stiff to limber, action is determined by taper, thickness, and blank composition. A stiff action rod offers virtually no tip flexibility. A fast action rod bends only near the tip, and works best for detecting strikes and setting the hook. A medium action rod is flexible further down the blank. A slow action rod is flexible, bending more than halfway down the blank. However, a slow action rod lacks sensitivity and makes hook-sets difficult.

Power: Often confused with action, power refers to the flex over the entire blank. Long, light power rods, flexible throughout the rod length, are good choices for live bait fishing because the rod absorbs most of the shock from the hook-set, or when jigging. Consequently, baits are less likely to come loose from the hook while fishing. Also, fish feel little resistance should they shake their heads or make unexpected moves after picking up bait.

Shorter, medium power rods don't flex as much, and work better for jigging larger, heavier lures. Heavy power rods feature little if any flex and are more limited in use. They often are

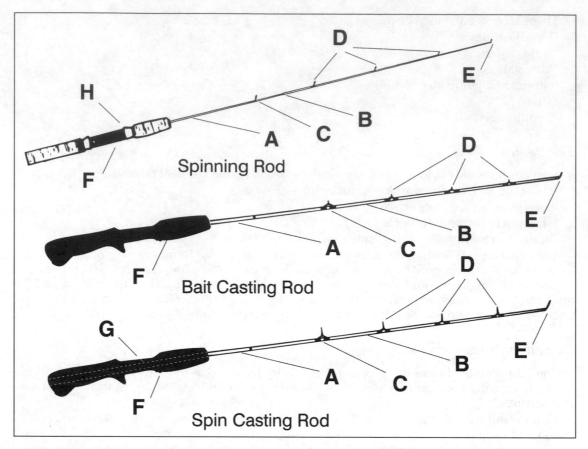

Anatomy of an ice rod

used for fishing heavy baits or thick cover, because they provide the leverage needed for presentation control, solid, quick hook-sets, and controlling fighting fish.

Weight: Obviously, a lightweight rod is easier to hold and fish, making a long day of fishing less wearisome. If you heft iron castings every day at work, weight won't be an issue for you. However, for a child or someone who doesn't do a great deal of heavy lifting, this may be an important factor.

Line guides: A quality rod features a greater number of guides than a cheap rod. These help keep line aligned with the blank for more precision. Quality guides are usually made of aluminum oxide or silicon carbide, affording less line friction when lowering your lure or fighting a fish. This minimizes line damage.

For light fishing, lightweight, single-footed guides are sufficient. Double-footed guides add weight and tend to restrict a lighter rod's action, but for heavier fishing applications, they provide strength and durability.

Handle design: (see F, above) Handle grips may be wood, cork, foam, or plastic. Wood is most sensitive, followed in order by cork, foam, and plastic. Although most handle designs feature attached reels or built-in locking reel seats, some models come with straight cork or corkalon handles with seat rings, called Tennessee-style handles. Longer foam handles are preferred for rods to be placed in rod holders.

Regardless of design, look for a blank that extends through the rod handle (see G, above). If the blank doesn't extend completely through, the handle will dampen vibrations before they reach your fingertips.

Most importantly, the handle reveals whether the rod is a jiggle stick, jig pole, spinning, or casting model. Jiggle sticks feature a simple line winder device for holding line, usually mounted on a plastic or wooden handle. Jig poles feature a plastic ice reel mounted on the same kind of handle. Spinning rods feature a straight handle and large, single footed guides (see H, page 150). Casting rods feature straight or pistol-grip designs with an underslung "trigger" and smaller, double-footed guides.

Jiggle sticks

A basic fiberglass jiggle stick, rigged with a simple line winder, is really all you need to catch fish through the ice. If you intend to keep your ice fishing simple, keep the gear simple, too. For basic, shallow water, active fish situations—farm ponds, river backwaters, and shallow, weedy lakes and bays—a jiggle stick will serve you quite well. The largest selection I've seen is available from **HT Enterprises**, although good models are available from several companies, including **Lakco**, **Schooley**, and **Northern Specialties**.

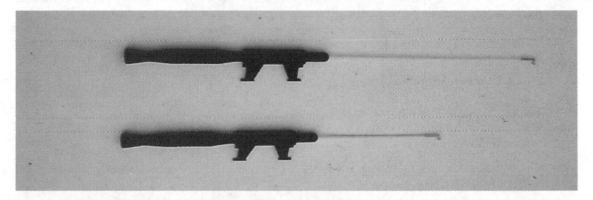

A pole and line winder are the only basics needed for fishing jiggle sticks.

Most such rods come spooled and rigged, so all you'll need to do is bait up, choose the depth you want to fish, and properly set your bobber. When a fish bites, set the hook, and, if fishing shallow enough, merely extract the fish from the hole. If the water is over six feet deep, you'll have to hand-over-hand the fish to the ice.

Examples of various common jig poles

Jig poles

Jig poles catch fish, and they are a step up from basic jiggle sticks. Jig poles are the "compact cars" of the ice rod world—reliable performance without overkill. They may not have all the features of the deluxe models, but they get you there without costing a fortune.

Jig poles generally offer more variety than jiggle sticks in terms of composition, strength, sensitivity, action, and power. Due to their ice reels, jig poles allow you to fish deeper water more easily because you can spin line from the reel to get your bait down, as well as reel fish up.

In addition, the drag control allows you to catch and fight larger fish more easily. If a large fish makes a run, you simply loosen this tension and gently "feather" the spool with your finger. This allows the fish to take line at a controlled rate.

Most ice reels also offer a depth marking system. After getting a bite, simply slip a depthmarker peg into the holes on the outside edge of the spool and reel up the fish. The line will wind around the outside of this peg. To reset depth, just lower your line until the peg is exposed. Simple, but effective.

Most anglers use a jig pole/ice reel combination in tandem with a spring bobber. This is an efficient system that allows sensitivity, strength, drag control, depth marking capability and the ability to reel up a line without interference from pegged bobbers. These are all the basic features needed in a versatile ice jigging system.

My favorite models are **HT**'s Little Jigger series, available in a variety of lengths, actions, styles, and compositions. Most of these models come spooled and rigged. Many similar models are available from companies such as **Schooley**, **Lakco**, and **Northern Specialties**.

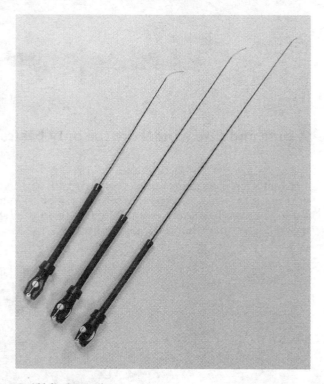

Stillfish rods

Stillfish rods

Popular in certain regions, hollow stillfish ice rods feature special stillfish reels. When using such a reel, the angler merely threads line through the inside of the rod and out the tip to a super-sensitive spring bobber. With no need for guides, the line follows the blank perfectly, and sensitivity is unsurpassed.

Because a stillfish reel has no drag, a low pick-up ratio, and a tendency to tangle, it is best used for smaller panfish in shallow water, and since the line runs through the thin blank where freeze-up

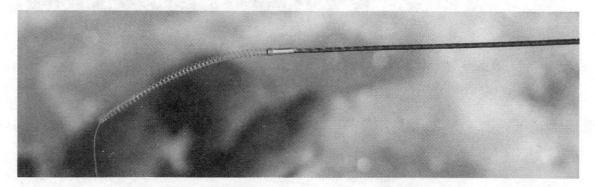

Stillfish rod tip with spring bobber

can occur, use is limited to warm days or shanties. These rods are made of fiberglass or graphite, and feature interchangeable spools.

Spinning rods

One of the most popular ice rod styles, spinning rods offer a variety of models and reliable performance with a few added goodies. They range in length from 12 inches to 6-1/2 feet, with two- to four-foot lengths being most popular.

Most spinning rods are made of fiberglass, graphite, or a blend of the two, with fiberglass models being least expensive, and graphite being most. Though graphite is the most sensitive material, a sensitive fiberglass rod will do the job for less money, and is more durable.

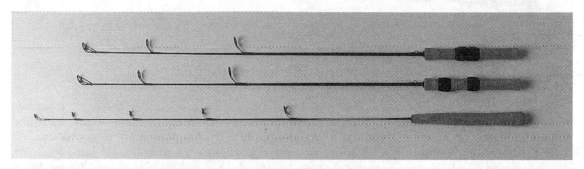

Spinning rods, walleye action

Most spinning rods feature straight cork, foam, or plastic handles. The most common fixed reel seats can be tightened on a threaded section to hold the reel firmly in place. However, some rods offer cork handles with metal or graphite seat rings. Foam and plastic are least costly, while cork handles appear on the more expensive models. As stated earlier, I prefer a handle onto which the reel can be taped, both for warmth and balance adjustment.

Want snob appeal? Try an expensive, 96 percent graphite rod with cork handle and gold-rimmed guides. If you do prefer a graphite ice rod, buy a good model, and give it special care. If you've never seen a grown ice angler cry, you will when he breaks his $30 graphite rod.

A spinning rod's stripper guide has a large diameter to gather the first large loops of line from the reel. Guides diminish in size toward the tip, though they are relatively large to minimize line friction and freeze-up.

Keep in mind action and power when choosing a spinning rod:

*Flexible, fast action, light power fiberglass rods work especially well for fishing lightweight and ultralight style lures.

*Fast action, medium power fiberglass rods, with a sturdy butt section tapering to a limber tip, provide the best general purpose action.

*Heavy action, heavy power rods are good for big fish/deep water fishing, such as when seeking lake trout.

*Spinning rods that are too flexible—slow action blanks—lack sensitivity and make hook setting difficult.

As for particular models, I prefer to make my own or go with custom designs. However, **Loomis**, **HT**, and **Berkley** produce some nice graphite models. As with any product, features and extras affect the usefulness and price of a spinning rod.

Bait and spincasting rods

Baitcasting ice rods are workhorses, designed for fishing larger, heavier baits and lures in deeper water. These rods range from two to six feet long, with power designations ranging from medium-light to extra heavy. They are especially popular among Western ice anglers seeking large trout in deep water.

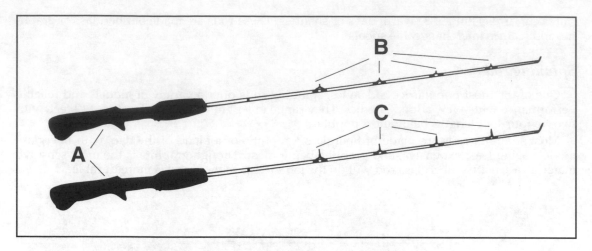

Baitcasting ice rod (top) vs. spincasting ice rod (bottom)

Spincasting rods, which accommodate a wide variety of lure sizes and weights, range from two to six feet long, and offer mostly medium and medium-heavy power designations. Both baitcasting and spincasting rods are usually made of fiberglass, graphite, or fiberglass/graphite composite.

The difference? Baitcasting rods are typically longer, heavier, and feature relatively small, low-set guides (see B, above). Spincasting rods feature shorter, lighter blanks, and larger, high-bridged guides (see C, above). Both types feature medium action that extends well down into the butt, although softer tips may be added to increase sensitivity. Most have offset handles of cork, foam, or plastic, with locking reel seats and an underslung "trigger."

Guidelines for Choosing a Rod

Your choice of rods depends on your fishing techniques. Anglers who regularly use several techniques may carry three or more rods, each set up with a different lure or live bait rig.

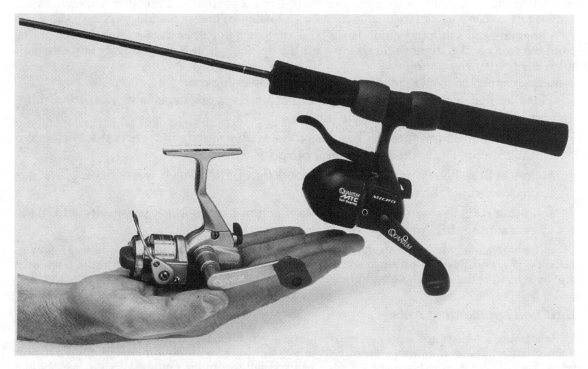

Micro rod (Zebco Corp.)

Panfish can be caught on almost any rod, but with the proper down-sized tackle, even a small sunfish may put up a respectable battle. For best results with panfish, therefore, select a fast action, light power jiggle stick or jig pole, or an ultralight or micro spinning rod with a cork or wood handle.

For larger gamefish such as walleyes that usually require lures weighing from 1/8 to 5/16-ounce, select a cork handled, two to four foot, fast action, medium power fiberglass or graphite spinning rod with larger guides. Because you'll be adjusting depth and reeling up frequently, the larger guides prevent frustrating guide freeze-up.

For live bait, a longer, cork handled, medium action, light power graphite spinning rod with large guides is a better choice than a shorter, stiffer model.

For working smaller jigs and other lures weighing from 1/16 to 3/8-ounce, a cork handled, fast action, light power graphite spinning rod is an excellent choice. It flexes easily, yet provides the power necessary to set the hook.

For working rigs weighing more than one-half ounce in deep water, a cork handled, 3-1/2 to 5-1/2 foot fast action, medium power fiberglass baitcasting rod with large guides is the best choice. Such a rod has more backbone than most spinning rods, making it better suited to fishing heavier lures and rigs.

Notice most of the rods recommended here feature fast action. Slower action rods are simply not as sensitive—an undesirable quality for light-biting winter fish.

Similarly, serious walleye anglers prefer cork handled graphite rods in most situations, because these rods transmit vibrations better than fiberglass. However, fast action compensates for sensitivity, and is found in fiberglass rods at half the price.

When fishing in timber, brush, dense weeds, or other snag-prone cover for bass, pike, or other larger gamefish, you'll need heavier gear to pull fish free of obstructions. This requires stiff action, medium and heavy power bait-casting rods.

If you pursue lake trout, especially on deep, big water such as the Great Lakes or lakes of the Canadian Shield, short, stiff bobbing sticks, or longer, medium action, medium power fiberglass spinning and baitcasting rods with long, durable foam handles will be needed. These can withstand the stress of hard-pulling, deep water presentations, and will allow solid hook-sets with long lengths of dacron or braided nylon line.)

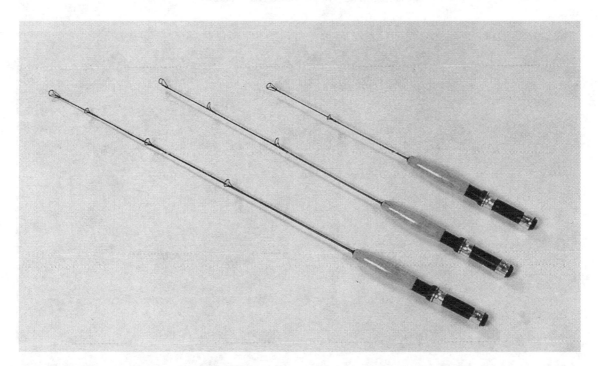

Specialty ice rods, such as HT's ice fly rods, require an ice fly reel to create the best balance.

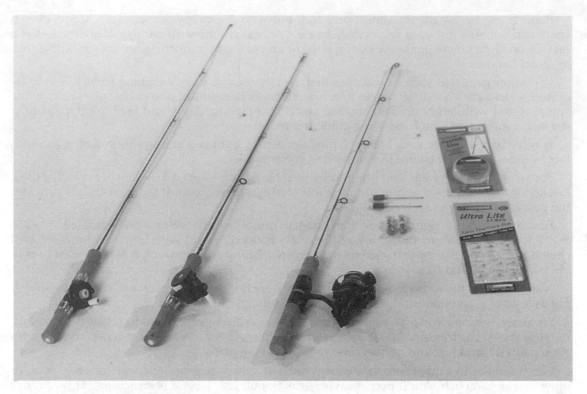

Rods, reels, lines, and lures must balance for best performance.

Tip: If the small guides of a micro rod are freezing up, try wiping a light film of petroleum jelly on the rod guides, or spraying the guides lightly with **Blakemore**'s Reel Magic. If you're worried the foreign scent might turn off fish, mix a drop of fish scent in the petroleum jelly. (The same techniques work on floats and slip-bobbers as well.

The author explaining rod action and balance at an ice fishing instructional seminar.

Lure Balance

Finally, be sure your intended lure balances with the rod you select. First, check the manufacturer's recommendations. Second, after the outfit is assembled, hang the lure about a foot below the rod to be sure the rod tip bends slightly. If the lure hardly bends the tip, or weighs it down excessively, you won't be able to work the bait and set the hook properly.

Building Your Own Rod

Some ice fishing fanatics insist on expensive, custom-built ice rods. Others are so fussy about action, power, and bend that they insist on building their own.

If you'd like to go this route, you will find a wide selection of blank styles, compositions, lengths, guide styles and sizes, handles, and reel seats available. If you don't find what you need, call a supplier such as HT Enterprises, and they will work with your sporting goods dealer to get you the supplies you desire.

Rod building can be a complex process, but for most ice rods, the key is finding a blank that approximates the action you desire, then painstakingly sanding the rod until its action is perfect for you. Next, the preferred guides and tip are neatly wrapped and glued in place, and the handle of choice is attached. A customized jig rod allows you to attain the exact blank composition, action, power, length, design, guide placement, and handle composition you desire.

The author with a customized rod

Choosing the Proper Reel

Despite the technological advances in ice fishing reels, the basic purpose of a reel remains the same: to store line, and to let it be released or retrieved as needed, smoothly and effectively.

Once you've narrowed your selection to the proper reel type, look closely at each model's construction. You will notice their housings, gears, and other parts may be made of aluminum, chrome-plated brass, graphite, or plastic. Metal or sturdy graphite housings, and machined metal gears are obvious choices for durability. Other than in specialized ice reels made of customized plastics, plastic (especially plastic gears) wears easily.

Next, consider balance. For maximum sensitivity and casting performance, a reel must properly balance your rod. Follow the manufacturer's recommended line ratings and lure weights on each respective model. If, for example, you used a reel intended for 14-25 pound line with a rod designed for 6-10 pound line, the outfit would be rear heavy. This would hamper sensations from subtle bites, reducing sensitivity.

Test the balance of the combination by mounting the reel on your chosen rod. Be sure that the reel isn't too large or small, heavy or light, and that the reel fits snugly in the reel seat. Of course, your reel's retrieve should also have a smooth, precise pickup. While not necessary, reels featuring ball bearing drives are a pleasure to fish.

Drag

Drag is possibly the most important feature to consider when purchasing a reel. When fighting a fish, a drag mechanism allows line to slip out from the spool if your quarry makes a sudden run. This reduces the chance of overstressing the line. But drag must be set correctly to function properly; it should be neither too loose nor tight.

On most ice reels, drag is controlled by a simple knob and two-washer system that applies pressure against the spool. This can be adjusted amazingly well. It offers good, reliable drag at a reasonable cost.

On baitcast and some spincast reels, drag settings are adjusted with star drag, a star-shaped adjusting wheel at the base of the reel handle. This tightens a series of metal and leather discs against the spool, causing the spool to slip less freely.

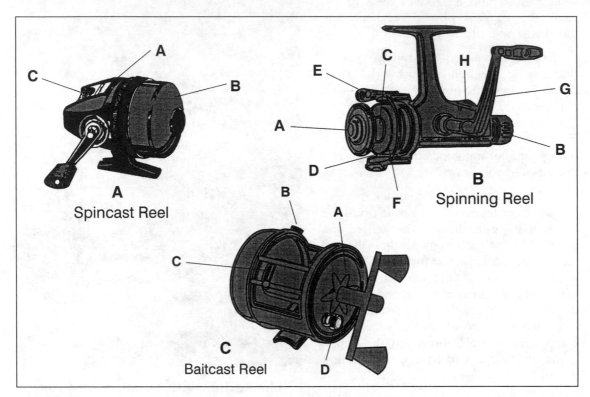

Spincast Reel

Spinning Reel

Baitcast Reel

Three primary reel types

Another type, dial drag, comes in three forms: (1) a simple dial located on top of the reel (See A on fishing reel examples, above), common on spincast reels; (2) front dial drag; and (3) rear dial drag (See B on spinning reel examples, above), both common on spinning reels. The principle is the same on all three: a series of washers either increases or decreases pressure on the spool. Front drag is typically the most precise, while rear drag is easier to use when fighting a fish.

Once you've identified the drag control, test it. If the reel doesn't come with line, have your bait shop operator wind on a few yards. Set moderate drag tension, tie your line around a solid object, and begin stepping backward, allowing the reel to spin out line. The spool should turn evenly and smoothly. Don't accept less; a sticky drag is the leading cause of lost fish.

Now turn the drag down tight, then check at various intervals as you back off the drag until the spool spins freely. You should be able to make at least two full turns (three is better) of the drag control between both extremes. A drag without such wide adjustment latitude may cause a snapped line when you're fighting big fish.

If you purchase the reel, have the dealer fully spool it for you. This can be done at home, but it may not be spooled with the correct amount of tension, causing problems later. If your reel comes with a spare spool, have that filled also.

To set the drag, tie your line to an accurate spring scale, place a moderate bend in the rod as line is paid out, and gradually adjust the drag until the scale reads approximately a third of the line test. If you're spooled with 10-pound test, the scale should indicate just over three pounds; if 6-pound test, the scale should register two pounds. By leaving two-thirds of the line strength in reserve, you dramatically reduce the chance of line breakage.

Ice reels

Ice reels

For most beginners, an ice reel is the easiest kind to use. Its function is simple: line is wrapped on a simple, single-action reel, and wound with a small handle. Drag tension is set using the adjustment knob located at the center of the reel. One nice feature to look for on an ice reel is a depthmarker system, which allows an easy return to the same depth. Simply insert a depthmarker prior to reeling up a fish. When putting the line back in the water, release line until the marker is exposed, thus stopping at the proper depth.

Spincasting reels

A spincasting reel's design is a compromise between spinning and baitcasting reels; hence its name "spincasting." Mounted on top of a rod, this reel features a spool enclosed in a conical cover (See B on spincasting reel examples, page 158). Line passes through a hole in the center of the cover, and a thumb-operated push button at the rear releases line for casting (See C on spincasting reel examples, on page 158).

When the release button is pushed, the spool moves forward so line can flow out. On the retrieve, a turn of the reel's crank retracts the spool and pops out a line pickup pin on the edge of the spool flange.

Spincast reel (Johnson Fishing)

The reel's design eliminates the release of loose coils prematurely, reducing snarls. However, because finer lines can snag inside, such a reel functions best with lines testing eight pounds or higher.

Make sure your chosen model has a smooth, reliable line pickup mechanism. On cheap spincast reels, unless the line is taut, the mechanism often fails to pick up line when the crank is turned.

Also consider the gear ratio. Modern reels are so efficient that the rate of lure retrieve is often between three and five spool revolutions for each turn of the reel handle. A high-speed reel has a gear ratio of 5:1 or 5.5:1. This is better for retrieving line quickly than a reel with a 3:1 or 4:1 ratio. Higher ratios provide better lure control, allowing you to crank fast or slow.

Spincasting reels come in a variety of sizes ranging from micro, a small panfish reel, to relatively large metal reels made for fishing heavy cover. All have dial drag mechanisms (See C on spincasting reel examples, on page 158).

Spinning reels

The spinning reel is the most popular of all reels, simply because it is the most versatile. The reel, which mounts below the rod handle, consists of an open-faced spool (See C on spinning reel examples, page 158). Line is wound on by a revolving bail, and the spool moves in and out on a center shaft for even winding (See D on spinning reel examples, page 158).

To release line, the bail is flipped back and the line is picked up with the index finger. When the line is released, it spins from the end of the open spool. With so little line friction, a spinning reel can be used with a wide range of lures and baits, including lightweight micro baits.

A quality spinning reel has a free-turning bail roller (See E on spinning reel examples, page 158) (made of stainless steel or hard metal alloy) mounted on a firmly snapping bail. Without this feature, line doesn't wind properly during retrieve, and roller abrasion wears the line unnecessarily.

A skirted spool (See F on spinning reel examples, page 158) is also necessary to cover the sides of the center shaft and rotor. If the spool has no skirt, line may slip between the spool and rotor, and tangle around the spool shaft.

Spinning reel (Silstar Corp)

Spinning reels also offer a variety of special features. Reel cranks are reversible, so they can be cranked with either right or left hand (See G on spinning reel examples, page 158). Interchangeable, pop-off spools allow line to be changed quickly. Anti-reverse devices prevent reels from backwinding when a fish is taking out line (See H on spinning reel examples, page 158). Beginners should leave the anti-reverse engaged. Experts often disengage the mechanism so they can backreel to assist the drag, should a fish make a fast run. A wide range of gear ratios are available, although 5:1 and 5.5:1 offer the most lure control.

Drag is usually regulated by a dial at the front of the spool or rear of the reel. While rear drag is easier to adjust while playing a fish, front drag is generally smoother. Either can be set to handle even large fish on light lines.

Spinning reels come in a variety of sizes: micro, ultralight, light, medium, and large. Micro and ultralight reels are designed for light line fishing. Light spinning reels are a good all around choice for panfish, small bass, and walleye, while medium reels are the choice for larger bass, walleye, and light pike. Large spinning reels are designed primarily for pike and muskie.

Underspin reels

This hybrid reel releases line with the pull of a trigger like a spincast reel, but mounts beneath the rod to balance like a spinning reel. Basically, it looks like an upside down spincast reel.

Baitcasting reels

A baitcasting reel acts as a winch to make retrieval of larger, heavier lures easier, as well as provide tremendous power. It works best with lures weighing more than 3/8-ounce.

A baitcasting reel mounts atop the rod handle and features a freespooling spool, meaning the spool revolves as the line runs out. A button releases the spool into the release position (See B on baitcasting reel examples, page 158).

Almost every modern baitcasting reel features a level-wind mechanism to spool line evenly, and an anti-reverse that can be set to keep the spool from turning backwards freely, (See C on baitcasting reel examples, page 158) since this increases friction when releasing line.

If you pull line from a baitcasting reel too quickly, the line will overrun itself, and cause the proverbial backlash. To prevent this, an angler must use thumb pressure to feather the spool and control the flow of line off the spool.

Some top quality baitcast reels have a magnetic anti-backlash device that places slight pressure on the spool (See D on baitcasting reel examples, page 158). Nonetheless, light thumb pressure further reduces the chance of backlash and enables the lure to be dropped quickly. Some baitcasting reels also come with interchangeable spools.

These reels come in a variety of sizes, ranging from small for relatively light fishing, medium for heavier jigging, and heavy for heavy jigging. On most baitcast reels, a star drag allows the line to be pulled from the reel when playing a large fish (See A on baitcasting reel examples, page 158).

Reel Care

Today's reels offer quality far superior to reels of only a few years ago. They're more reliable, and using them is easier and more pleasurable than ever. Nonetheless, they need proper care and maintenance, and most of this care reflects common sense. Ultimately, such effort will make your fishing more efficient and effective.

*Always keep a reel clean and dry, by keeping it free of water, slush, and snow.

*Fill the spool properly. Most manufacturers recommend to within one-eighth inch of the spool's lip.

*Periodically lubricate the reel. On a spinning reel, apply silicone spray to each side of the bail assembly to prevent binding. Do the same for the worm gears on a baitcast reel. On any reel, lift off the spool and coat the spindle with light machine oil, then remove the housing cover and spread a few drops on the internal gears. In really cold weather, replace heavy gear lubricant with freeze-proof tip-up lubricant.

Lines

In recent years, almost every kind of line has been changed dramatically for the better. Lines have gotten thinner and less visible, yet stronger, and with high knot strength and low memory.

Line is the only connection between you and the fish, so don't skimp with bargain brand lines, especially when ice fishing. Monofilament lines get stiff and coiled, and generally act strange in cold weather. In such weather, a bargain brand can be a disaster. So stick with premium, proven brands:

*Berkley offers an excellent lineup, including Trilene XL and XT, which are specially designed for ice fishing applications, and Gorilla braided nylon line.

*DuPont's fine lineup includes Stren, Magna-Thin, and Kevlar braided nylon. DuPont and Berkley each

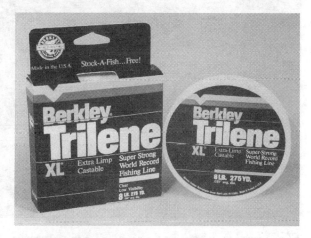

Standard monofilament line, Berkley trilene (Berkley)

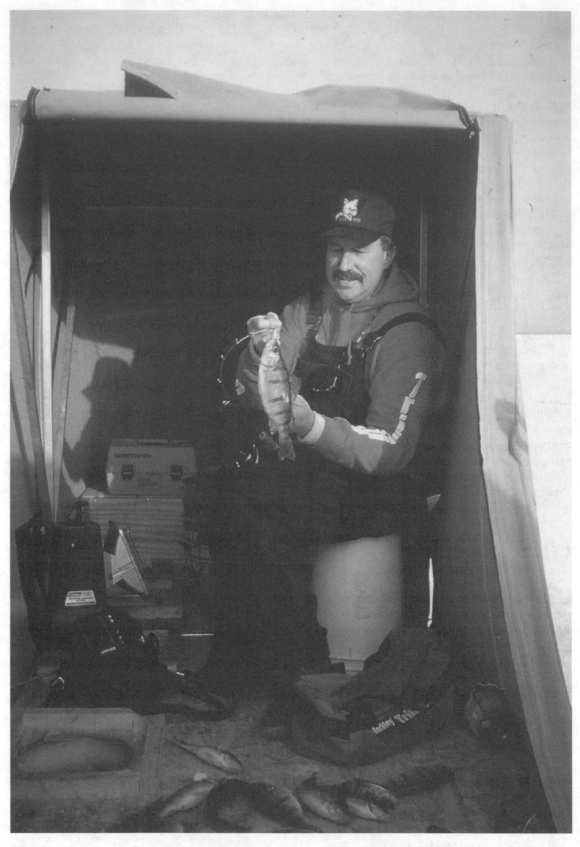

Electronics have led many jig fisherman to one of the most sought after panfish, the jumbo perch.

offer low-visibility clear or green line, and hi-visibility fluorescent line.

*__Bagley__ has an exceptional all-weather formula line under the Silver Thread label, as well as Super Braid braided monofilament.

*__Gudebrod__'s one-half pound Micro Mono, and __HT__'s one-half, three-quarter, one, and two pound Panfish Line are among the best ounce-rated lines I have seen on the U.S. market.

*__Cortland__ offers Miracle Mono, a high-visibility fluorescent yellow monofilament that makes seeing light strikes easier.

*__Fenwick__ also offers very good line.

Micro/panfish lines

Years ago, some veteran ice anglers who realized the value of low-diameter micro lines began using nylon sewing thread. Although this thread works, its diameters aren't always consistent, and thread isn't subject to standardized diameter or pound-test ratings.

Now that micro and panfish lines are commercially available, I've grown fond of them. Such lines for ice fishing may include, but are not limited to, fly fishing leader material. Fly fishing brands such as __Aeon__, __Cortland__, __Climax__, __Dai Riki__ and other premium tippets make excellent micro ice fishing lines.

I listed the best domestic brands earlier, but a number of micro monofilaments are imported from Europe. These are excellent lines, but be warned: they are labeled in diameter, rather than pound or ounce-test ratings, so unless you have a cross-reference table, you'll have to be careful when choosing the right line for your ice fishing application.

Ultralight lines

Ultralight lines, by my definition, are those of two, three, and four pound test. The brands listed at the beginning of this section are all excellent. In addition, __R.J. Tackle__ and __Cabela's__ offer very good products.

When choosing ultralight lines, look for low diameter, high strength, superior knot strength, shock resistance, abrasion resistance, and low memory. Lines with these qualities won't easily weaken, break, or tangle, and will provide the ultimate combination of control and sensitivity in your presentation.

Standard monofilaments

Standard monofilaments are the commonly available 5-40 pound test lines. These cover most ice fishing situations, and any angler who fishes open water is familiar with such lines. Just keep in mind that ice fishing, like open water fishing, demands use of the lightest line possible, although heavier monofilaments may be used on handlines or tip-ups.

Braided nylon

Misinformation regarding this line is common. Anglers who try fishing braided lines just as they do standard monofilaments are in for trouble. This relatively new category of ice fishing monofilaments is growing in popularity, and braided lines are available from the above-listed makers, as well as Spiderwire and others.

Braided lines should be limited to specific uses. If used incorrectly, this line can slice rod guides in two. In fact, it's so strong that anglers who have applied excessive pressure have broken their ice rods!

The reason is that braided lines hardly stretch. Conventional monofilament lines stretch between 22 and 30 percent, while braided monofilaments stretch only three to four percent. This aids in better hook-sets when fishing bony-mouthed fish, especially in deep water jigging situations.

Braided monofilaments work well for precision jigging of hard-mouthed, deep water fish. They offer exceptional lure control, low stretch on the hook-set, superior sensitivity, and quick, solid hook-sets.

However, braided line has some serious drawbacks. First, because the line has low shock resistance, if a fish hits hard or runs fast, the line is much more susceptible to breakage than standard monofilament unless the ice rod has plenty of "give." Therefore, braided monofilaments are *not* good line for stiff jigging rods, and they make poor tip-up leader material. Second, "flat" braided lines twist easily if used on spinning gear, although the conical cross-section lines seem to be better.

Third, if a fish suddenly runs toward you, you'll see approximately 25 percent more slack in your line than with monofilaments. A monofilament's line stretch works in your favor by holding the bend in your rod.

Fourth, because the line doesn't stretch, a hook is more apt to come loose. For instance, in soft-mouthed fish such as a crappie, a hole may actually form around the hook, making it vulnerable to coming out. A longer, lighter ice rod can compensate for this tendency.

Fifth, knot strength is difficult to attain with braided monos. Knots tied with these lines can slip easily, so tie knots carefully. Many ice anglers experienced with braided lines recommend double-line knots such as the Palomar, or modified, improved clinch style knots featuring double loops through the hook-eye. Special adhesives are available to strengthen knots in braided nylon.

Braided lines (Berkley)

The advantages of ice fishing with braided lines are clear, but limited. Anglers must use and rig them properly in the correct situations.

Balanced Tackle

A brown trout caught jigging

Ice jigging requires balanced tackle. Don't make the common mistake of placing heavy, bulky reels on lightweight ice rods. Instead, use the smallest reel you can find, making sure it has a smooth drag and a silky retrieve.

Always choose the lightest line possible. Line tends to magnify underwater, and looks larger under the ice than on top. In addition, water under the ice can be exceptionally clear because particulate settle and many algal blooms die off.

Don't give yourself too little line. It's the only thing between you and the fish, and while small line diameter makes your lure appear more natural and increases your sensitivity, underpowered line leaves you at serious risk of breakage.

A good compromise is a fast-action rod, a quality reel with a light, reliable, precision drag, and a slightly lighter line. The fast rod tip will absorb some of the hook-set shock, and the smooth drag will relieve line stress during hook-sets and while fighting fish.

Jigging Sensitively

Winter fish hit subtly and you'll feel almost nothing when they strike. Therefore, learn to *see* strikes, rather than feel them. With each slight movement of the rod, make the lure quiver slightly when jigged. Should a panfish strike, the quivering will stop and register a strike at the rod tip. This is especially true of big fish, so rather than waiting for a smashing hit, look for tiny differences in feel. This is a key to winter jigging success.

Sensitive ice rods certainly help, but you must develop a seventh sense, maintaining an eagle eye on your rod tip and line. By concentrating on your rod tip and line, no matter which style you are using, you will notice subtle twitches and tension releases caused by slack line, or you may sense a slightly different "feel" of your jig. If this happens, don't hesitate; set the hook immediately! Even if you were mistaken, giving your jig an extra hard bounce probably will attract fish.

Fish displayed on electronics

Evaluating Ice Jigging Presentation

Many ice anglers are good at reasoning why fish *don't* bite when fishing is bad, but neglect to consider why the fish *do* bite when the fishing is good. Don't fall into this pattern. Always question and experiment regardless of how many fish you are or aren't catching. Remember, the fish are always telling you something.

After a fish hits, evaluate. Did the fish hit hard or light? Were you jigging up or down? Fast or slow? The answers to such questions will help piece together the fish's mood and activity level—a critical part of choosing the best jigging pattern.

Vertical jigging probably is the most exact way to fish a structural element, for several reasons. First, such jigging keeps your bait within the cone of your depthfinder. This lets you know where your jig is in relation to the fish below, and, more importantly, how they're responding to it.

Secondly, you will be working a precise location, thus presenting your lure exactly where you want it. Your line will remain straight below you.

Thirdly, if you're fishing from a shelter, or your rod tip is held near the water with a minimum amount of line exposed to the wind, your sensitivity is increased dramatically. That boosts your advantage when fishing a neutrally active school holding tightly to secondary structure such as pockets in weeds, a turn along a prominent weed line, or an opening between large rocks.

However, these advantages also conceal one major disadvantage: vertical jigging can't cover much area at one time. In summer, you can slow troll, work a shoreline or depth contour with an electric motor. In winter, you're strapped to one hole in the ice. You'll therefore have to beat

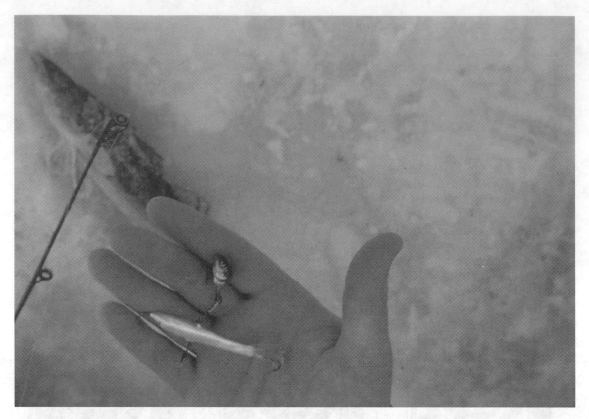

Tipping lures such as this Rapala can be a very effective presentation.

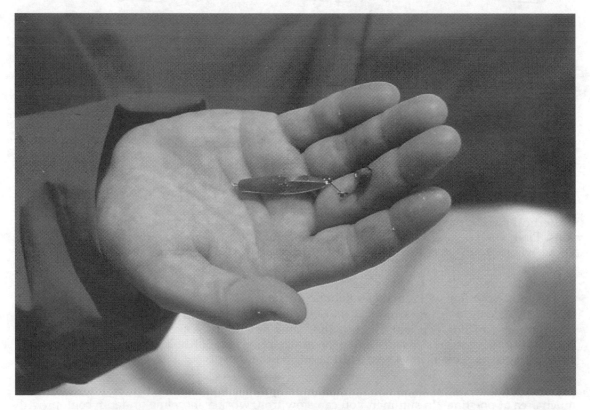

A Marmooska spoon tipped with a minnow head

the odds with mobility, electronics, and experimentation with jigging techniques to attract and trigger fish.

The standard winter jigging method of working your lure a foot or so up and down, while using a medium-speed lift, and a fall-and-drift-back pattern is often effective. The lift creates fish-attracting flashes and vibrations, and the drop triggers hits.

However, this traditional method is merely the foundation of a complex series of jigging systems. Just as fish prefer different sizes, styles, and colors of jigging lures at different times, for different activity levels, various species often show preferences for different jigging speeds and jigging motions.

Speed control depends primarily on how fast you jig, but also is controlled by factors many ice anglers often overlook, including lure size, shape, and line diameter. Simply put, heavier lines are thicker and offer more water resistance than light lines, thus slowing a lure's fall. In deep water fishing, water resistance becomes a major

When jigging from a shelter your jigging control is increased dramatically, because the effect of the wind is eliminated.

factor, especially when fishing a heavier, thicker diameter line. On the other hand, light line increases lure action and your sense of feel, so carefully balance these variables of your presentation for the best results.

Large, round, heavy-bodied lures drop relatively fast, while smaller, lighter, flat, or bent-shaped, finned lures tend to flutter down slowly and enticingly, or glide out to the side. Always try a variety of jigging methods with each lure style and jigging speed:

*Repetitious, rhythmic movements interspersed with erratic lift falls

*Wide rocking motions

*Short fluttering movements

*Various swimming retrieves

*Bottom-bumping presentations

*Slight shimmying or shivering motions

Remember, while "hard" jigs—quick, short hopping motions interspersed with big jumps or "ripping" motions—may attract and trigger active fish, "soft" jigs—less aggressive jigging methods—tend to work better for neutral and inactive fish.

The most productive jigging methods also depend on the primary forage of the fish you are seeking. For example, if the fish are foraging in thick cover on or near bottom, they're likely feeding on slow-moving bottom roving insects or worms. In such a case, slow, meticulous jiggling motions with small lures directly on the bottom often will attract the most attention.

Given such a situation, try bottom-skipping first. Drop your bait to the bottom and gently "skip" it to attract fish, then gently tick the tops of the cover or bottom while jigging in a steady, rhythmic shimmying motion using short one-sixteenth inch movements. Gradually work your way up and back down again. You will not only catch more fish by covering water more effectively, you will sense strikes better as well, because this technique prevents slack.

Presentation by rod and reel can yield large walleye during peak periods.

For active fish, bottom-dropping is a productive technique. Allow the lure to settle to bottom, pause, sweep it up a short distance, then pause again before lowering it back to bottom. Repeat the sequence.

Variations of these soft jigging tactics also work well at various depths when fish are feeding on slow-moving, suspended plankton. However, when your quarry is actively foraging on baitfish, wider fluttering motions with larger baits usually work better. Drop the lure to bottom, or any depth where fish are feeding, then abruptly snap or work the lure upward and back down again, pausing for fairly short periods of time between such movements.

These snap-jigging modifications are excellent beginner's techniques. New ice anglers often experience subtle strikes, but, unaware that a fish ever struck the lure, never set the hook. The art of snap-jigging compensates for such errors, because the angler often inadvertently sets the hook while merely working the lure.

At times, aggressive, flashy "pops" of the bait, interspersed with a slight jigging motion are good. In fact, thousands of variations of these basic techniques can work well, depending on the conditions. Therefore, experiment constantly in numerous locations, using electronics to monitor the fish's responses to each lure and every movement. Match your jigging motions and actions to the conditions at hand and thus maximize your catch.

Short strikers

Winter fish occasionally short strike. Each time this happens to me, I wonder, if a fish strikes, it must want to eat, so why doesn't it take the whole thing? The answer is fairly simple.

When a fish approaches a bait, it flares its gills, expecting the bait to drop into its mouth. However, if the jig is too heavy or the line is too tight, the bait moves only part way, unnaturally, resulting in a short strike.

To counteract this problem, you sometimes can tease a fish into taking a bait. Try pulling gently on the line to make the fish worry about the bait getting away, then suddenly go slack with it, but don't overdo it and spook the wary fish.

The right rod and reel combination, with a selection of successful jigs, can be used to catch fish such as this trout.

Also try running the line between your fingers while lifting slowly with the rod tip. Lifting the rod places just enough pressure on the bait so the fish feels insecure about its grip and moves in for a better bite, while your fingers can feel the action through the line. When the fish hits, set the hook immediately.

Many more such techniques, especially regarding lure modification, will be discussed in the chapter on ice lures. For now, let's look at a common topic of discussion among modern ice anglers.

Jigging or tip-ups—which is better?

Which is the superior method of ice fishing—jigging or tip-ups? After thousands of hours of experimentation, my answer is: "It depends." Some days, under some conditions, jigging will outproduce tip-ups 3:1. Other days, tip-ups are a sure bet, while jigging won't buy a fish.

I've found that the best way to obtain solid facts about this topic is to use both approaches side by side, under the same set of variables. Do this repeatedly, and keep notes. Eventually you will have some clues for predicting the right presentations for a variety of situations. Of course, such predictions will never be fully accurate, but the more you do it, the more consistent your fishing will be.

The following are my observations of the advantages of each system.

The advantages of tip-ups

During winter, predators such as perch, northern pike, walleye, and lake trout scatter and move often, usually in search of food. A presentation with the right bait, offered in a high-percentage area, is the best way to catch these fish. And when you know fish are present because electronics have revealed them, a tip-up will wait until they become active.

If a location isn't holding fish, but is along an identified migration route or in a spot where fish may eventually concentrate, a tip-up will announce when they have arrived. Unlike an angler, a tip-up has infinite patience. It will sit and wait until the fish are willing to cooperate.

By setting several tip-ups in a high-percentage area, you will cover a lot of water thoroughly. The tip-ups that are most active will help you establish a pattern.

Although a tip-up is "old" technology, its common use in modern ice fishing proves its effectiveness. Consider, for instance, a live minnow rigged below a fixed position tip-up. The minnow fins gently in place until a fish approaches, when it will try to escape. This is a realistic presentation. Even the most advanced jigger would have difficulty duplicating such movement.

The jigging enthusiast will argue that a set bait is a disadvantage, because motion is needed to attract distant fish to the bait. With the motion, flash, vibration, and action of a jig, nearby fish might not even see a bait finning gently below a tip-up.

The tip-up angler may counter with wind tip-ups, noting that they keep the bait moving and struggling, drawing fish in from a distance, whether the bait is live or dead.

Of course, the jigger will point out that constant movement could be considering "overjigging," whereas jigging allows precise control of motion imparted to the jig.

Set correctly, however, the wind tip-up can achieve almost any amount of movement. If the wind fan is positioned parallel to the ice it catches little wind, imparting only slight action to the bait. An increase of the angle to the arm increases the amount of jigging action.

I use tip-ups most of the time, but I'm not a "single method Sam." Because jigging is more versatile than tip-ups, I refuse to limit myself to a tip-ups-only approach. When the time is right, I jig.

The advantages of jigging

Using a wind tip-up is like using the automatic pilot on an aircraft. It works fine when cruising, but you can't use it when details are critical, such as during take-off or landing. In these instances, there's no substitute for a manned cockpit and manual control. That's jigging.

Wind tip-ups will function in certain situations just fine, but when it comes to the ultimate in control, the wind tip-up—the "automatic pilot"—must be set aside for the refinements offered by manual jigging.

A lively minnow suspended in one spot below a tip-up may trigger a fish into hitting, but lacks the power to draw fish in from a distance the way a precisely controlled, moving minnow can. Thus, jigging can be a more effective approach than tip-ups when seeking active fish. Just as a spin-

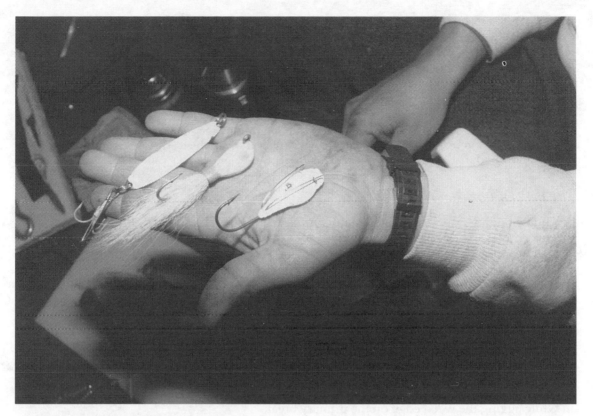

Commonly used lake trout jigs

Jigging presentations can offer variety. This rattlebait uses sound to attract or tempt fish to bite.

nerbait often outfishes a bobber and minnow during summer when the fish are active, the jig covers more water than just one depth strata. It enables you to draw the bait past more active fish.

The only difference between the spinnerbait and jigging lure is that the jigging lure works vertically instead of horizontally. This is good, because the fish are less active in winter, so a fast-moving bait zipping by probably wouldn't draw much attention.

Another, obvious reason a jigging lure outproduces a stationary minnow is that the lure is controllable. You dictate when the lure moves, as well as how fast, and how far. By experimenting with a combination of movements and pauses, you can determine precisely which is drawing the most hits. If the fish stop responding, you can change any of the variables. The key is finding the right combination, and that's up to you.

The best of both worlds

Understanding how to apply the right approach, in the right location, at the right instant, is what separates the average ice angler from an expert. The process of deciphering this proper ratio of movement to pauses can be complex.

Suppose you are ice fishing for walleye, and have just marked a shoreline bar covered with weeds. It is 10 feet deep, and drops off quickly into 30 feet of water to create a distinct weed line. Walleye will normally hold on such a weed line, though they may move up onto the flat or down on the base of the break. Even if several anglers were working together, that is a great deal of water to cover, which brings us back to the question at hand: what's the best approach, tip-ups or jigging?

In most situations, this one included, I feel it's best to combine the advantages of both approaches rather than limit myself to one. If my electronics had revealed fish in the area, I would set tip-ups baited with minnows on the weed line, the flat, and the base of the drop-off, all while jigging the weed edge on the primary break.

If I don't happen upon a pattern at the weed line because the fish are feeding on the flat at the base of the drop-off, I needn't worry. My tip-ups in that area will clue me in.

If the fish move onto the flat, other tip-ups will indicate the change. If a fish is caught on a tip-up, I might decide to jig in that area, and move those tip-ups elsewhere to catch another movement. If a tip-up trips but misses the fish, I usually pull the unit and begin jigging in the same hole, knowing that at least one active fish is nearby. If I haven't spooked that fish, this often works.

When using this strategy the primary approach is jigging, but tip-ups are used to establish exactly where the fish are and where they are moving. This approach works best when fishing with a group of anglers. By setting numerous tip-ups and leaving plenty of extra holes for jigging, you increase your coverage area tremendously and are more likely to latch onto the pattern more quickly.

Even when one approach is working far better than the other, I assume that nothing is ever 100 percent. Rather than risk missing fish, I keep the odds in my favor by keeping both approaches, and ultimately, catching more fish. That, after all, is the reason I'm out there in the first place.

An angler reaching for a walleye

Chapter 7

Ice Lures

*F*or the open water season, many anglers purchase a wide variety of lures in different styles, sizes, and colors. They buy stick baits, topwater plugs, crankbaits, spinnerbaits, jigs, spoons, and plastics. From these they select the baits needed for particular purposes, yet many of these same anglers don't think twice before purchasing an ice lure. They buy teardrops or spoons but pay little attention to their design, style, size, or color. They give the same lack of consideration to any other baits they might purchase. Same lakes, same fish. So why the lack of careful bait choice?

Knowledgeable, successful ice anglers don't make lure selections based on whim. Instead, they carefully match lure styles, sizes, colors, and designs with jigging methods that best suit the given conditions. They change as fish activity levels and moods change, which can be sudden and frequent.

Too often, ice anglers scramble to find what the nearby "lucky" angler is having success with. However, by the time others discover what he or she is using, that lucky angler may have already switched to a different presentation or moved on to another location, following the active school.

Ice lure versatility is to presentation what mobility is to winter location. You already understand the importance of moving from structure to structure and hole to hole to find the best combination of structure, cover, and forage. The same principle applies to lures. You must shift strategically from lure to lure to find the best combination of lure style, size, color, and jigging action.

Most anglers simply don't understand modern ice lure technology. Many continue using the same presentations that have produced results in the past, without being versatile or innovative. A mistake.

Consistency in winter catches requires carrying a variety of lures and knowing how to use each lure most effectively. Aids such as lake maps, electronics, specialized rods, reels, and lines are great, but they're a waste of money if you lack one critical variable: lure choice.

For consistent catches, the ice angler must rely on an organized system for determining the best combinations. A key step in accomplishing this feat is categorizing jigging lures. This can be complex, and like summer lures, would require an encyclopedia to detail all the classifications, designs, styles, and types. Here we'll cover the basics—even some of the details—and once you're on the ice, you can pick up the rest on your own.

Ice Lure Classification

Seven general ice lure groups exist, each with its own actions and designs that best suit specific sets of conditions. The groups are:

1. Swimming minnows/side planing lures and swimming jigs
2. Jigging spoons
3. Vibrating blades
4. Rattlebaits
5. Teardrops, leadhead jigs, and ice flies
6. Plastics
7. Micro baits

By understanding these basic classifications, you can build a diverse, structurally sound system for patterning most species of fish consistently throughout the winter. Here's how the system works.

Swimming/side-planing lures

There are two types of swimming or side-planing lures: jigging minnows and swimming jigs.

Jigging minnows have cylindrical, minnow-shaped lead bodies with an attachment eye molded in the center of the back, an ultra-sharp rig hook pointing up on each end, and one loose treble dangling from the center. Examples include **Normark**'s Jigging Rapala, **HT**'s Walleye Ice Jig and Marmooska Minnow, and **K & E**'s Nordic Minnow.

Jig these baits by lifting the lure with a sharp twitch, then lowering the bait and pausing. The lure will swim up and out and return in a quarter or half-circle before gliding back to its original position. This will allow you to cover a much larger area than can be done with live bait or most standard ice lures.

Experiment with various height lifts, then pause for different lengths of time between movements. This gives fish a chance to strike, and will help you determine their activity levels. When fish are aggressive, high lifts and short pauses generally produce best.

One of the main reasons for lost fish is dull hooks, so after selecting a swimming lure, sharpen each hook to a fine point, particularly the center treble on a jigging minnow, as fish often strike such a lure in the center.

Always attach a swimming lure directly to the line, tip it with a grub, minnow head, or (better yet) a live minnow. Match jig weight to minnow size, using the largest minnow you can effectively fish and still keep lure action realistic. For example, a large minnow will actively swim on a one-eighth ounce swimming lure, but likely will twist the line and ruin the action of the lure.

Choosing lures in the store

Swimming jigs generally take two forms: a winged leadhead jig, or an elongated, bent spoon shape.

My favorite examples of winged leadhead jigs include **Northland**'s Airplane Jig and **System Tackle**'s Walleye Flyer. These baits are jigged much like a swimming minnow, respond similarly, and also are capable of swimming in complete circles when worked. However, they pro-

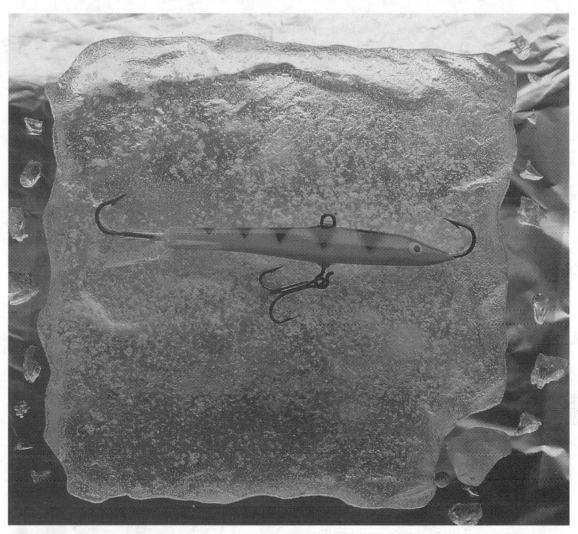

Jigging minnow style lure, the Jigging Rapala

duce wide, relatively slow falls, which are better suited to fishing less aggressive fish, or unschooled, less competitive fish.

Elongated bent spoon designs include:

***HT**'s Ice 'N' Spoons, which feature a lifelike swimming action.

***Bad Dog**'s Crippled Willow, that flutters with a realistic motion. Its offset hook angle and reversed bend deliver excellent hooking percentages.

***Custom Jigs and Spins**' Striper Special, **K & E**'s Super-Rocker and Walleye Jigger, and **Northland**'s Fire-Eye Minnow are fished similarly and produce similar reactions. While capable of swimming in tight, complete circles, they generally dart out just to the side, and wiggle or swim back to their original position in a quarter or half-circle.

To create maximum action with a bent spoon, sweep the rod tip upward a foot or more and allow the lure to settle, following the lure down with your rod tip. Pause for a few seconds, then make another sweep. In response, such a bait will flutter down actively, much like an injured minnow, thus attracting virtually any gamefish.

For best results, always tip a jigging minnow or swimming jig with a grub or minnow head, and attach the lure directly to the line.

Jigging spoons

Jigging spoons are the largest lure category in ice fishing, and next to teardrops, offer the largest selection of models from which to choose. Jigging spoons for ice fishing are similar to the jigging spoons for open water fishing, but usually are smaller and narrower. They feature little if any action when pulled upward, but tumble seductively to the side when allowed to sink under a slack line.

Examples in this category include:

*HT's Marmooska Spoons

*Bay de Noc's Swedish Pimples, Vinglas and Flute Spoons

*Acme's Kastmaster and Fjord Spoons

*Fred Arbogast's Doctor Spoons

*Williams' Ice Jigs, Dartees and Wabler

*Bait Rigs' Willospoons

*Bass 'N Baits' Rattlin' Snakie Jigging Spoons

*Jig-A-Whopper's Hawger Spoons

*Luhr Jensen's Crippled Herrings, Mr. Champs, Super-Dupers and Krocodile Spoons

*Normark's Pilkies

*Mepps' Syclops

*Reef Runner's Slender Spoons

*Eppinger's Dardevle

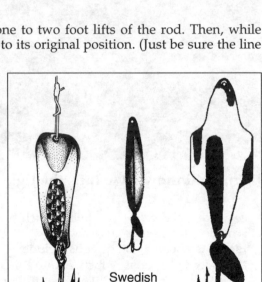

Swimming style lure, Northland Airplane Jig

To work a flash lure, jig upward with sharp, one to two foot lifts of the rod. Then, while keeping the line tight, immediately return the rod to its original position. (Just be sure the line isn't so tight that it interferes with the action of the jig.) The lure will respond by erratically fluttering and flashing its way down, while allowing you enough contact with the jig so that you can set the hook if a fish should strike. Wait for your lure to settle, then lift the lure a few feet before dropping it again.

The resulting flash and movement will resemble a wounded minnow that attracts fish. This action often draws and triggers strikes from fish that would refuse other presentations. The tantalizing up and down motion is hard for a fish to resist.

Anglers usually tip these lures with whole or cut minnows, pork rind strips or fish eyes, and attach them with a split ring to maximize lure appeal and action.

As a rule of thumb, use lighter, small lures in shallow water or for panfish. Use heavier lures in flowing water, deep water, or for large game-fish. The chosen lure always should be heavy enough to reach the desired depth, but not so heavy that it sinks too fast, especially if the fish are being fussy. As a general rule, allow about one-eighth ounce for every 10 feet of water.

Slender Spoon

Swedish Pimple Spoon

Vingla Spoon

Jigging spoons

Vibrating blades

Vibrating blades, or bladebaits, feature a heavy head and thin steel body with a treble hook attached at each end. A series of line attachment holes at the top of such a bait allows changing of the balance and action of the lure. Be sure to experiment with different positions to see which will produce best.

Examples of bladebaits include:

Blue Fox's Wiglstik

Reef Runner's Cicada

Heddon's Sonar

Cordell's Gayblade

Bullet Lure's Bullet Blade

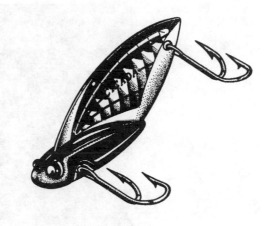

Reef Runner's Cicada

The best way to fish such a lure is to jig gently on bottom, then rip the lure rapidly upward. As the bait rises, fish are attracted by its intense flash and vibration. Fish usually follow these lures up, then strike on the pause or drop. Best of all, bladebaits usually work well in clear *or* turbid water.

To increase hook-ups, try bending the hooks out 5-10 degrees to widen the hook gaps, and make sure the hooks are sharp. Also use a ball-bearing swivel two feet up from the bladebait to reduce line twist, especially when fishing deep water.

Try tipping the center hook with a grub or small minnow to add the smell and taste of live bait. And be prepared as you jig such baits; fish usually hit them hard.

Here's a warning: The experts at Reef Runner Tackle advise that most anglers tend to over-work a bladebait, ripping it too hard upward and thus spooking the fish. Scott Stecher notes, "The ripping action should only be used to attract fish, then your motion should be slowed down to trigger hits. Attach [the lure] with a snap—not a snap swivel—and add just a minnow head or plastic curly tail to the center hook. This adds a splash of color and slows the fall of the bait without affecting the lure's action."

For your reference, ice anglers normally use bladebaits weighing from one-eighth to one-fourth ounce for white bass and crappies; from one-fourth to one-half ounce for walleye, bass and pike; and one-half to one ounce or more for lake trout in deep water.

Rattlebaits

Rattlebaits, while having limited use for ice fishing, are another unique bait gaining acceptance on the hardwater scene. Examples would include smaller versions of **Normark**'s Rattlin' Rap; **Bill Lewis**'s Rat-L-Trap, Spin-Trap, Spark-L-Trap, Mini Rat-L-Trap and Tiny Trap; and **Cordell**'s Rattlin' Spot.

A rattlebait can be an excellent attractor bait when rigged with a short dropper line to a small ice lure, or hook-tipped with a minnow or grub. This is especially true when working deep suspended schools or murky water.

For best results, work such a rig conservatively with sharp, sporadic 6- to 18-inch lifts of the rod tip, interspersed with long, gentle, jiggling pauses. The sound and vibration of the bait will draw fish, and the wiggling dropper will do the rest.

Such a rig seems to work by playing on the naturally competitive instincts of the fish. When a gamefish sees the rattlebait move, it thinks another fish is feeding and comes over to investigate. The fish then sees the tiny dropper lure, apparently thinks this is another fish's food, and promptly steals the tiny bait.

Teardrops, leadhead jigs, and ice flies

Teardrops get their name from the shape of the lure body, even though some lures classified in this category may be round, elliptical or elon-

Rat-L-Trap Jig

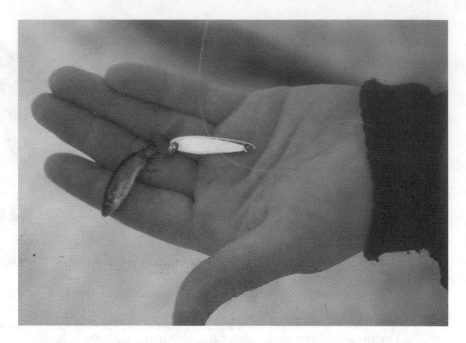

Baiting of Flash lures.

gated. A typical teardrop, weighing less than 1/32 ounce, consists of a thin, painted, teardrop-shaped lead body molded around a #6 to #14 light wire hook. Each variation, of course, is designed for a specific purpose.

*HT Rockers are vertical riding baits that work well for active fish, especially when rigged with a swivel spliced onto the line to prevent line twist. Other HT models include the Daphnia, Teardrop, Fish Eye, Golden Lite, Helicopter-Jigs, and Ultra Glows.

*K & E Tackle's lineup includes the phosphorescent Moon Glow and the sparkling Moon Glitter. As you may have guessed, these short, heavy-bodied teardrops are moon-shaped. They work vertically. Other K & E models include the Rocker, Glo-Top, Flipper Jig, and Gold Rush Jig.

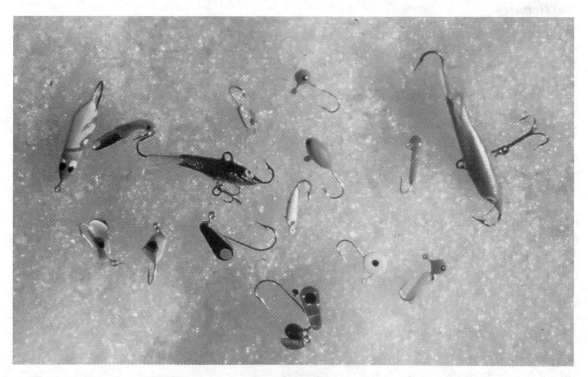

A vast assortment of teardrop and Rapala jigs

*Custom Jigs and Spins** offers several teardrop lures: 2-Spot, a traditional tear with a large profile and slow-fall motion; Rocker, a slim curved spoon that falls quickly and erratically; Poppee, a teardrop with a slow-spiral fall; Demon, a uniquely shaped slow-falling lure; Purist, a lightweight teardrop with a soft plastic body molded over the hook; and Rembrandt, a large-profile, spoon-type body covered by a plastic sheath.

*Bad Dog's** lineup includes Water Fleas, which features an epoxy body (instead of lead) that changes colors as it falls slowly; Four Eyes, a wide teardrop blade with a hammered nickel back and painted front; Waxy Rig, a single painted ball-head teardrop with prism glitter back; Bug, an oval teardrop with prism glitter back; Hot Shot Tear, which features hot glow colors; Featherlite Grub, a larva-shaped body with glow body and prism glitter back with

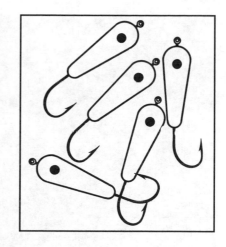

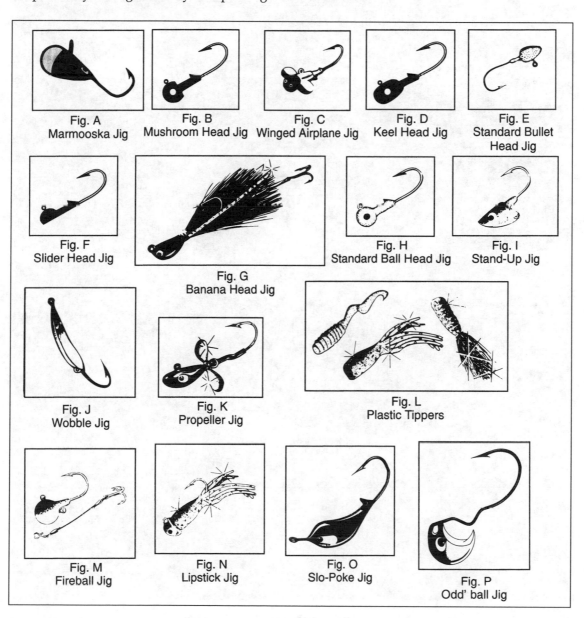

A variety of leadhead jigs and various additions to enhance presentation

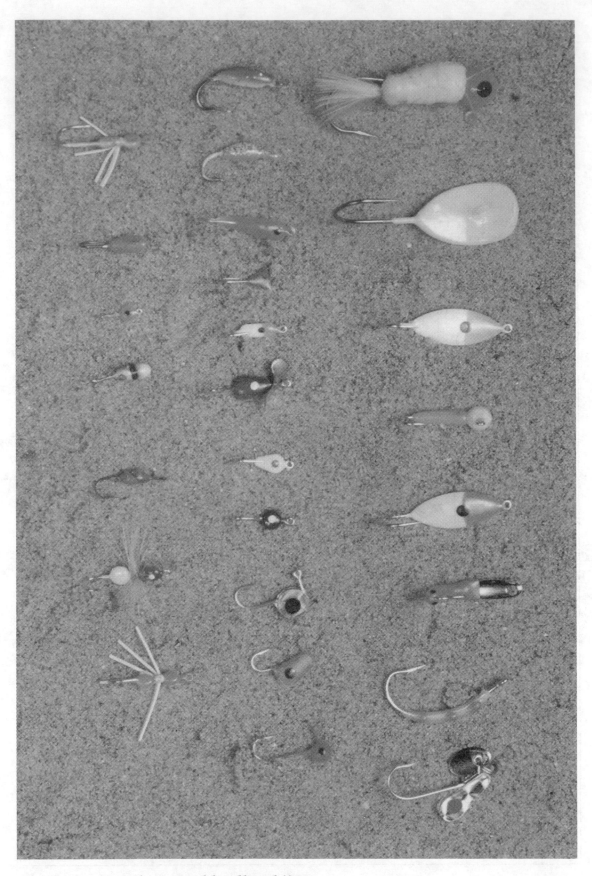

A variety of teardrops and leadhead jigs

an extremely slow fall; Rockers, Measle Tears, Flipper Tears, and Bullies, which feature helicopter-style props at the top of the lure; and Sparkles, with a hot sparkle finish.

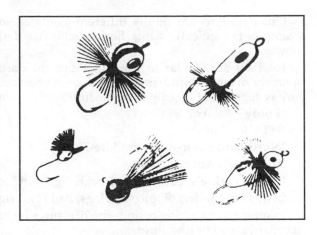

Ice flies (K&E Tackle)

*The **Dickey** Pearl is a vertical teardrop jig that fishes stiffly, but has a unique pearl color that imitates the flash of a wounded minnow.

*The **Killer Binkle** is perhaps the most unique teardrop variation. This lightweight teardrop is bent, so it settles slowly and wiggles on the fall to create a tantalizing action.

*Other excellent products are the **Jig-A-Whopper** Flutter Bug; **Lakco** models; **Northland** Jig-A-Bit and Bob-A-Bit; **RJ** Ladybug; and **Shearwater** Starlite.

Teardrop lures also come in medium and larger sizes for larger gamefish. Though similar in design to smaller teardrops, they are larger and heavier. Many are made from a diverse array of wobbling blade designs. Examples include:

***Custom Jigs and Spins'** Striper Special, a heavy, slim- tapered spoon that fishes heavy for deep water use, and Willow Spoons, a weighted willow leaf blade for diving and darting action.

***HT**'s Ice 'N' Spoon, a weighted willow leaf blade that offers a unique swimming action, and Walleye Spoon, that offers a slow fall, painted front, and silver plated back.

***Bad Dog**'s Crippled Willow features an offset hook angle and reversed bend that make it flutter like an injured minnow, and the Willow Hot Tail features a unique football bend that creates an ultra-slow fall.

The list, of course, could go on. So evaluate each lure and its design. And most importantly, read the package. Most manufacturers list a lure's design features, including the best situations and tips for fishing them. After all, they want you to catch fish with their lures so you'll buy more. Most teardrops work best when tipped with a grub, maggot, or small minnow, and when jigged gently with slow lifts and drops with frequent, lengthy pauses.

Leadhead jigs, or roundheads, are probably the most simple, yet most effective lures.

***HT**'s Hothead is conducive to fishing smaller panfish, white bass, crappie, and perch. The small plastic grub on the hook is impregnated with fish attracting scents, and though the lure fishes somewhat stiffly, it can be jigged aggressively for active fish, or more subtly for less active fish. The Ultralite works well when tipped with just a hint of live bait for fussy or neutral fish. The Football offers a slight swimming action when jigged.

***Bad Dog**'s Slo-Dog features a point under the jig head that facilitates better hooking of tippers and trailers.

***Northland**'s Sink 'n' Jig and **Jack's** Jig.

You also may choose from a variety of modified and specialized leadheads:

***Custom Jigs and Spins**' Purest sports a flat head, and a slightly bent teardrop body for unique action that seduces fussy panfish. "The Rat Finky," one of my favorite small profile horizontal baits, is similar to the Hothead, though more petite and lightweight.

***HT**'s Marmooska is perhaps the most innovative jig design. Its light wire, small barbed hook with a special bend increases hook-ups dramatically.

***Northland**'s Whistler, has a propeller blade that sends out vibrations when jigged.

***Bait Rigs'** Mini Slo-Poke Jig features a large, more open gap and stand-up for better hooksets when fishing the bottom. Odd'ball Jig, also a stand-up head design, fishes horizontally, but stands up when on bottom.

*Dressed leadhead jigs can be worked using the "finesse" method, or jigged aggressively. Dressings tend to slow a jig's fall, and in cases such as bucktail, absorb and retain natural or added fish scents, helping draw fish. Examples include **Northland**'s Sting'r Bucktail, **Lindy**'s Fuzz-E-Grub, **HT**'s Ultralite Ice Lure, and Blue Fox's Foxee Jig, among others.

Other designs are simply different leadhead shapes. Keel or bullet-shaped leadheads, for example, fall quickly, while horizontally flat designs create more water resistance and fall slowly.

Ice flies are similar to teardrops and standard ice leadheads, but have tiny lead bodies sparsely dressed with hair, feathers, or rubber legs. These dressings add lifelike action as the lure is jigged, and usually slow the lure's fall. Examples include:

***Lindy**'s Ice Ant

***HT**'s Ice Ant

***Northland**'s Gypsy Jig and Fire-Fly Jig

***Bad Dog**'s Ant and Spider

***K & E Tackle**'s Ice Nymph, Hackle Jig, Mini Jig

***Ant**'s Nu-Spider, Bippie with legs, Bait Fly, Wiggle Rocker, Flash Ant and Fluster Bug

In addition to giving action, the dressings on these lures absorb fish scents better than do standard metal or lead lures.

Teardrops, ice flies, and leadhead jigs generally work best when jigged gently up and down with three inch or smaller movements, and long pauses in between. Don't be afraid to use the bottom. Fish will often pick up these lures right off bottom.

For best results, tip them with live bait such as waxworms, mousies, wigglers, grubs, or small minnows.

Live bait tipping of teardrops, leadheads, and ice flies

These lures range from about one-sixteenth to three-fourths ounce, depending on the depth you are fishing and the fish species you are seeking. However, to properly present a jig and live minnow, rig your jig with a minnow hooked through the lips or in the back near the dorsal fin. Work the bait by easing it up a foot or two, then allowing the minnow to swim and flash as it falls back to its original position.

Always match jig weight with minnow size when fishing live minnows. To keep your bait alive and active, use the lightest jig you can effectively fish. Just make sure you remain in control. For example, a large minnow will actively swim on a 1/32-ounce jig head, but you easily can lose control of this presentation because the bait takes so long to drop. In fact, if not weighted properly, the minnow may swim out of the zone you are trying to fish.

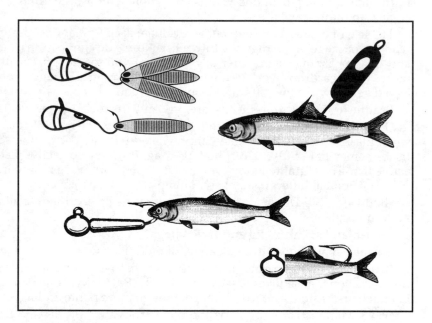

Bait tipping

For best results, use a one-sixteenth ounce jig in water of 15 feet or less; one-eighth ounce down to 30 feet; and one-fourth ounce and heavier in deeper water or in current. Heavier jigs also should be used when trying to "anchor" live baits for less active fish.

In addition, teardrops, ice flies, and plain leadheads usually should be tied directly to your line. The only exception would be when using large jig and minnow presentations for pike. In that situation, a light wire leader may be a good idea.

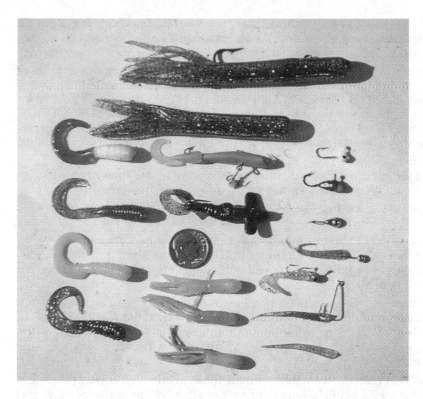

Various plastics

Plastics: A revolution in ice lures

My experience with plastics on the ice began just a couple years ago. With one lake trout on the ice and fish still registering on my electronics, I quickly lowered my Marmooska Minnow toward the school and watched on the screen as a fish charged my bait, then stopped short and swam away.

Thinking my bait was tangled or my minnow gone, I began reeling up, and watched as another fish approached the bait. To trigger that fish, I experimented with a number of lift-drop and wide-swinging swimming motions. Nothing.

I reeled up and tried several jigging lures in various styles, sizes and colors. It didn't seem to matter. Whatever I did, fish would look and follow, but did not strike.

I then decided to try a relatively new lure on the ice fishing scene; a large plastic tube jig. I watched my electronics as the lure slowly whorled toward bottom. Again a fish rushed the bait, but this time it connected, and in short order I had landed a respectable seven-pound laker.

More and more anglers are employing the benefits of plastics on the ice. Not only are these lures cheaper and more durable than live bait, they also are versatile. Available in an infinite variety of styles, sizes, shapes, and colors, they feature natural texture and action; can be worked at virtually any depth or speed; offer excellent hooking qualities; work for a wide variety of species including lake trout, northern pike, walleye, crappie, and perch; and they don't have to be kept alive in extreme, frigid temperatures.

Innovative manufacturers have been quite successful in designing plastic baits that feature a compact, naturally streamlined appearance, and soft, natural, "lifelike" textures.Today's ice anglers can find plastics that fall quickly or slowly, that provide maximum action with fast or slow jigging speeds at a variety of depths, and that tantalize with built-in fish scents and amino acids.

Good ice plastics include **HT**'s Softies Tails; **Cy's** Flies; **Falls'** Flicktails; **Creme Lure Company**'s Super Tubes; and **Mr. Twister**'s smaller Twist Tails, various tube jigs, and curly tails.

How to Fish with Plastics

Strikes on plastics are seldom rod-busters, so select a rod with delicate touch and maximum sensitivity for feeling light, subtle bites, yet with the strength necessary to drive a hook. For best results, I recommend fishing a 30- to 44-inch light-action rod with solid backbone and light tip action for panfish, or stiffer actions and powers for larger gamefish. Combine this with a spinning reel featuring reliable drag, and spool it with the lightest line possible for the situation.

Lure size and shape are critically important. Plastics for winter panfish, for example must wiggle enticingly, so short, thin plastic strips rigged on tiny #12-14 dry fly hooks get the nod of most ice pros. (Examples include **Falls** Flicktails, **Cy's** Flies and **HT**'s Softies Tails.) Rig your lure by heating the hook or jig head just prior to sliding on the plastic, because the heat melts the plastic down, helping hold it in place. Some anglers rig their plastic bodies on tiny teardrops or leadheads, or use specially designed shapes that resemble teardrops, spikes, spiders, bloodworms, or hair shrimp.

Plastics should always be rigged on hooks or lures tied directly to the line, unless fishing large-tube jigs for pike, when a light wire leader may be needed to help prevent bite-offs.

The most effective ice plastics consist of three styles: thin plastic strips, twist or curly style tails, and tube jigs.

Plastic strips are short, thin plastic bodies fished horizontally on thin, light wire hooks or tiny micro jig heads for panfish (see C and D, Figure 7-10). They feature slim, translucent horizontal or vertical tails that quiver slightly when jigged softly, and are extremely effective for inactive or heavily pressured panfish.

Curly tails, on the other hand, work best when tipped on a standard jig head, or on the front treble of a vibrating style action lure such as a bladebait, or (best of all) on the rear rigid hook of a swimming style lure such as an airplane jig or jigging minnow (see A and B, Figure 7-10). Curly tails wiggle enticingly when jigged aggressively, which often is the trick for increasing catches with action-style lures.

Tube jigs offer many advantages for ice fishing. Small tubes work well for crappies and perch, because they resemble small baitfish. Larger tubes are effective for walleye, pike, and lake trout, because they sink slowly with realistic, lifelike motions, enhanced by unique tentacles that shimmy when jigged. Tubes can be fished in a number of ways to attract fish through the ice.

Be sure to experiment with various lure weights, plastic styles, lengths, and colors, as fish preference can vary greatly from day to day, even hour to hour.

Fishing plastics for larger gamefish

Consistent success begins with the right ice rod. For best results, use a longer, 36- to 54-inch rod sturdy enough at the butt to set the hook and control heavy fish, yet sensitive enough at the tip to provide the right lure action and enable detection of subtle strikes.

I prefer shorter ultralight or light action rods with super-sensitive tips when fishing tiny plastic strips for trophy panfish; 36-inch medium action ice rods with good tip action for small tube jigs; 48-inch medium-heavy rods for smaller curly tail baits; and longer, heavy action rods when fishing larger curly tail rigs and tube jigs.

Balance is particularly critical when fishing plastics, so be sure the reel properly matches the rod, and offers a smooth, reliable, easily-adjustable drag system. A spinning reel should feature a solid snapping bail mechanism and smooth turning bail roller to help prevent unnecessary line twist or breakage. A casting reel for larger gamefish should have a level wind mechanism, especially when fishing deeper water, so the line doesn't bunch up, twist or tangle.

As for line, choose fresh, smooth, low-memory premium monofilament for added strength and sensitivity. Because hook-sets and line retrieval through icy guides place great stress on line, check often for abrasion, then re-tie or re-spool as necessary.

To decrease line twist when using larger, heavier baits in deep water, use a small #14 black barrel swivel to splice a slightly heavier leader between your line and lure. The leader will help prevent line breakage.

A good electronics unit is helpful as well. Of course, electronics are most often used to find primary fish-holding structures, cover, forage, and fish. But many anglers overlook using electronics to monitor fish response.

By carefully watching your screen, you can determine if the fish are spooking, turning away, nipping, bumping, or aggressively striking your presentation, then adjust to whatever bait combination seems to produce best.

Rigging and fishing ice plastics

To make your plastic bait presentation appear most natural, work the bait with slow, deliberate swimming motions to create subtle, tantalizing lifelike action.

When fishing plastic strips and smaller tube jigs, use properly balanced rod combos and light line, and tie your hook or jig with a loop knot, always using the least amount of weight necessary to get the bait down. Then fish slowly.

When fishing more active, minnow-feeding fish (such as lake trout), use larger action lures and curly tail rigs, or large tubes, along with heavier tackle and more aggressive jigging approaches.

The biggest mistake I see most first-time plastics users making is fishing with a single, repetitive, jigging motion. Because fish activity levels and responses vary from day to day, you must experiment. Try various rigging techniques and jigging methods in a tub of water prior to fishing.

Tube jigs, for example, are usually rigged by slipping a thin, cylindrical tube jig head into a soft, hollow plastic body. When jigged vertically with a gentle lift-drop motion, this design produces a distinct, slow spiraling fall that fish find irresistible.

However, by experimenting with various style jig heads, you can attain various actions. Wider, flat-bottom designs slow a bait's fall tremendously, and enhance the lure's swimming action. Round or keel-head style jigs, however, tend to lessen the lure's swimming effect and cause the bait to sink faster, which is useful when target fish are holding in deep water, or are less active and unwilling to chase a wide-swinging bait.

Tubes also can be specially rigged. For instance, try leaving a little plastic sticking out at the head instead of snugging it against the front of the hollow tube. This way, the lure will swim farther to the side as you work it. Some anglers even pack this area with fish attractant.

Plastics should always be tied directly to the line unless fishing for larger gamefish when wire would be better in preventing bite-offs.

Another variation is to tip a tube on a swimming style airplane jig. Rigged on the rear hook, the tube slows the lure as it falls, and when jigged, the tube will stay on the hook better than live bait. When a fish bites the plastic, the tube flattens against the hook shank, exposing the hookpoint. To improve this effect, try bending the hookpoint up about five degrees. It helps!

Tube jigs also make an effective addition to various size jigging spoons. Many such spoons will fit inside some tube designs, allowing the tube to form a sheath around the lure body. This gives the spoon a slower fall, as well as a hint of contrasting color, a more natural feel, and more subdued flash.

Soaking or tipping your plastics with a touch of fish scent or attractants isn't a bad idea, either. My personal favorite is **Wisconsin Pharmacal**'s MAX, which also releases metalflake "scales" that resemble loose scales from an injured baitfish. Many anglers add a touch of pork rind to their plastic presentation for enhanced natural texture, taste, scent, and action. Although I haven't tried them, salt-impregnated baits seem to have a similar effect.

When taken, lightweight plastics tend to drop right into fishes' mouths gently, so strikes can be casual and light. Therefore, keep the rod tip low for better control, and maintain constant contact with the bait.

Subtle is often the name of the game with fussy winter fish. By using a sensitive, properly balanced ice rod outfit, and experimenting with various styles, sizes, colors, rigging strategies, and jigging actions, all while using electronics to monitor fish responses and pinpoint the best presentation, you'll increase your winter catches tremendously. That is why plastics are fast becoming one of the most productive weapons in the modern ice fishing arsenal.

Micro Baits

When using ultralight rods and reels with line the diameter of a human hair, it only makes sense to balance the system with baits of 1/32 ounce or less—much less, in fact, for most "micro" lures weigh between 1/100 and 1/256 of an ounce!

Many such lures are homemade, although some commercially produced models are available. High quality, #14-#22 or smaller straight-eye dry fly hooks, such as **Mustad**'s Accu-Points, **Bad Dog**'s Micro Trebles, or hooks produced by **Tiemco** or **Orvis**, teamed with a precisely placed ultralight, fly fishing style shot, make excellent micro ice bait. Hooks may be the cheapest and a seemingly insignificant part of these systems, but they are a vital link in micro system performance. Therefore, use only ultra-sharp quality hooks, because you won't be able to set the hook aggressively with this downsized tackle.

Commercially made micro lures are also available:

***HT Enterprises** offers Tiny Tears, Marmooskas, and Darter Jigs.

***Turner Jones** offers Micro Jigs and One Half Micro Jigs.

***K & E** offers Tiny Tears and Micro Jigs as well as Micro-Trebles.

***Bad Dog Lures** offers jigs in sizes from #10-#18, and weights of 1/128-1/256 ounce.

Consistent hook-sets are the biggest problem with any of these tiny baits. For best results, bend the hookshanks out 40 degrees, turn the hookpoints up five degrees, and tip them with a single, tiny grub or maggot. While splitshot take away some lure action, they do help get lightweight baits down, especially when fishing deeper water.

As with any ice lures, tie micro lures with loop knots for maximum action and highest hooking capabilities. Always tie knots carefully, by first wetting the line, then patiently tightening each down slowly and smoothly.

As in summer, fish during the winter prefer specific sizes and styles of winter lures and jigs, given various situations and conditions. The greater your knowledge and versatility, therefore, the greater your chances of consistently catching fish.

Vertical, convex, concave, and bent-spoon shapes offer the most action and flash. Slightly bent-bodied vertical designs produce a slight bobbing motion, while long, thin bodies create a different rocking action.

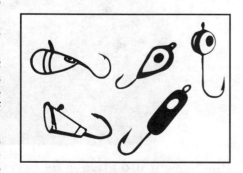

Micro ice lures

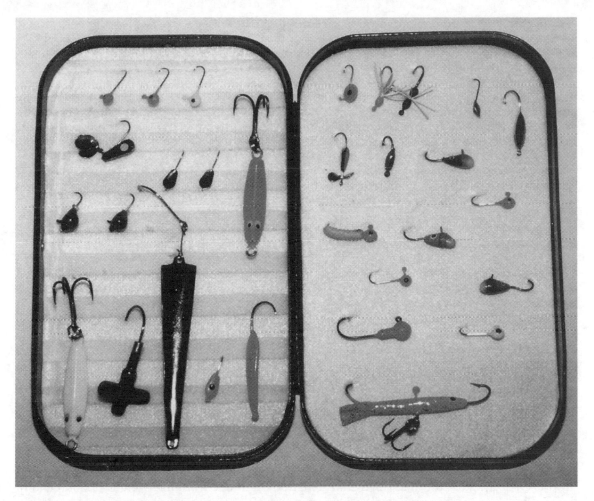

A fly angler's box makes an excellent storage box for ice lures.

Several specialized micro jigs exist. Examples include **System Tackle**'s Fat Boy, a vertical design that features a flat top to enhance visibility on electronics, and **HT**'s #16 Marmooska and #14 Marmooska Jewel, horizontal micro jigs that pivot the hook toward a biting fish.

Ironically, there also exist many micro jigs, such as Tiny Tears, Micro Flies, Copepods, and Rat Finkees, that offer almost *no* action except what is imparted by the user. Remember that actions of tiny micro baits vary with even the slightest difference in design. Therefore be sure to experiment, because these subtle variations, in specific sets of conditions, can make a huge difference in results.

Carry a full spectrum of lure colors, including intermediate colors such as subtle chartreuse, white, gold, and glow-in-the-dark. Also try tipping your jigs with short, thin strips of soft plastic shaved from various colored plastic worms. These shimmying, colored strips drive panfish crazy, and help slow the fall of a jig, offering many new and effective presentation options.

Many anglers have never even considered the difference between horizontal and vertical micro ice jigs, much less understood the various uses and advantages of the two. Horizontal micro jigs are better. These rock gently when jigged, providing additional feel for the angler and added temptation for the fish. More importantly, a horizontally exposed hook turns in the direction from which a fish is biting, reducing missed hits. Vertical jigs don't normally offer this advantage.

Micro baits are meant to imitate tiny food items such as zooplankton, so use a jigging method that closely mimics the actual movements of these critters. For example, to best imitate Daphnia, which are most active and available to winter panfish during twilight hours, try a slight one-sixteenth to one-eighth inch vertical motion with a bulbous, slightly bent-bodied jig during low light periods.

Copepods are a more aggressive species of plankton that is active during daylight hours, and is the primary daytime winter forage of panfish in many waters. To imitate Copepods, switch to a thinner, more erratic, spoon-shaped rocker style ice jig, and use an aggressive jigging action interspersed with long hops.

As for rods, the lighter the better. **HT**'s 19- or 24-inch Micro Ice Rods are ideal. As for reels, quality micro spincast or spinning reels are excellent choices. Just be sure the drag is smooth, and (on spinning models) the bail rollers spin freely. For line, two-pound test is good, one-pound is better, three-fourths or one-half pound is best. A micro bait presentation requires the ultimate in finesse, so there's no room for error. Make sure your equipment works with you, rather than against you.

If you've enjoyed ultralight in the past, you'll find micro to be even more fun and effective. There are times you'll fish without a single bite using heavier tackle, but get near-limit catches using ultralight. The difference between ultralight and micro can be equally rewarding.

Colored Hooks

If micro baits have been the newest wave in ice fishing advancements, what's next? Colored hooks. Simple concept? Yes. Effective? Very! The key is the combination of slow fall and attracting color.

Painted hooks are available from two sources: **Northland Tackle** and **Hawg Wild Enterprises**. To rig such hooks, sharpen the point with a quality sharpener, and tie the hook with a loop knot to provide a loose, natural fall. Add an ultralight splitshot 6-12 inches up the line, and add bait.

For crappies and perch, gently nip the hook through the tail of a one- to two-inch shiner or fathead. The added flash of the colored hook makes a difference.

For bluegill, nip a waxie through the tail, or try two wigglers lightly nipped through the nose. Either way, this presentation allows maximum exposure of the hook's color and flash, and maximum liveliness from the bait.

Colored hooks can also be tipped with thin strips of plastic—a deadly technique for "pressured fish." A small colored hook can also be rigged as a stinger or dropper below a larger teardrop used as an attractor. Just run a short length of light line from the eyelet or hook bend of the lead lure, and tip it with a small grub or minnow.

Colored hooks aren't the answer to everything, and are not a magic bait, but in certain conditions, they can be a highly productive alternative that you shouldn't overlook.

Hook Style

Most ice lures are molded onto or incorporate light wire aberdeen, sproat, or model perfect hooks. The sproat and model perfect are good for general applications. The sproat, when made of light wire, is an excellent ultralight ice jig hook because it is a strong design with a smooth, parabolic bend. The model perfect features a wide gap, and the round-bend design reduces the hole made in the jaw of a fish, thus preventing escapes when vertical jigging.

In most situations, however, light wire aberdeens perform much better. These thin wire hooks dig home readily, so you can embed the barb even with a light, ultralight, or micro ice rod.

For larger, active fish, choose larger, thicker-bodied hooks. For smaller, less aggressive species, choose smaller, lighter hooks.

Don't hesitate to remove a lure's standard hook and replace it for a more refined presentation if the situation demands it. Standard hooks usually are fine, but sometimes a special hook can mean the difference between catching only a couple of fish and catching a limit.

Hook Adaptation and Alignment

A serious open water angler rarely leaves shore without a hook sharpener, yet I've met only *one* angler who claims to use a hook sharpener on his ice lures consistently, even though cold-blooded winter fish often mouth ice jigs subtly, and a bent out, ultra-sharp hook can make all

The author's ice lure tackle box

the difference. Bending hookpoints out 5 or 10 degrees, or replacing round bend trebles with longer shanked trebles, can greatly increase your advantage. Take a standard treble and gently tap your finger on its hookpoints. You will feel little more than a slight poke, if that.

For a prominent hook point, always stroke toward the tip with a premium file, or you'll leave metal burrs along the hook edge that will decrease your percentages.

Sharpen the hook in this fashion, and bend the jig's hookpoint up a few degrees. Then grasp the shank just behind the head with a needlenose pliers and bend the shank down about 35 degrees. Finally, replace the spoon's standard treble with a round bend treble. Now tap your finger on the hookpoint carefully. If you tap too hard, you'll have a hook imbedded in your finger.

As for stinger hooks, most open water walleye anglers always carry several, just in case the fish are short-striking. These same anglers, when faced with the same conditions under the ice, seem to forget everything they've learned. Any time fish are just nipping at a presentation may be a good time to set up a stinger. Reliable commercial stingers, which come with a variety of convenient adjustable loops, vinyl-dipped eyes, or snaps, are available from suppliers such as **Northland Tackle**.

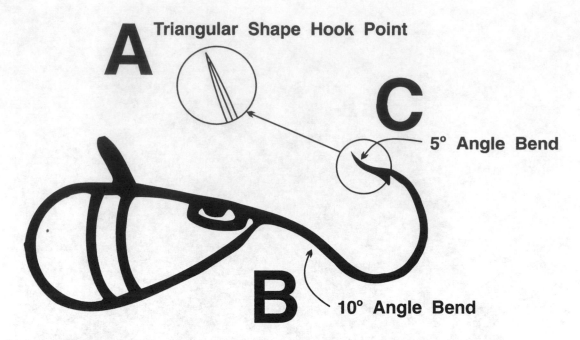

A Triangular Shape Hook Point

C 5° Angle Bend

B 10° Angle Bend

Bending hooks

A stinger can be made by attaching a light monofilament or wire leader to the eye of an ice jig or fly, or to the split ring on a jigging spoon. In either case, attach a sharpened, small, round bend bronze treble to the opposite end, and embed it near the tail of a live bait tipper, barely nicking the bait's skin. (Always position the hook so the hookpoint aims away from the minnow's head.) Should a fish short-strike or casually nip at the bait, the stinger will drive the hooks home.

Two variations of this stinger hook technique are growing in popularity: the free-style stinger hook, and the dropper line system. The free-style stinger consists of a stinger hook completely separate from the bait. In my opinion, this actually improves bait action hooking.

A dropper line, on the other hand, consists of a short length of monofilament rigged with a hook or tiny ice jig. This is tipped with a grub or maggot set beneath an attractor, such as a jigging spoon, hanger rig, action jig, or even another tiny ice jig.

One of my favorite rigging methods is reverse-hooking my lure through the tail of a minnow, and placing a fairly long-leadered light-line dropper hook near the head. This rig allows the bait to remain more active.

Also, a snap, #10 snap swivel, or short three-fourths inch light wire extension from the lure body to the center treble on a jigging minnow will avoid the twisting and tangling that occurs with mono. This improvement can increase hooking percentages by a considerable margin. This tactic can work on blade-baits and rattlebaits as well.

Tipping

When tipping your lures, experiment with various bait types, sizes, colors, and rigging methods. Versatility is a virtue.

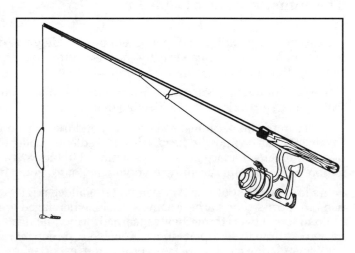

Dropper rig

One trick is to shorten your offering. For example, try cutting a minnow in half before hooking it, or use just the head. With grubs, try tipping your jig with one or two tiny spikes or wigglers instead of a fat waxworm.

Sometimes adding a tiny attractor to the front of an ice lure helps. A small spinner, shred of yarn, or slice of plastic can make an attractive target for hungry fish.

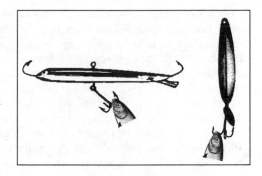

Tipping with minnow heads.

Plastics, such as swimming, gliding, reaper, or thumper tails, as well as grub bodies with tentacles, tube jigs, and assorted scented plastics can be quite effective.

Also experiment with various sweeps of your rod tip. Work the bait with medium slow lift-drops, occasionally varying the action with slight jiggling, swimming, gliding, or hopping motions to trigger fish, depending on their mood.

Lure dressings play a significant role in lure action and fish catching abilities. Feathers, for instance, slick back so the lure falls faster and deeper. However, when fished with a slow, methodical vertical drop-and-jig motion, the plume puffs out and quivers to attract fish.

Tinsel, another dressing, enables even a small jig to sink fast. Because it isn't buoyant and doesn't trap air bubbles as fur or feathers might, tinsel provides a distinctive, fish-attracting, pulsing motion.

Color Schematic Conversions

Suppose you're marking fish, but they won't bite. Perhaps you can even see them, yet they refuse to bite. This means something is wrong with your presentation. You have several options. You can try switching lures, weight, jigging action, or even color. Sometimes, a color change can be the key to making reluctant winter fish strike.

Research has shown that reds change to brown at 10 feet beneath the surface, then to black at 30 feet. Blue, with the shortest wavelength, shows up best in deeper water, and fluorescent colors remain the same at most depths. Unfortunately, this data was collected and interpreted by human eyes, which are structurally different than a fish's eyes.

So how does the angler choose the right color? Frankly, there are no rules. I will provide some general guidelines, but the only way to find the right color is experimentation. Anything else is an educated guess.

Fishes' color preferences can change throughout the day, even by the hour, depending on various factors. Some days, color changes seem to make little difference. But when the fish aren't active, which is a large amount of the time, definite color patterns often emerge.

When experimenting with color preferences, be sure to determine if color is the only variable making the difference. Only if you use the same lure in the same weight, style, and size, work your bait the same way, and fish the same area at the same depth and speed, will you know if color is the factor.

In addition, study fish and their eye structure. Research has shown that many fish have acute vision, including good ability to recognize a variety of shapes and colors. In fact, most species have specialized vision that allows them to feed best in certain intensities and wavelengths of light.

Trout, bass, bluegill, and pike, for example, are primarily daytime feeders, while walleye are primarily night feeders. Crappies feed both day and night. The eyes of daytime feeding fish are equal in size to about 20 percent of the overall head length.

The night-feeding walleye, however, has eyes that are considerably larger: 40-50 percent of the overall head length. The larger eyes gather more light, making vision fairly good even in the dark. Crappies, which feed mostly at twilight, but can be active either night or day, have eyes larger than most members of the bass family, but smaller than the walleye's. Most baitfish have small eyes.

Because of these differences, various species feed during different times, and see color differently. For example, researchers have discovered that the color receptors in the walleye's eyes are sensitive to reds/oranges and greens/chartreuses, while bass see red more distinctly than other colors. Although we still know very little about these differences, we do know that fish see color, that they see some colors better than others, and that they feed during particular times of the day.

The effectiveness of colors will vary according to light intensity, water clarity, water color, depth of the fish, and a host of other factors. Water clarity, because it affects all the other variables, will therefore be used as a general guideline.

In clear water, subtle colors usually perform the best. These include white, brown, black, chartreuse, dull green, and purple.

In dark, turbid water, black, bright orange, green, red, chartreuse, and hot fluorescent colors are good choices. (My favorites are the hot fluorescents.)

At night, black and hot phosphorescent (glow-in-the-dark) colors are best. Black creates a silhouette against the lighter sky, helping fish see the bait. The hot and glow colors help fish find a jig even if it's on bottom. **HT**'s phosphorescent Nuke Tape and **Witchcraft**'s glow tape work great under these conditions.

Stained water is an in-between condition, requiring greater care in choosing color. For instance, if the water is turbid, start with bright orange or fluorescent lime greens. Silver tinsel jigs work well in stained water; sunlight reflecting off the tinsel surface makes it look like an injured minnow.

A dark back and white belly is standard coloration for most fish, including minnows. If a minnow is injured, becoming an easy target for a predator, it usually turns on its back or side, thus flashing its contrasting dark and light sides. This rings a dinner bell to any hungry predator. A jig with contrasting colors provides a similar effect, and I've had good luck with the principle.

Similarly, a fluorescent head with a white body might work well in stained water because it offers two good color selections in one shot. Likewise, a phosphorescent jig head with a hot green body may be quite effective in a turbid water situation.

Of course, you can't carry 100 styles of lures in every conceivable color combination. Instead, carry a good variety of standard sizes and styles, a few colored permanent markers, a package or two of Nuke Tape, various colored prism tapes, maribou, and bucktail. This way, a lure may be altered into almost any color quickly.

Through experience, you'll gain a feel for which colors produce best on your favorite lakes and in various situations. Take color seriously enough, and you'll see an improvement in your results.

Scent

Although scents have not increased my catch, they have increased the overall size of the fish I'm catching. I believe this is so because fish gain a more keen sense of smell as they get older. Fish scents and attractants cover up enough foreign odor to tempt those larger fish.

As mentioned earlier, **Wisconsin Pharmacal**'s MAX formula also releases silver glitter into the water as you jig, to mimic scales falling from an injured minnow.

Berkley's Power Bait and **Baitmate**'s Ultimate Bait are two prime examples of new impregnated and flavor-enhanced plastic soft bait technology. Each gradually releases scent, dispersing it as you retrieve slowly. This can attract inactive fish and trigger them into biting.

Action Distortions

When used regularly, action modifications can be highly effective, and they're easy to make if done before hitting the ice. Simple modifications such as flipping a flash lure and reversing the line-tie and hook ends can add a whole new dimension to your jigging approach.

Adding a plastic sleeve to slow lure motion and presentation speed (or removing it to increase lure motion and presentation speed) can be highly effective. Slipping a tube jig over a flash lure, such as a Swedish Pimple, slows the lure's fall, reduces flash slightly, and adds a different texture to the bait.

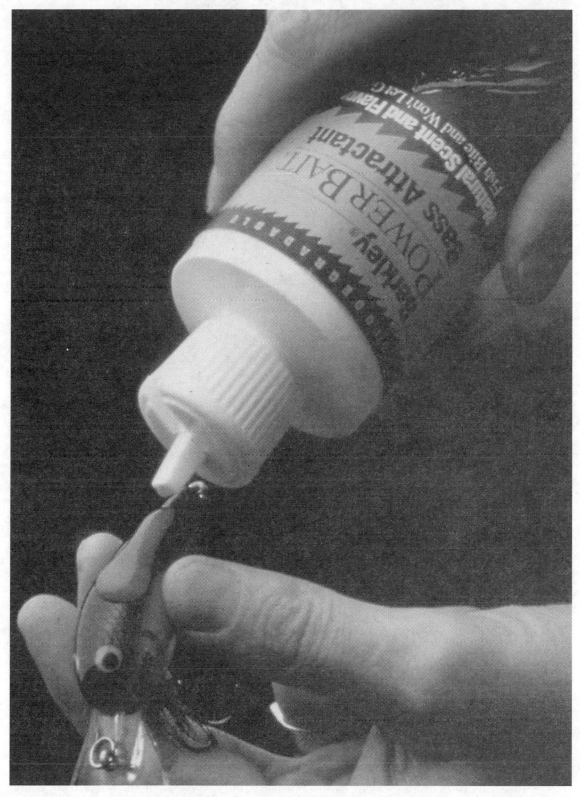

Berkley scent (Berkley). Use of scents may not necessarily increase your catch, but may increase the overall size of the fish you're catching.

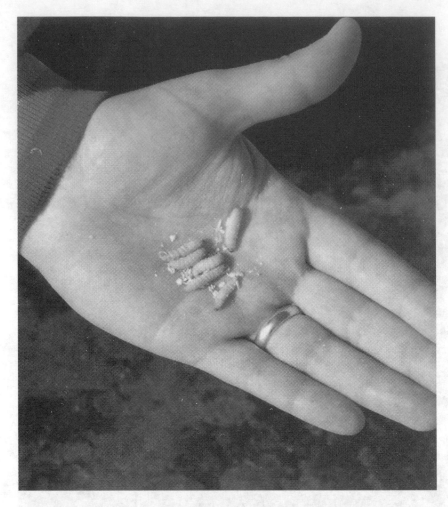

Waxworms are a commonly used bait for panfish.

Adding or removing a few strands of bucktail, feathers or hair can work well in your favor, because their natural buoyancy slows sink rates. And don't forget to experiment with various colors.

There are even more highly dramatic lure body variations. A relatively fast-falling ball-head jig, if slightly flattened horizontally (with a needlenose pliers on both sides of the line tie) falls more slowly. In addition, the flat surface causes the lure to show up better on electronics.

Bending or trimming lead from a jig is also an innovative tactic. This creates a unique fluttering action "swimming" jig, an effective stand-up jig, or a compact ultralight bait for fussy fish.

Lure Size Refinements

Often, simple changes of lure size are the key to catching winter fish, particularly when the fish are super active or fussy. New large baits such as **Normark**'s #11 Jigging Rapala and **Bay de Noc**'s #14 Swedish Pimple are great for large, aggressive fish because of their large profiles and aggressive motions.

At the other end of the spectrum, tiny micro lures in size 16, 18, and 20 (weighing less than 1/256 ounce) are available from **HT Enterprises** and **Turner Jones**. Smaller jigs enhance lure sensitivity and action, and tend to more accurately match the size of prey that winter fish often prefer.

Innovative ice lure designs such as the ultralight European Marmooska jigs incorporate many of these high-tech features. The concept is simple: they consist of a light wire, and a small-barbed hook with a precisely balanced, relatively heavy head. The advantages are threefold. First, the large, heavy head is easily visible on electronics. Second, constant contact with the bait provides better "feel." Third, the small light wire hook and tiny barb facilitate better hooking.

In fact, a sharp hook requires only a tiny barb to hook and hold a light-biting fish. And the smaller the barb, the less "punch" it requires to get a solid hook-set. (For winter fish, never set the hook with a sharp snap; an authoritative lift of your rod tip will suffice.)

The small hook/tiny barb concept also helps in another respect: fussy winter fish generally inspect baits and lures closely, rejecting anything of the wrong size, shape, color, or action. For instance, squishing the end of a maggot or grub with an oversized, unsharpened hook often kills the bait, and turns off fish. With a sharpened light-wire hook, however, you can easily nip a maggot just through the skin, thereby keeping the bait active and increasing your catch.

In addition, a small, light wire hook aids lure performance. Because the hook is so light, it actually pivots toward a biting fish's mouth if the fish strikes the lure opposite the hook. This, of course, dramatically increases hooking percentages.

Such small design modifications can make a big difference. In the strange world of refined ice fishing, simple, tiny details are often, and usually, the keys to more consistent catches.

Live Bait Tippers

Under most conditions, artificial lures alone can't imitate the scent, texture, taste, and action of live bait. In fact, many of the gamefish caught through the ice are likely taken on live bait or lure/live bait combinations.

Nonetheless, consistent success with live bait requires precision and finesse. A fish may instinctively be attracted to a fast-moving lure and strike for any number of reasons, but it usually takes more time inspecting a slowly fished natural bait. An angler must therefore exercise special poise in order to take fish consistently.

Minnows

Choosing a minnow. There's a difference in hardiness among minnows. Emerald shiners, for example, are not hardy. Fatheads, however, can withstand dramatic temperature changes, low oxygen levels, and rough handling. Generally, the hardiest species are the liveliest on a hook, and this can make a difference in success rates. However, if the fish aren't active, an emerald shiner might be a better bet.

Also consider size, shape, flash, and smell. A golden shiner has a different profile than a fathead. Shiners give off a great deal of flash, and smelt and other oily baitfish give off a stronger odor than lean-fleshed fish. Experiment to see if the fish show a preference for a particular species or quality, and (more importantly) try to determine why.

Strike indicators. When selecting a float, consider the size of the bait, the species you're seeking, and how well the float's resistance can be felt by the fish. Today's super-sensitive balsa floats have changed ice fishing "bobber" methods dramatically. With the correct number of properly positioned split shot, these low-resistance designs can be fine-tuned to attain neutral buoyancy.

Terminal tackle. If a sinker, hook or jig is too large, fish may feel too much resistance and quickly drop the bait. Choose shot that will properly "load" your float, and will get your minnow down and keep it at your chosen depth. Sinkers should be attached far enough from the bait to not interfere with the desired swimming action. A minnow weighted with a small split-shot, lure or jig can swim in a large circle, while a minnow "anchored" with a larger, heavier shot or lure covers less territory. Adjust according to the activity level of the fish.

Hook styles. Your hook should be large enough so the point protrudes slightly from the minnow, but no larger than is needed for the method of hooking. Proper wire thickness depends on the size of the bait. When using smaller baits for smaller fish, a thin, small-barbed light wire hook keeps bait lively and enables a slow falling presentation. However, when fishing larger minnows, a heavier, larger-barbed hook is stronger and holds more securely.

Be mindful, too, that hooks with short points penetrate more easily, while long points hold better. Spear points are stronger, while hollow points are thinner and sink better. Turned down eyes and bent shank designs such as the Tru-Turn direct the point into the fish upon hook-set. As for hook color, at times, red, silver, or gold help attract fish, while bronze or green hooks are less visible.

As with tip-ups, gamefish usually eat prey head first, so hook a minnow with the hook point toward the tail. The hooks will thus always be in the optimum hooking position. Also, position the hook so the bait balances properly and has freedom of movement.

Modifying bait. To improve your chances of attracting fish, inspect the bait often. If a minnow is not working well, replace or modify it. Many ice anglers use special live bait modification techniques when fishing is slow. Some clip a small portion of a baitfish's tail, thus causing the minnow to swim erratically. Others hook a minnow upside down on a jig head, so that as the minnow tries to right itself, its struggling movements attract fish. A few anglers even dye their minnows with different colors!

Sometimes, just *part* of the minnow works well. Strips of minnow belly meat work well when filleted into a V-shaped pattern. These add natural scent, taste, and texture to the bait, and create a unique swimming action when tipped on a jig.

Grubs and maggots

Although most worms, grubs, and maggots will attract winter fish, there is a difference between them. Maggots, for instance come in different sizes, shapes, actions, textures, and scents, and each may generate a different fish response. Sometimes I've seen fish snub their noses at a waxie, but inhale a gallworm grub or a lively red wiggler. You don't have to carry two dozen types of live bait on the ice, but be aware that doing so might give you a distinct edge.

A mousie, a fat grub with a long "tail," is actually a crane fly larvae. (The long tail is its breathing apparatus.) While highly effective, the mousie often is hard to come by. So try traditional waxworms, spikes, and mousees, because they'll usually produce.

Don't ignore specialty baits such as goldenrod grubs or acorn weevils. Both can be hand collected: goldenrod grubs from goldenrod galls from late fall through spring, and acorn weevil grubs after acorns fall.

When tipped on a small ice fly, jig, or teardrop, tiny insect larvae are often ideal ice-fishing baits, especially for panfish and trout. Another method is to barely nip a fine wire hook through the tip of a single grub or larva. Clear liquid will ooze out, but their internal organs won't be injured and they'll keep wiggling.

Use the smallest, sharpest hook you can. I often pinch the barbs on my hooks slightly down if they seem too big for the size and style bait being used.

You also can hook a grub with a light wire hook threaded through the tail and out through the head, then turn it inside out to release body juices and attract fish. Or, rather than removing a larva mangled by biting fish, leave it on when you add fresh bait. The additional scent permeating the water often attracts fish.

As for color, some bait shops offer live, colored grubs (the color coming from dyed food). While many anglers may disagree, there are times when color can make a difference.

Mealworms, larger, wiggly grubs, work for larger,

Berkley Power Baits (Berkley)

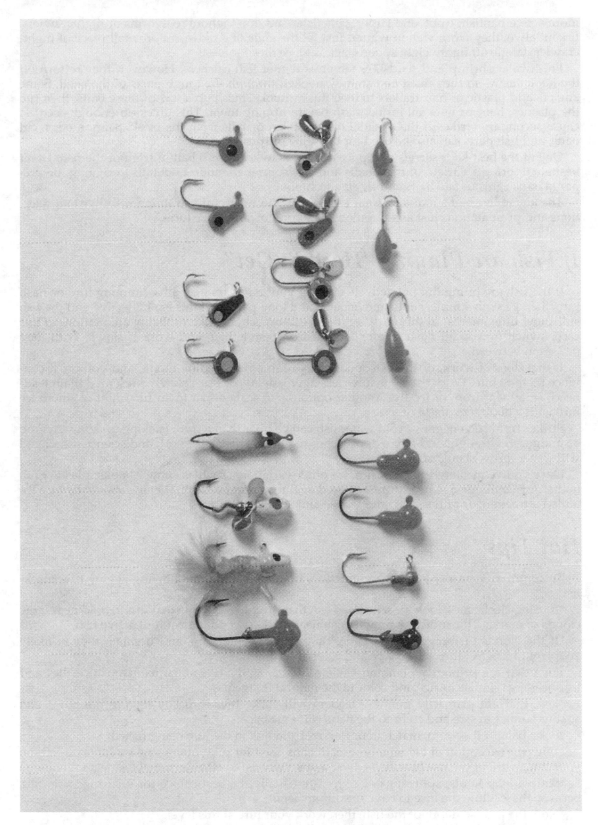

A variety of jigs used for specific fish and conditions.

more active panfish, trout, and larger gamefish. And don't ignore redworms or nightcrawlers. If kept alive, they work well in winter. Just let the ends of a redworm or small piece of nightcrawler dangle off lightweight spoons, jigs, and ice flies.

Freshwater shrimp and scuds are fabulous winter fish catchers. However, they're torn off the hook easily, so they must be carefully hooked through the tough parts of the shell. Some anglers add plastic or hair trailers to their jigs or hooks, mash up a few of these baits, then rub the plastics, hair, or bucktail in the mash before tipping them. This gives off enough scent to cause secondary strikes if the original bait is stolen or falls from the hook. Salmon eggs, cut baits, and fish parts can also be used for the same purpose.

One of the best-kept secrets of top ice anglers is to keep fresh bait in front of the fish. Don't hesitate to bring a variety of fresh baits and pay special attention to details in rigging. Be prepared to use any and all baits and rigging techniques.

The key to live bait success on ice is experimentation! Carefully examine your live bait selections and presentations just as scrupulously as you do various ice lures.

If Fish are Playing "Hard to Get"

If the fish are biting but not actively chasing your baits, try a small swimming lure or flash lure, then jig with simple, subtle movements and long pauses. If this isn't effective and the fish still show little interest in this fairly aggressive approach, the fish probably are neutral. In this case, switch to a small flash lure or large teardrop-style bait, and work it slowly with long pauses in between.

If that doesn't work, or the fish spook, they're in a non-feeding mode, and you must convince them to bite. Work the same lures less aggressively, or use a slowly presented plain leadhead, small teardrop, or ice fly. Another option is to scale down to an ultralight or micro ice lure with a hook size of #14 or less.

Strikes from such negative cold water fish can be finer than a trout sucking up a tiny nymph or midge, so ultralight and micro approaches require all the skill, sport, and science associated with other forms of angling.

Once you've mastered these basics, try other variations, such as stinger hooks; plastic grub bodies for "bulk" and slower drops; colored or fluorescent beads on the line above the lure for added attraction; or rattles, fins, and visible and audible attractors.

Hot Tips

To summarize proper jigging presentation, I've assembled the following jigging tips checklist.

*If using electronics, look for schools of fish that produce squiggly marks and hold near large clouds of marks. This indicates moving fish near food—a good indicator of active fish.

*If the clouds of forage appear large, they're likely minnows, and if small, they're likely zooplankton. Select lure size, shape and color accordingly.

*Fish that are primarily plankton feeders usually will strike small teardrops, ice flies and leadhead jigs similar in size and color to the natural forage base.

*Fish that are primarily minnow feeders will strike mostly flashy jigging minnows and spoons similar in size and color to the natural forage base.

*For a balanced system, match your rod, reel and line to the lure being fished.

*With the exception of bladebaits or leadheads used for pike, always tie ice lures directly to your line, without the use of wire leaders, snaps, swivels, or other terminal connectors.

*Simple loop knots, split rings or snaps are usually the best choice for securing your bait, because these allow the lure to have maximum action.

*Note the precise depth of the fish, then work your lure at this level.

*Watch for fish appearing near your lure, and observe their reactions to various lure styles, sizes, colors, jigging motions, and live bait tippers. This will help you pattern the fish more quickly.

*When using a wide-angle cone, not all fish will appear on your electronics at the exact depth they're holding due to distortion or placement within the transducer cone. Therefore watch

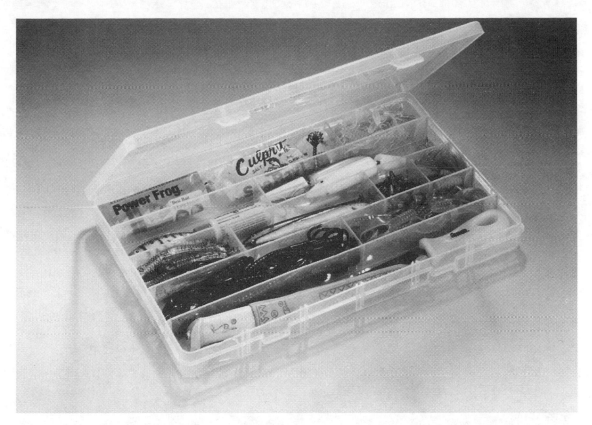

Companies like Plano are now making tackle boxes suited especially for ice fishing.

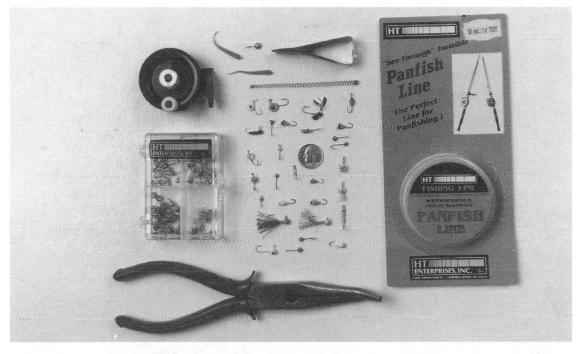

A variety of Micro Tackle items.

your line and rod tip for any twitches or unusual movements that may indicate unexpected strikes.

*Modify your lure as necessary to best match the conditions at hand.

*Always maintain close contact with your jig, especially as the lure sinks. However, don't keep your line so taut that it inhibits the action of your lure.

*Experiment with various line colors, line test ratings, live-bait lure "tippers", and methods of hooking your bait.

*Always set the hook at the slightest indication of a strike. Because winter fish aren't very active, if you hesitate, a fish may expel a small bait or ice jig before you react.

As I said at the beginning of this chapter, it's truly amazing just how many types of ice lure classifications and derivatives of each are available to the ice angler.

Believe me, if you combine this organized, highly versatile lure presentation and modification scheme with the proper jigging approach and methods, and you'll see your ice fishing success improve dramatically.

So prepare yourself! You'll soon see the challenge, fun, and undisputed effectiveness of various lure modifications, and realize how they truly increase the quality of your hard water fishing adventures.

Chapter 8

Winter Camping/Ice Fishing Adventures

*T*hanks to immensely advanced improvements in cold weather clothing, equipment, and knowledge over the past decade, folks are finding outdoor winter recreation more inviting than ever. Not just ice fishing, but snowshoeing, cross country and downhill skiing, snowmobiling, ice skating, ice boating, and even dog sledding are increasing in popularity.

Winter camping is another such activity. Ten years ago, this unique sport was limited to the folly of a few hardy individuals looking for adventure. It was virtually unheard of among the general public, and even today when explaining winter camping, my words are occasionally met with raised eyebrows and a great deal of skepticism.

But attitudes are changing. With amazing technological advances in lightweight and durable outdoor gear and an increased awareness of advanced cold weather skills, winter camping is gaining interest among outdoor enthusiasts, especially adventurous ice anglers. Just keep in mind there are some differences between summer and winter excursions and these are best learned through proper preparation and planning.

Preparation and Planning

I highly recommend hiring a guide your first time out, but if you insist upon setting out on your own, stay close to home; the backyard would be a good start. Attempting a solo, long-distance excursion into the backcountry your first time out is foolhardy.

Start by taking inventory of your equipment: food, water, clothing, and tackle. Begin with a checklist, and make sure it's complete. For your convenience, a winter camping checklist is provided at the end of this chapter. If you forget the fire starter or frying pan when summer camping, even in a fairly remote area, you can usually find a supply store or another camper nearby that can help. However, in winter, you'll find fewer convenient options, and if you are unprepared such a situation can have grave consequences.

Next, test yourself. Set up a mock camp at home using the gathered equipment to double-check yourself; then prepare to actually spend a night in the backyard. Be sure your tent is dry and includes all posts, ropes, and anchors. Also take inventory of sleeping bags, blankets, pillows, clothing, your cook-

Winter camping is something for every outdoor enthusiast to try.

stove and cookware, food, water, matches, lantern and extra mantles, candles, hot water bottles, first-aid items, and ice tackle. Almost without exception, you'll discover a missing item that you didn't think of while making up a checklist in the confines of your warm living room.

Don't forget handy items such as plastic garbage and ziplock style bags, a snow shovel, cross country skis, snowshoes, and if you're snowmobiling, an extra drive belt, spark plug or two, and a few basic tools. Other important items should be kept in a handy pocket at all times: a compass, a map, matches, fire starter tablets, a knife, sunglasses, a filled water bottle, facial tissues, lip balm, sunscreen, a watch, a pocket sewing kit, a whistle, and a sandwich bag stuffed with raisins, nuts, and candies.

At the same time, you'll do yourself a big favor if you pack only items that are necessary to keep you warm and comfortable. Extra equipment is only a burden.

Finally, take inventory of special skills. What relevant winter field experiences exist in your group? Are the members of your group familiar with the area you intend to camp and fish? Who has appropriate winter safety and first-aid training for preventing and treating cold-related injuries and afflictions? When satisfied you've got everything together, you're ready to begin the winter camping adventure.

Setting up Camp

The ideal winter campsite is a small, flat clearing in a wooded, wind protected area. Overhead tree branches or pine boughs should be stripped of snow to prevent surprise tent flattening ceremonies.

Secondly, use your snow shovel to remove snow from central traffic areas and the fire pit. Snow can also be piled into a large dome on a deep snowdrift, allowed to settle for an hour, then hollowed out to create a snug igloo-style sleeping shelter. This eliminates the need to pack or carry a tent, thus lightening your load.

Otherwise, level a sleeping area away from the fire and cooking spot, build a tent-high "snow wall" around the leveled area, and suspend a large plastic tarp over the future site of your tent. Both will help shed snow and deflect wind away from your shelter. Spread a second tarp under the future location of the tent floor to help minimize moisture seepage, and while setting up, keep all posts, ropes and anchors together to prevent loss.

As for tents, I like lightweight, peaked, non-waterproof dome models, which can be set up without removing mitts. Peaked dome designs also reduce snow buildup, decreasing the likelihood of collapse. Non-waterproof is important, too. Unless you intend to hold your breath, each person releases a minimum of one pint of water into the air each night, forming condensation. Condensation can be minimized by opening the top of the door on one side and the bottom on the other side to facilitate cross ventilation, but if the tent is waterproof from outside in, it's also waterproof from inside out, leading to the formation of ice crystals inside the tent ceiling and walls. Of course, this will happen to some degree with any tent, but using a lightweight, non-waterproof dome tent, you can simply invert the unit and dump out any accumulated frost each morning.

Winter tenting equipment is different than that used in summer. Anchors, for example, should be discs that can be buried in the snow. Standard anchors are impossible to work with in rock-hard frozen ground. Other good features include tunnel entry, helpful for keeping out wind and providing a place to brush snow off outer clothing layers prior to entering the tent, and a cook hole, a zippered hole in the tent floor that allows you to set up a gas stove for inside cooking and heating. *Be sure to light your stove outside, then bring it in, so in the event of a flare-up caused by spraying fuel during the priming process, you won't start an undesired blaze.* Always be sure to have adequate ventilation anytime an indoor cook stove is lit.

Next, spread a thick, full-length Ensolite pad between your bedding and shelter floor. This will add an effective barrier against condensation, and an added layer of insulation between your sleeping bag and the cold ground. Sleeping bags should be chosen based on their insulating capability. "Just remember," claims Paul Schurke, a recognized winter camping expert and guide from Ely, Minnesota, "most heavy-duty bags feature a fleecy mass that must become the same temperature as your body in order to keep you comfortable. If you simply crawl into a cold sleeping bag, no matter how good it is, this mass will do its job and draw heat, and should you go to bed groggy and cold you will chill, or worse yet, acquire hypothermia shortly after settling down because the bag is absorbing your body heat."

"Rather," Paul recommends, "warm your sleeping bag by the fire or stove prior to settling down for the evening, sip hot liquids, exercise heavily to get your blood pumping, and carry a hot water bottle and warm blanket to bed with you. If you wish, a small pressurized white gas stove can also be used in your sleeping quarters prior to retiring. Just be sure to have adequate ventilation and be sure it's turned off at bedtime for safety."

Where legal, a warm fire is always welcome at the end of a cold winter day, so if land use permits, bring a sturdy folding saw for gathering and stockpiling dead, dry wood. And no matter how dry, use fire starter tabs, which will catch immediately and burn hot. If wood is scarce or isn't legal to use in your area, invest in a heavy-duty camp stove. Either way, stoking up a warm fire or stove to help warm yourself, and your clothing, bedding, hot water bottles, snacks, and drinks before retiring is a winter treat you'll come to appreciate as much as a hot bath.

Remember, the key is to be warm, safe, and well-prepared. Winter camping is not meant to be a survival trip, but rather an enjoyable recreation alternative.

Clothing

The secret here, like preparing for any cold weather experience, is to remember the layering concept. Your clothing system should again be based on the "WWW" layering strategy, the acronym standing for "Wicking, Warming, and Wind," introduced in Chapter One.

The wicking layer is closest to your body, and should be comprised of polypropylene or other similar synthetics, designed to keep you warm even if they get wet by wicking moisture away from skin. They dry fairly quickly because they are made of hollow-core fabrics that act like straws to move moisture out through osmosis.

The next layer is the insulating, or warming layer, used to capture warm body heat. Lofty materials such as down, hollofil, or synthetic fleece are good examples. All help create dead air space that traps heat yet allows moisture to escape, without being bulky.

The third layer is the wind protective layer. This layer is designed to cut the wind and keep water from soaking in, yet remain breathable and release moisture vapor from inside out. A good example of such material would be Gore-Tex. Otherwise, go with a one-piece system such as Northern Outfitters's unit, made for just such usage. One of these units plus a few changes of synthetic long underwear will keep you comfortable, warm and dry for extended periods, even in extreme cold.

Remember, damp skin is much colder than dry, due to the cooling process of evaporation, and if your clothing traps moisture, these materials become useless, if not dangerous. The real secret is to stay dry, block the wind, and remain "comfortably cool." Should you cross the threshold of perspiration while winter camping, you're in serious trouble.

To avoid this, you must use different combinations of clothing depending on the conditions. Being dynamic is especially important when spending extended periods exposed to cold weather. Layers of clothing should be added or removed, depending on the air temperature, wind, and your level of physical exertion. Every ten or fifteen minutes, evaluate whether you feel hot or cold, then add or strip layers, adjusting outside jacket zippers, cuffs, hats, and scarves to either close warm air in or allow cool air to rise through the clothing and out at the neck. Also make sure you have warm footwear, mittens, and a stocking cap.

The cap is especially important because your head is the body's heat regulator, either releasing or holding heat depending on your headwear. Remember, as the head and vital organs begin cooling, the body reduces and slows blood flow to your extremities. If your head is warm, however, blood flow increases. Toes cold? Put your hat on! You'll be surprised how quickly they'll warm.

Once back in camp and preparing for bed, strip down to a second, dry wicking layer, stocking cap or face mask, socks, and mitts. Dry the other layers overnight, and yes, if hung out, they will dry though sublimation, a process where water goes from solid to gas, even in extreme cold.

This may all sound like a lot of work, but rather than look at these tasks as chores, view them as enjoyable. Be prepared to allow more time for everything you do since organizing for the trip, setting up camp, getting dressed, preparing meals, and travel time simply take longer in winter than summer. With the acceptance of this preconceived mindset, it's much easier to enjoy each task as a part of the overall experience.

Drinking/Eating

Next to clothing, the trick to staying warm while winter camping is to drink and eat a lot, and do it frequently. As with any extended cold weather activity, drinking is most important, as dehydration is a significant concern in cold, dry air. Without adequate liquids, your body's metabolism slows, producing less heat. Remember, as pointed out in Chapter One, drink a lot of liquids of the non-alcohol and non-caffeinated variety. Stick with water, juices, and non-caffeinated herbal teas, preferably warmed.

As for food, eat a lot, often. I haven't seen anyone gain weight while winter camping. Drink and snack frequently, and shift to a diet rich in fatty foods. Fat has three times more calories than carbohydrates or sugars. Furthermore, fried, high-calorie fats provide more energy with less volume than other foods, plus burn slow and steady as opposed to carbohydrates, starches, or sugars that offer quick bursts of energy and heat, but burn fast.

Camp meals must be hearty, but keep cooking simple. Before a trip I fully prepare, then freeze, items such as fried bacon, sausage, scrambled eggs, fish and other meats, instant potatoes with butter and sour cream, and stews and soups. All we must do in camp is mix them with water or milk at the evening meal. I supplement this with heavy bread, butter, doughnuts, and frequent snacks comprised of beef jerky, cheese, cookies, hearty meat or peanut butter sandwiches, hard candy, dried fruit, caramels, instant oatmeal, freeze dried foods, and hot beverages. You'll have no problem keeping foods, as they'll freeze solid and remain that way until you warm them.

In terms of cookware, a large aluminum frying pan and pot with lid serve the group, and an individual needs only a cup, bowl, plate, and utensils. To clean your cookware, scrub with warm water. Soap should be avoided, because if not rinsed properly, which is hard to accomplish correctly in the field, soap residue can bring on a case of stomach cramps you'll never forget.

Next to clothing, the trick to staying warm while winter camping is to drink and eat a lot, and do it frequently.

Snowmobiles aid the transportation of camp's necessities.

Getting Around

Once set up, you'll be ready to relax and enjoy the peace of winter solitude. However, if you're like me, sitting still isn't something that comes easy. When I'm on a winter camping/ice fishing trip, I like to explore, hike, fish, ski, and snowshoe. Yet if not done correctly, such movements can be dangerous.

On most winter camping trips, you'll want to travel on cross country skis or snowshoes. Without these aids, legs "post hole" through deep snow. Perspiration, dehydration, and exhaustion quickly follow from the heavy exertion, and damp clothes and sapped energy quickly create a cold body.

The best way to reduce this risk is to adjust the clothing you're wearing, drink often, and decrease the amount of effort needed to travel by using your snowmobile, cross country skis, or, my favorite method, snowshoes. The basic premise behind snowshoeing is to spread body weight over a larger area than is provided by boots alone, keeping you from sinking in deep snow. Aside from walking with your legs a little further apart, not only do snowshoes provide an easy method of travel, they also make remote winter camping and fishing hotspots more accessible.

An important item for hauling gear is the "cross country sled." This is a light, narrow, boat-type equipment carrier with a slick outer shell that glides through the snow with a minimum of resistance, and can be attached to the body via a specialized harness designed to relieve the strain and fatigue caused by carrying heavy loads over the shoulders. Be sure to pack heavy items first, keeping your shovel on top so it's the first item available at your campsite. The sled will also come in handy in camp for storing accessories and ice tackle, which you can't leave outside at risk of being buried by falling or blowing snow.

Where to Go

State and national parks and forests are good bets for places to take your initial winter camping/ice fishing excursions. Often, book authors, chambers of commerce, tourism associations, outfitters and guides are at your disposal and will help you book reservations. If setting out on your own, be sure to check into permit requirements and local land use practices before leaving. As a final precaution, always tell someone where you're going, your anticipated route, and when you plan to return.

If a winter camping/ice fishing adventure sounds appealing to you, I would highly recommend reading any one of the numerous books and handbooks now available on the sport, then try writing the publisher or author for a current list of winter camping guides that might assist your party on your first trek. Believe me, there are many "tricks" and secrets these experienced guides utilize and will offer that make the winter camping experience more enjoyable. Having a guide will virtually ensure a successful first trip, and many thereafter.

Summary

While still in its infancy, winter camping/ice fishing trips are growing in popularity, namely because they offer a closer, richer, more fulfilling look at this enchanting, icy, marvelous season, leaving life's winter wonders open to great contemplation.

And as those who respect and appreciate the winter outdoors already know, if you're prepared, traveling, fishing, and living directly within the winter elements comprise some of those distinctive activities that enliven our senses and awaken us to another world—a world all too many folks shut out.

Winter Camping Checklist:

   *Map, Compass
   *Snowmobile, Skis or Snowshoes
   *Sleds, Bungee Cords, Backpacks
   *Snow Shovel
   *Tents, Poles, Ropes, Anchors, and Tarps
   *Sleeping Bags, Blankets, and Mats
   *Hot Water Bottles
   *Clothing, Mitts, plus Extras
   *Stove, Lantern, Fuel, Mantles, Funnel
   *Folding Saw, Matches, Fire Starter Tablets
   *Food, Cookware, Paper Towels, Plastic Bags
   *Toiletries, First Aid Kit
   *Flashlight and Batteries, Candles
   *Sunglasses, Water Bottle, Lip Balm, Facial Tissues, Watch, and Emergency Rations
   *Ice Chisel or Drill
   *Ice Fishing Tackle and Safety Gear
   *Tools
   *Personal Items

Chapter 9

Ice Fishing Tournaments

*T*here are mixed opinions regarding fishing tournaments; always have been, probably always will be. Many anglers simply don't approve of the competitive side of fishing, or the big money promotions and purses. I can relate. Fishing, especially ice fishing, is seemingly designed to be a relaxing, social, peaceful sport, not a competitive big money event. Nonetheless, ice fishing tourneys and competitions have appeared and become a part of the scene.

Fisheries

For years ice fishing remained a social, peaceful sport that offered no reward other than a bucket of fresh fillets. That was until the advent of locally organized ice fishing events consisting largely of "fisherees," low key, local fishing contests set up by the town's sportfishing clubs and civic organizations. Primarily set up as fund raisers, these fisherees have become annual traditions that get friends and families together for a day on the ice. They have become a part of ice fishing tradition throughout the ice fishing belt. There's nothing wrong with the idea, either. After all, this gets people interested in the sport, and being around those familiar with the ins and outs provides a learning opportunity for those curious about the sport. It also offers anglers a chance at some give-aways and door prizes, while helping a good cause at the same time.

Ice Fishing Derbies

Ice fishing derbies soon began appearing, too. These are often organized by regional sportfishing clubs or related chapters of such, and sponsored by tourism bureaus or chambers of commerce organizations trying to promote winter sports within largely summer tourist areas. Others are established with the intent of getting children or non-fishing adults interested in this unique sport. Most are designed to offer a variety of prizes for many contestants, not just those catching exceptional fish or the most fish. Often prizes are given for various placements. The angler with the twelfth largest fish, the seventeenth largest catch, the first perch, or the third pike, may take home the prize. That's good, because it offers a good chance of any individual winning something. A four year old who wouldn't likely outfish the local ice fishing wizard, may catch the first perch, for example, and win a major prize. It's a nice format that fills a niche.

But times are changing. Today's veteran, advanced anglers and ice pros are looking for bigger and better challenges, and it appears their wishes are coming true.

Local, State, National Ice Fishing Tournaments

Since ice fishing is not only a highly regarded sport in isolated areas, but popular throughout various areas of the United States, tournaments are appearing at the state and national level. Each year, for example, the Brainerd, Minnesota, Jaycees put on a "$100,000 ice fishing extravaganza." The event draws casual anglers just there to socialize, husband-wife and adult-child teams and groups. The lowest turnout ever, the winter of 1994, had only 4,800 contestants show. The temperature was minus twenty-five degrees Fahrenheit.

In other years, the event has attracted as many as 7,000 ice anglers. The Brainerd Jaycees and neighboring chapters, along with the help of other volunteers, put on the one-day event, which brings an estimated two million dollars or more to the area economy, as contestants purchase gas, sporting goods, clothing, bait, food, and lodging. Eighty percent of the proceeds go to the Confidence Learning Center, a camp for mentally and physically handicapped children. The remaining twenty percent goes to local charities. This has brought a new level of interest to the sport from ice anglers of all skill levels, businesses catering to the tourist industry, communities, and ice fishing tackle manufacturers.

A DeForest, Minnesota, enterprise also holds a one-day ice fishing event, providing prizes ranging from new trucks to portable shelters and ice augers. It, too, draws contestants from all over the ice fishing belt.

This isn't uncommon. In 1992, another tournament, held on the waters of Lake Michigan's Green Bay in Door County, Wisconsin, attracted support from local businesses, the chamber of commerce, and several major ice fishing tackle manufacturers and retailers. The tournament drew 4,300 contestants to the frozen waters of the bay in its first year.

People of all ages, from all walks of life, from all over the country appeared, some from places you wouldn't expect. Anglers from eleven states, including Missouri, Arkansas, even as far away as Florida, turned up to participate in the event with their friends and families. "It was like sittin' on a giant ice cube," exclaimed one excited Florida resident.

While this tournament is no longer held, with this kind of enthusiasm, you can bet currently organized ice tournaments will grow, and that more are sure to appear.

One such tournament is Dave Genz's competition held each year on Lake Okojobi in Iowa, a popular ice fishing lake for residents of that area. While kept informal, don't let the participants fool you. These folks are serious about their sport, and about exchanging cutting edge ice fishing information.

One of the longest lasting, well-organized ice fishing tournaments I've seen is Norb Wallock's Icemasters Classic, held each year in Eagle River, Wisconsin. Norb limits the contestants to three hundred, because the after-tournament banquet facility accommodates only that number of people. Wisconsin now requires a permit for any organized winter tournament, which Norb obligingly applies for. He has support from several manufacturers of ice tackle, Eagle River's Chamber of Commerce, and local businesses.

I questioned Norb about the organization of such a tournament; how to make it fair, and have as little negative impact on the lake being fished as possible.

"We're careful to run a fair tournament with solid rules. We've disqualified a few participants for not complying with our standards and rules, and through such close monitoring, have made this an excellent tournament. We inspect all vehicles thoroughly before contestants leave shore, and have a hired staff to watch all participants. We also plow roads around the lake for added accessibility, and provide tags for each tip-up or rod used by every individual, so we can monitor the number of lines being used to ensure no one is using an unlawful number of lines.

"Of course, the tournament isn't just about rules. We allow each angler to pick their own partner so that adult-child, husband-wife or fishing partner teams can spend time together. The response has been so good that I'm considering a couples tournament!"

Any troubles from local landowners or anglers?, I question.

"No, I invite any of them to participate, or come to watch the tournament. Many have come to watch; some have even brought camcorders to document events. After a short time, they see the positive attitude, our commitment to catch and release, and respect for the lake. And this, combined with the positive economic boom to the area, brings good relationships with the community."

Norb's emphasis and commitment to catch and release is a major positive point. All anglers bring their catch to the weigh station in plastic bags filled with water. They're handled as little as possible, and with the cold water, survival rates are excellent, but just to make sure, captured fish are weighed, then held in a holding area prior to release to monitor the fish's condition. The system seems to work well, as few fish have been lost throughout the history of the event.

Norb, well satisfied with this outcome, invited the Wisconsin Department of Natural Resources to witness the procedure, welcomed them to provide any further input on winter catch and release, and offered to help with any scientific or environmental impact studies. No doubt, such cooperation will foster new knowledge—another benefit of winter tournaments.

Curious, I question Norb about the changes he's seen in fishing methods over the sixteen-year history of his tournament.

"The biggest change I've seen in the sixteen years of the tournament is the move toward finesse," Norb pointed out. "And the number of caught fish has gone up each year, dramatically in recent years. And I don't think this trend has peaked." This says a lot, seeing as winter fishing pressure gets tougher each year, and lakes usually "cycle" in productivity. But it places emphasis on the impact of electronics, new and lighter tackle, and techniques.

"Ten years ago, everybody fished with ice sticks and bobbers," Norb commented. "Today, less than 10 percent of the contestants fish this way. Ice anglers are learning to read the water and adjust to the conditions, just like in summertime. They fish with open minds, and let the fish tell them what they want."

Competition is fostering new and advanced equipment, methods, and techniques, which is yet another advantage of the competitive environment for anglers wishing to learn more about the sport.

International Ice Fishing Tournaments

Ice fishing is not only a highly regarded sport across the northern third of the United States and high elevation areas throughout the lower 48, but also throughout Canada, Finland, Sweden, Norway, Russia, Iceland, Luxembourg, Italy, Japan, and Korea. Many of these countries have already begun to organize highly acclaimed ice fishing events.

In fact, it's not unusual to find 5,000 or more ice anglers in Scandinavian countries participating in an ice fishing competition on any given winter weekend.

That's right, 5,000; and on a single lake, mind you.

Organized ice fishing tournaments exist close to home, but unfortunately, these widely scattered, local events have largely remained small and haven't set the pace for the creation of more

Weigh-in at the 1991 World Ice Fishing Championships

advanced competition. That's discouraging because the folks that consistently place in these events often utilize some innovative, extremely effective tackle and techniques and the word isn't being spread among many other anglers, but only among limited groups of curious anglers in specific areas.

In contrast, European and Scandinavian tournament anglers are aware of the benefits derived from organized competition and angler communication, because they've had representatives competing in open water "Match Fishing" and ice fishing competitions for years. These events draw together thousands of highly innovative, skilled anglers from all over Europe to challenge each other and share ideas, thereby advancing their approaches, philosophies, and angling techniques well into the future. To reach the prestigious world championship, anglers must

The author with a Russian ice fishing professional

fish a series of local, sectional, regional, and national tournaments. Of course, similar results have been attained by organizations such as the Bassmasters and MWC groups right here in North America.

Yet "hardwater" fishing competitions and tournaments were never actually recognized by a centralized, sanctioned organization capable of bringing global ice fishing talent together. That was the case, at least, until 1990, when CIPS (the Confederation International de la Peche Sportive), the official world governing body of international fishing competition, held the first formal world ice fishing event in Finland. Competing countries included Canada, the United States, Russia, Norway, Sweden, Luxembourg, Italy, and Finland. The interest was so strong that another international competition was held in Sweden in 1991, and in Canada in 1992.

In March of 1991, I participated in the 1991 World Ice Fishing Championships in Lovanger, Sweden, as a member of the United States Ice Fishing Team, providing my first taste of real ice fishing competition. What an experience!

I'd never been to Europe, nor had I ever fished in a formally organized ice fishing competition. I had a lot to learn. I was fishing in a foreign country, on unfamiliar waters, several thousand miles from my home in southeastern Wisconsin. It soon became apparent that my ice fishing strategies were as diverse from theirs as the number of miles between our favorite lakes.

At first sight, I stared blankly at their equipment, scarcely believing my eyes. By our standards, they carried relatively little tackle. Their ice rods appeared too short and insensitive. Their lines seemed too heavy. Even their lures differed from ours.

Competitions are a different type of game that is not at all unfamiliar to the Soviet, Swedish, Icelandic, or Finnish teams. In fact, thousands of Europeans participate in ice fishing competitions each winter, many with the ultimate goal of having a crack at the gold in the world championships. Through such experience, they've carefully refined their equipment and techniques to become adept ice tournament anglers.

The more I watched these European competition style methods in practice—and more importantly, saw them work—the more intrigued I became. Not because their approaches were so foolproof, but so different.

Ahh...refreshing new concepts! Suddenly like a child in a candy store, I wanted to know exactly what everything was and what it tasted like, and I soon found out.

I can't possibly list everything I learned in this chapter; a book could be devoted to the subject. I can say that the experience taught me a greater level of versatility and open-mindedness, which I otherwise never would have attained.

In fact, I'll never forget my first day of competition in Sweden...

The sun is about to rise over the Swedish village of Lovanger. Like every morning for the past week, I'm up early, fully awake, still suffering from jet lag and not yet accustomed to the seven hour time difference between the United States and Sweden. As I'm about to learn, I'm

The author visits a Swedish sportshop.

not only behind the Swedes on a time frame, but behind in their carefully refined skills of ice fishing as well.

It's Saturday morning, 4:30 a.m. Quietly I sneak out the door of our peaceful, rustic cabin, careful not to wake the others. Standing on the porch taking in the peaceful serenity of the predawn darkness, I watch as large heavy flakes settle calmly amidst the tall, majestic pines. It's hard to believe that in just a few hours, I'll be among the crowd at the Second Annual World Ice Fishing Championship.

After a light breakfast and an hour or so of brief preparation, the five of us arrive at the weigh-in site and find ourselves standing among hundreds of interested observers, waiting near the snowmobiles

A Swedish competitor's tackle box

that are about to take us to our designated fishing areas. We sign a few scribbled autographs for Swedish children as we wait in the cold, shake hands, and wish each other the best. This is it.

They call my section over the loudspeaker, and suddenly I'm sitting in a sled with five strangers from an equivalent number of countries. One of them is Per-Olof Antonsson of Sweden, who at the end of the day will become the new world champion.

As we bounce along in the sled, I glance into the eyes of my Finnish competitor. Prior to the tournament, these highly secretive but friendly Scandinavian experts say very little about ice fishing to me. Today is no exception. He only nods his head to acknowledge my presence and wish me luck. I return the gesture with a smile and a "thumbs up" sign. My Soviet competitor, sitting next to me, smiles and shakes my hand energetically. A smile is all I'm allowed; he speaks no English.

The sled comes to a stop. Grabbing our equipment, we quickly run to our hopeful hotspots. Shortly thereafter, the sharp crack of the opening gun echoes through the Swedish hills to open the tournament. "Next time I hear that sound," I think to myself, "we'll know who won the competition."

It wasn't until after that final gun sounded and the competitive curtain was lowered that I was able to openly discuss with these foreign experts the unique Scandinavian techniques that led the Finnish team to first place, and the Swedes to a close second.

Our results? We fell just short of third place, beaten by the Soviets who managed to edge us out by just two points.

The Advantage of Participating in Ice Fishing Tournaments

I have to admit that one of my favorite pastimes has always been organizing my tackle box. More fun yet is the chance to have someone else share their tackle box with me. The opportunity to catch a glimpse of someone else's world of fishing—their favorite lure styles, colors, and sizes; their lures with the most teeth marks; and with which lures they've caught their biggest fish, the most fish, or maybe no fish at all—is one of the most enjoyable of all learning experiences.

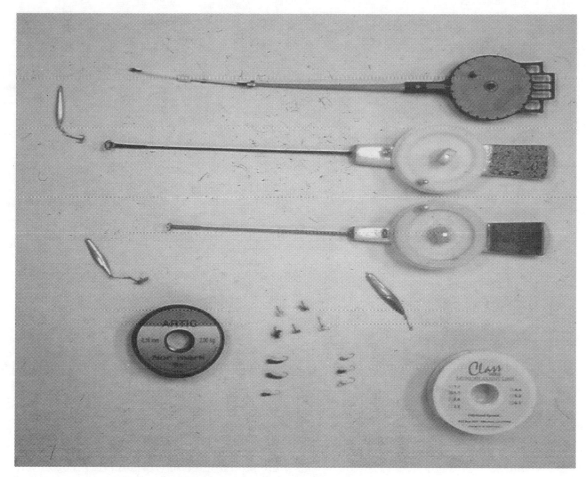

Several European ice rods, lines, and lures

My desire to peer into the boxes of the world's most elite ice anglers intrigued me during the entire ten day trip to Sweden. Prior to the competition, they were essentially closed to view, so when the final guns of the contest shot down the competitive wall that had prevented the exchange of information between competitors, I quickly began speaking with the Swedes and Finns. The most in-depth and interesting conversation was a long one with Per-Olof Antonsson.

I asked Per-Olof if he would explain his strategies and show me a few of his favorite baits. He agreed.

Before continuing on, however, I should point out that power augers and electronics are not currently allowed in World Ice Fishing Competition, so mobility becomes the key to consistent success. In fact, during the four hour competition, I drilled close to one hundred holes. Many of my competitors outdid me.

In addition, predetermined fishing areas are divided out, encompassing a total area approximately the size of a football field, greatly limiting the area that can be legally fished. Each team member must fish in the small segment he or she is assigned to, along with one representative of each of the competing countries. Thus, the mobility factor is critically important, yet ironically, limited.

With all this activity focused in one small area, fish often move or become spooky, limiting successful presentations to highly sophisticated techniques. The experienced Swedes and Fins are masters of these highly sophisticated ultralight ice fishing techniques, all of which are highly refined for tough fishing situations. Much can be learned by carefully evaluating these highly refined techniques, and when applied toward tough or "slow" fishing situations here in the states, ice fishing success can be increased tremendously.

Swedish gold medalist with the author

Their systems begin with the boxes that hold the Scandinavian's equipment and double as a seat. As Per-Olof opened his box, revealing the mystical tackle, I peered eagerly over his shoulder. Within it, I learned, twenty or thirty rods were stored, precisely organized according to aggressive approaches, ultralight approaches, and negative approaches. Within each "sector" were five or six rigged rods, each carefully coordinated and adorned with lures of various sizes

The United States, Canadian, and Russian ice fishing teams at the 1991 World Ice Fishing Championships

and colors and spooled with various line tests. I had three. Of course, they also carry boxes of well-organized accessory lures and hooks.

"Heavier lines," Per-Olof explained, "particularly in deep water, offer more water resistance than a light line. This slows the fall of a tiny jig enough to make a negative fish suck in the easy offering."

I, too, had realized the fish were negative, and had chosen HT's three-quarter pound panfish line and #14 Darter Jig. I figured the lure would fall slowly (which it did) and be lightweight enough for the inactive fish (which it was).

My technique worked, the problem was whenever I tried to drop this ultralight presentation into fifteen feet of water, the process took several seconds to reach bottom. At home, I never think twice about spending an extra thirty seconds to drop my lure into the strike zone. During world competition, however, time is of the essence. The extra seconds wasted each time I lowered my lure added up over the four-hour competition period, and I lost ground. So Per-Olof had me convinced—almost.

I understood that the heavy line created a slow fall, but I had to wonder why the heavy line didn't spook the wary fish.

Per Olof answered without a word. He just pulled a rig from one of his tackle boxes and handed it to me. What he showed me was a Pirkar Spoon, (pronounced Pilkey Spoon) somewhat similar in design to a Swedish Pimple, rigged with a split ring and a six to seven inch light line monofilament leader tied to—get this—a #22 hook.

As Per-Olof explained this system, it suddenly made sense. The heavy line between the rod and flasher spoon slowed the lure's fall, while the light leader was practically invisible to the fish, and the bait with the tiny hook floated safely down behind it.

"When the Pirkar reaches about a foot off bottom, I stop the lure, allowing the tiny hook to float slowly down in front of negative fish. Believe it or not, even negative fish can't resist a tasty bloodworm floating right down in front of them on a light wire #22 hook. They slowly approach the bait, flare their gills—and boom!" Per Olof explained, "They're weight in favor of the Swedish Ice Fishing Team."

"The heavy line also slows the erratic action of the Pirkar, which shouldn't be overdone with spooky fish," Per-Olof added.

I noticed that not only did the heavy Pirkar spoons drop quickly, but my competitors didn't have to stop and skim their holes to drop an ultralight lure into the hole. Every time I drilled a hole and stopped to skim ice chips I was losing ground. My competitors simply dropped their

Snow sculpture at the 1991 World Ice Fishing Championships

People gathered at weigh-in of 1991 World Ice Fishing Championships

presentations through the ice chips, and were consequently able to spend more time fishing, and less time skimming holes. In addition, they used barbless hooks. "Can take fish off very fast this way," Per Olof emphasized.

In the states and Canada, barbless hooks accentuate faster releases if you're practicing catch and release. This is important in cold weather, where damage to the fish's eyes is caused by overexposure to sub-freezing temperatures.

I also determined that tiny, lightweight hooks are easier for negative fish to suck into their mouths. A heavy teardrop or spoon is just too much for negative fish to suck in with the subtle, half-hearted flare of their gills, and I pointed this out to Per-Olof. "Of course," Per-Olof smiled brightly, realizing I was catching onto his reasoning.

Another thing I noticed was after a Scandinavian caught a fish, they'd immediately drop their line back down. I asked Per-Olof why.

"The sight of a feeding fish often draws other fish into the area in a feeding frenzy, which is essentially what the Pirkar Spoon imitates in the first place." Unquestionably, the system works.

This brings us to the lure itself. Pirkar Spoons are fascinating lures; perhaps the most fascinating ice lures I've ever laid eyes on. At first glance, it appeared that each Pirkar was the same, but I couldn't have been more wrong. Each is different, and works differently, depending on its own unique weight and shape, and how you jig it.

I also learned that my competitors spend many hours watching each of their lures respond to various jigging actions in a clear plastic pail. Each lure was then labeled: the most wide wobbles for active fish, and less vigorous ones for neutral fish. The ones that fished "stiffly" were reserved for negative fishing situations. I suppose in some respects, the Pirkar could be considered somewhat akin to a Heddon Zara Spook. The lure does little by itself, but the subtle design differences between Pirkar Spoons enable the angler to make the lure respond differently to each angler's individual jigging motions.

The Scandinavians also choose their Pirkar Spoons based on the depth they're fishing. "Lighter spoons in shallow water, heavier spoons in deep water situations," Per-Olof explained. If the fish refuse to bite, he bounces the lure off bottom, "one time, not very many," Per-Olof emphasized, "or boom, you'll scare the fish away. But once you're in the right area, shake the lure in place gently, trying to tempt them to hit the tiny hook dancing seductively in a puff of silt stirred up from the bottom, allowing the bloodworm to fall in front of them."

Differently designed lures have different actions, and therefore have different applications. Learning to apply the correct action to the correct situation is an extremely important facet of jigging. Using this knowledge in the right place at the proper time, I'm convinced, is what separates a good ice angler from an expert one.

So what benefit are ice tournaments? An education. Pirkar Spoons aren't all that different from a Bay de Noc Swedish Pimple or Mepps Syclops. With each of these lures, and similar jig-

The author lifts a perch during international competition.

ging spoons, taking the time to study the various actions that result from different jigging methods and modifications can reveal the available options and the lure's true overall versatility.

After all, the flash created by a spoon plays on the naturally competitive instincts of active fish. When a fish sees flash, they think other fish are darting toward a food source and feeding actively. Essentially, these fish become competitive and swim over to get their fair share. When they do, your hook sticks them. However, fish feed differently, depending on their mood. Active fish may move around aggressively, while inactive fish may not move at all. So experiment with your lures before fishing to decipher which of your lures are best designed for various fishing situations and particular conditions.

In world competition, for instance, the best action for the first portion of the competition (while the fish were still active) was a wide, wobbling flash that darted out and looked like another fish feeding. After the activity on the ice spooked most other fish fifteen or twenty minutes into the competition, a slower action spoon with less wobbling gradually became more effective.

Obviously, the Scandinavians understand that mobility and versatility are critical to consistent tournament success. Regardless of whether or not you fish tournaments, you should, too. Such practice will allow you to pick up on the background knowledge and subtle details necessary to catch winter fish under tough or high pressure conditions

Maybe you're not a tournament angler. However, popular lakes being pressured by sophisticated anglers create a similar situation. The ability to make that subtle change that leads to more strikes can mean the difference between a fish or two and a limit.

European strategies work, and so do ours. The bottom line is fish are fish no matter where you go. Anglers all around the world face the same sets of challenges; they just respond to them in different environments, and consequently, use different approaches and ways of thinking to solve the same sets of problems. It's seeing, realizing, and understanding these changes that allows us to modify our approaches, become more versatile, and catch more fish.

There's always room for trying something new. And combining the best qualities of various productive strategies and concepts will always put you on the trail toward becoming a better ice angler.

Catch And Release Ice Fishing

The rapid sophistication of today's snowmobiles, four-wheelers, electronics, tip-ups, rods, reels, lines, and lures, and their effect on new-found ice angler mobility, knowledge, and techniques is unquestionably leading to increasing advanced ice angling skills, and correspondingly, increased pressure on our fisheries. As pressure becomes greater, and as advanced ice fishing tournaments are established, the argument for successful catch and release methods on the ice presents itself.

Given these higher levels of knowledge, ice anglers must have an increased awareness of environmental responsibility and ethics. Included on this list of ethical responsibilities is the catch and release issue. From a proper management standpoint, I feel ice anglers have advanced in stature faster than fisheries officials have been able to compensate, further adding to this responsibility. Without cooperation on both sides, the effects of possible winter under-management, overharvest, and ineffective catch and release practices could seriously harm segments of our fisheries.

Although we don't have all the answers, resourceful anglers must use common sense and act responsibly until more information can be attained. For instance, fish intended for release must be reviewed carefully to see if they're likely candidates for successful releases. If a fish is hooked in the tongue, gills, or stomach and is bleeding, it stands little chance of survival. Furthermore, fish shouldn't be dropped on the ice or handled with dry gloves, which remove layers of protective slime and increase the chance of delayed mortality.

In addition, fish should be returned to the water as soon as possible. If fishing in a hut with a large hole, fish intended for release shouldn't be removed from the water at all, but rather unhooked and released immediately. If extra time is required to unhook a fish or you're in doubt about a fish's chance of survival, the best bet is to have a water-filled cooler or temporary holding pen drilled into the ice, where fish can be momentarily held for review prior to release. Gaffing, of course, is out.

If conducted properly, there are some distinct advantages to winter catch and release. First, cold water temperatures decrease the number of organisms living in the water, which lessens the chances of parasitic, fungal, or bacterial infections, even if fish are pulled from the water for short periods of time. Secondly, cold water holds more oxygen than warm water. This reduces oxygen deficits, and furthermore, reduces the metabolism of fish thereby slowing their "respiratory volume" or the amount of water being pumped through the gills, allowing them to absorb greater amounts of oxygen from the water before it circulates back out.

This ability varies with many factors, including the standard metabolism of the species, its size, length of time it was hooked, the actual temperature and oxygen content of the water, the depth the fish was hooked, and even the lake type being fished. A deep, cold oligotrophic glacial shield lake in northern Ontario will likely hold more oxygen throughout the winter than a shallow, eutrophic prairie lake in southern Wisconsin. And we're just scratching the surface. Many other variables exist that must be studied.

Every species, condition, and lake is different, and many variables must be reviewed and carefully studied before positive conclusions can be made. Unfortunately, winter catch and release studies monitoring such factors have been minimal.

Thankfully, some research is now getting underway. One such investigation was completed by Alan J. Dextrase and Helen E. Ball of the Ontario Ministry of Natural Resources. They studied delayed mortality of lake trout caught through the ice in relatively shallow water (two to seven meters) with live minnows fished on still lines. Fifty trout were caught and held for a 48 hour period. All of them were hooked deep in critical areas (gills, deep mouth, and stomach), and showed signs of bleeding. Three of four fish hooked in the gills died. Of the twenty-three fish hooked superficially in the mouth, none died.

The importance of the study is simple. New regulations such as reduced possession limits and trophy size limits are being introduced for lake trout to protect this precious resource for future generations of anglers. Yet the success of these regulations depends on the survival of released fish, and anglers must realize what conditions are suitable for successful releases in order for the new management to work. Of course, future studies comparing the use of live bait with artificial lures, which aren't as likely to be taken deeply, could be organized and would probably generate some interesting data.

Another such study was completed in the states by Paul Cunningham of the Wisconsin Department of Natural Resources, who studied winter pike releases. The experiment reviewed ice anglers on three separate lakes. Again, all fish were caught on stillfished live bait methods. Anytime an angler caught a pike, a fisheries biologist recorded the size of the fish, the type of hooking method used, how and where the fish was hooked, and the length of time it was held before being released. The fish were then marked for later identification and released into underwater cages where they were held and observed for forty-eight hours.

In this study, the most important factor determining successful releases was based on the type of hook used to catch the fish. "When we combined results from all three lakes, we found that less than one percent of the pike caught on treble hooks died after being released, while one-third of those caught on Swedish Hooks died," Cunningham reported. "Those caught on Swedish Hooks tended to be hooked deeply in the mouth or gills, which probably accounted for a higher mortality."

These results would indicate—given the right conditions and provided we follow the correct procedures—that pike caught ice fishing stand an excellent chance of surviving when released, a plus for fish managers and anglers alike.

"Of course, the success of new size limits and reduced bag limits for increasing northern pike populations would depend on the survival of any fish released," Cunningham added. "The results of this study simply indicate that such proposals could help increase both fish size and populations, but could be undermined if anglers released fish that were caught using Swedish Hooks."

The study, among others, has caused the department to change length limits and enforce reduced daily bag limits on some Wisconsin lakes to increase the pike's overall size and population. Previously, no winter size limit existed for pike in southern Wisconsin and the bag limit was five.

Chapter 10

Hardwater Secrets That Provide The "Edge"

*T*he revolution in ice fishing has brought new found knowledge to the sport, resulting in better catches, and in turn, creating higher levels of fishing pressure than ever before. Depending on your viewpoint, this could be good or bad.

The bad side is that if you don't keep up with the times, your ice fishing will become more difficult and less productive, especially on popular waters where fishing pressure may become intense.

Armed with the right knowledge, however, this pressure works like a capitalistic society: it pushes people to delve into the matter at hand more efficiently, look at it differently, and try to provide a creative edge.

No one can argue that things have changed dramatically in the ice fishing world over the last ten years. Ice anglers are now more knowledgeable than ever in how to find and catch fish through the ice. Many of the tactics being used could even be considered high-tech.

Fishing in mobile, versatile groups can help you cover water and put you on fish fast.

Mobility is one of the keys to modern day success.

Many of you, for example, have probably used such "edges" as a lake map and sonar unit to find potential location hotspots, and to pinpoint primary combination hotspots—the "spots on the spots"—that feature secondary cover.

Understanding the basic concepts involved with using sonar on the ice, I'm presuming you also stand ready to move as necessary in search of just the right combination of structure, cover, forage, and other factors that attract and hold the largest, most active groups of winter fish.

You also likely realize you can't play the presentation game right without using your sonar unit to its fullest capacity, either. So after finding primary combination hotspots, you begin carefully experimenting with various presentations, observing where your lure is positioned in relation to bottom and which depth fish are coming through. Then you meticulously monitor fish reactions to your presentation, doing whatever it takes to correctly pattern them and turn what could otherwise be a "slow" day for many into a highly successful outing.

The problem is, with so many anglers now using such strategies to their advantage, it's becoming increasingly difficult to stay ahead of the crowd and keep an edge. The more anglers and the more advanced techniques fish are subjected to, the faster this change occurs and the tougher fishing becomes.

However, it's not impossible.

Keeping Your Edge

With such high-tech pressure creating increasingly "educated" fisheries, if you want to stay ahead of the crowd, you must work extra hard to keep your edge. This requires refining your approach and paying special attention to subtle, yet important details that most anglers overlook.

In order to gain an edge, today's truly advanced ice anglers are paying attention to things they wouldn't likely have even thought of, much less implemented, only a few years ago. Tournament fishing will promote such cutting edge advancements and technology.

Competitive anglers will find that focused mobility is the first key edge. To be consistently successful, you must keep moving strategically from lake to lake, and from high percentage spot to high percentage spot, always experimenting, observing, concentrating, and searching for clues that lead to patterns. If you notice fish relating to a specific area, responding to a particular presentation, or biting on a certain live bait rigged just so, turn on an analytical mind and try to determine why.

The same thing also applies if they're not in a specific area or reject a certain presentation. Never overlook a single clue. If the fish demonstrate that they do or don't like something, make it your mission to find out why.

This means paying attention to details most other anglers miss. Some days weeds might be the location key to catching fish, but a good angler will notice whether these weed patches are on shoreline flats, or on points or humps. Observant, detailed anglers might also note that the most productive weeds consist of cabbage, are located near current in fourteen feet of water, and hold the most fish in bright conditions during the late ice period. Furthermore, the most active fish might hold on the shaded side of these clumps, and bite best on slowly jigged, #3 silver Swedish Pimples.

You must identify specific feeding patterns that may change throughout the winter, or within a week, a day, an hour, or each jiggle of your rod tip. This means you must concentrate and experiment, and be observant and detail oriented. Using the proper tools, learn to be precise, as described in various methods throughout this book. If you do not, you won't be as successful as the angler who does.

Secrets that Offer an Edge

Today's Global Positioning Systems are one modern edge. These units, especially on big water, allow you to electronically mark your specific hotspots, and return to them quickly, accurately, and repeatedly on an infinite basis. Once near these marked hotspots, you can use sonar to pinpoint secondary features, to locate schools of the most active fish within these areas, and ultimately, to monitor their specific activity levels.

For this last purpose, I feel flashers perform better than LCRs, simply because they provide instantaneous readouts, enabling you to monitor immediate fish movements and reactions that pro-

An angler with a GPS unit

vide clues that indicate the fish's specific activity levels. While LCRs have been dramatically improved in recent years and will tell you a great deal of information, they still don't provide instantaneous readouts.

Either way, you'll want to make sure your electronics are properly adjusted for maximum performance. A properly positioned transducer placed horizontal and level in the hole, for example, ensures the best possible signal from what's below: depth, bottom, secondary cover, your lure, forage, and fish. If your transducer is not placed properly, your true reading's precision is reduced.

Vexilar's FL-8 is an outstanding unit for maximizing precision monitoring, especially when specific, detailed presentations must be carefully watched. As mentioned earlier, the FL-8 offers a color readout that indicates whether your lure, bait, or

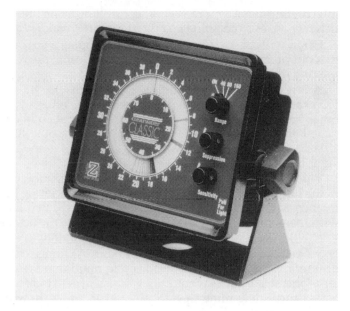

Used correctly, a flasher is the ultimate ice fishing tool. (Zercom)

target fish is near the center, middle, or outside edges of your cone, via color separation of red, orange, or green, respectively. You can easily spot fish as they move toward or away from your bait, even those coming through tight to bottom, because the red bottom signal intensifies.

Thanks to the instantaneous readouts, you can also monitor fish positioning and movements, even speed, given the changing color and intensity of the signals received. This not only makes the FL-8 one of the most precise information providing units I've ever used on the ice, but also the most decisive.

While Zercom's Clearwater Classic lacks color readout, these units offer similar precision. With these flasher units, you not only see your lure and its movements, you can see your split shot and your bait clearly at any depth. In fact, you can actually see a minnow wiggling on your hook or lure, as the signal marking the bait flickers intensely. If your minnow comes off the hook or is stolen, the mark becomes less intense and the flicker stops. These flashers are so exact that you can differentiate a fish hiding among thick weeds, or even tell when a tiny maggot has been stolen from tiny micro ice lures.

Reading these units requires study. Even with such precise units, you must concentrate until you know what each signal looks like and what it represents. You must know your unit—regardless of what model you use—and understand its capabilities and limitations. Once this is fully understood, your unit is properly set, and signals are correctly interpreted, you'll begin the learning process of pinpointing definite patterns on a consistent basis. You'll be able to read depth, mark structure, and note bottom content, such as rocks, weeds, and other forms of secondary cover. You'll also be able to determine the presence of forage and fish, and even analyze the instantaneous responses of the fish to specific presentations.

After you have a pretty good idea what the fish are up to in terms of location, positioning, movement, and activity patterns, find a comfortable position for holding your rod, and begin experimenting with various lure styles, sizes, types, colors, and actions. Go slow and be specific. You need to be consistent and organized to get a feel for the exact presentations fish will respond to, particularly when you make precise jigging motions.

This brings you back to interpreting what you're seeing. Whether working aggressive jigging lures or subtly fishing live bait, you must have just the right blend of attraction and triggering motions to tempt the most strikes. So fine-tune your presentation. Just as you'd experiment with crankbaits, spinnerbaits, plastics, or slip bobbers in summer, working the highest percentage areas and experimenting with various styles, sizes, colors, and actions to cover more water and maximize your catching percentages—try to accomplish the same with your winter jigging. Experiment with a variety of lures, always watching your screen, carefully interpreting what you're seeing, controlling your presentation, and monitoring instantaneous fish responses to combine just the right lures, actions, and movements to maximize your catch.

Often with pressured fish, you can instigate a strike by making them snap at a fast-moving bait out of anger or instinct, or just the opposite, by tempting them with a light, gentle, barely-moving live bait rig.

A Bay de Noc Swedish Pimple or William's Ice Jig worked with a flashy, aggressive action, for example, will often trigger strikes from otherwise completely uninterested fish. On the other hand, a lightweight, slow falling jig or plain hook tipped with a small minnow or grub fished on light tackle is often more effective. In some situations, blending the two by combining a flashy jigging spoon rigged with a long, light monofilament leader tipped with a lightweight jig or hook can be the right combination.

The basis for making these determinations is knowing exactly where your lure is in relation to the bottom and to fish. It is also important to know how your lure is moving. It makes a difference whether it moves a fraction of an inch, two inches, ten inches, or a foot. Experiment with them all, and note which seem to produce the best results.

Next, continuously try different jigging motions at various depths. Fish may change preferences each week, each day, or each hour. At times, each fish from one school may even react differently. So experiment, and keep in mind that the process of pinpointing presentation patterns and strike zones is continual. The goal is to look for general location and presentation patterns, then determine specifically what the fish will consistently go for. Proper use of electronics makes this possible.

If the fish are holding in cabbage patches on the edges of hard bottom main lake points in fourteen feet of water, and aren't moving from one depth to another, and you must jig right in front of them with a #3 Swedish Pimple to provoke a strike, sonar will tell you. If the fish won't hit a bait placed directly at their level but can be teased up to provoke strikes, you'll see that, too. And if they prefer a fast jigged silver Swedish Pimple to a slowly worked, prism pink one, you'll know. Either way, once you get them moving, there's a better chance of patterning the fish and increasing your catch.

Exposed structure and cover is easy to find, but most winter cover, hidden by a thick layer of ice, is visible only to ice anglers knowledgeably using electronics.

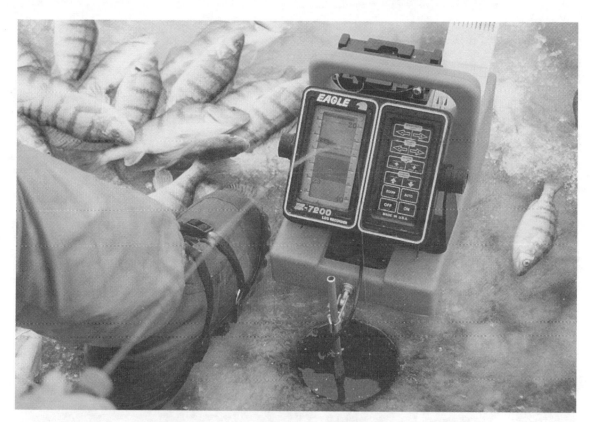

Today's LCG's are an easy way to find depth, structure, and fish.

Don't stop here. Also experiment with different knots to see which provide the loosest, most natural action. Always sharpen your hooks to a fine point, and reduce the barb on small micro and ultralight jighooks to a tiny bump. If you wish, try bending your hook shanks and/or hookpoints open slightly to increase hooking percentages—it helps. On larger, active swimming, vibrating or flash-type ice lures, experiment with different hook styles, sharpen your hooks to a fine needle point, and don't be afraid to try stinger hooks. In either case, consider dropper lines to a smaller, lighter hook as well.

Regardless of lure selection, be sure to experiment with various live bait and artificial tippers. Sometimes a certain bait type or specific method of rigging can mean all the difference in the world, simply because the bait offers a certain shape, profile, color, flash, motion, taste, scent, or drop rate the fish find irresistible. It can make a difference with pressured fish.

Try considering and experimenting with such things next time you ice fish. Become intimately familiar with your electronics and utilize them to their fullest capacity to find and mark specific high-percentage locations, and pinpoint the best combinations of secondary features, cover, forage, and other parameters. Effectively monitor specific fish positions, movements, responses, and reactions to various presentations, focusing carefully on suspending your bait precisely within the highest percentage strike zones. Always pay attention to detail. It pays!

Competition is tough, so today's ice anglers must practice highly advanced techniques. They mark, locate, and pinpoint primary fish producing structures using lake maps and electronics that bounce signals off satellite constellations orbiting the earth to reveal precisely where their hotspot is positioned on the planet. Many watch and interpret as modern sonar reveals the lake bottom, depth, bottom content, weeds, rocks, wood, forage, and fish.

Once location patterns have been determined, these anglers experiment with a variety of presentations until they decipher a specific, high-percentage presentation. Many also check to see what the fish are feeding on, then experiment with highly specialized rods, reels, lines, and hundreds of ice lure designs, styles, sizes, colors, and actions, tipped with a variety of baits. Some innovative ice anglers even use select gear to read water temperatures, oxygen concentrations, and pH factors.

Using electronics, catches like this are possible.

Consistent ice anglers have realized the benefits of such systems, and are taking full advantage of them. In addition, each year more people learn, refine, and become more detailed and skilled with their approaches, maximizing their percentages. On heavily pressured waters, those who don't take full advantage of such systems, re-evaluate their efforts, keep an open mind, and pay special attention to detail, will fall behind. I've experienced many tough days on heavily pressured lakes the last three winters, even when using advanced electronics, equipment, and techniques. Most days, however, I'm able to catch fish—sometimes limits that leave others using similar methods and techniques shaking their heads and asking how.

The key? Mobility, focus, and attention to detail. On most pressured lakes, if you pre-plan, study the lake, try structure after structure, and always fish the best combinations of secondary cover and available forage, you'll often mark fish. There they are, right where they're supposed to be, clearly defined on your electronics. Heart beating fast, you lower your favorite lure to them, but to no avail. They might ignore most everything in your tackle box and versatile bag of tricks. But if you fish effectively and precisely over large schools, concentrating carefully with a truly versatile, innovative variety of subtle, detailed approaches, typically at least a fish or two from each school will bite. Do this in ten or twenty spots, and things will eventually add up.

The author with a trophy brown trout

However, on some intensely pressured waters, you may not find concentrations at all. The combination of fishing pressure, activity on the ice, and conditioned fish break up schools, leaving only scattered, inactive fish. In such situations, move until you locate areas holding or funneling the largest number of fish through them, then proceed to stick it out, carefully fishing the same general area with the largest variety of innovative presentations as possible to maximize your catch.

Try thinner lines, and lighter, smaller lures and baits. Work them slower. Experiment with tiny, thin plastic strips in various colors. Sharpen your hooks. Be sure to bend your hookshanks and hookpoints out slightly to increase hooking percentages.

Tough fishing? You bet.

On pressured waters in today's world, fish populations can catch serious cases of lockjaw for any number of reasons. But don't let this scare you. When possible, try other areas, or if you must, other lakes.

In short, it's you, your knowledge, and your advanced equipment and techniques against "educated" fish. This is not always the most appealing situation to face, but it is among the most challenging, and with success, the most rewarding.

If you love a challenge, try applying mobile, versatile, innovative, focused strategies when fishing pressured waters. You may find these conditioned populations tough, but not impossible. As you learn and refine your techniques, you'll find yourself on the cutting edge of modern ice fishing, catching fish consistently. Should you wish, you may even be capable of participating in full-blown professional ice fishing tournaments that will perpetuate your desire to remain on the cutting edge even further.

Chapter 11

Ice Fishing With Kids

I'm not sure what they were for, or how they got there. I never cared. All that mattered was that panfish were attracted to them, and as I watched the kids catch several bluegills from beside them, I suddenly felt young again.

The rotting, algae covered, eight-foot 4x4 boards were perhaps parts of an old dock, long since forgotten, or remnants of a bank reinforcement project undertaken by a property owner or conservation minded sportsman of years past. Maybe they were shanty blocks left by a thoughtless ice angler, which soaked up water and sunk.

It doesn't matter. The boards stuck out firmly off bottom among a large patch of vegetation, and were easily recognizable on electronics. They held panfish periodically throughout most of the winter, and I could rely on the spot to allow the kids to sit there and catch fish for an hour or so, easily keeping them occupied until their attention span waned.

This was always a rewarding hour; a time for reflecting back on my childhood, my life, and my fatherhood, in between untangling lines, baiting hooks, and chasing escaped food wrappers across the lake's snowy surface, lost by a child during the excitement of hooking a fish.

It was such reminiscing that recently brought me some refreshing thoughts. For the last several winters, I've spent many hours ice fishing using thousands of dollars worth of electronics. My global positioning system locks onto satellites in interstellar space to accurately convey the exact coordinates of my hotspot on this planet. I fish one-half pound monofilaments and incredibly strong braided monofilaments that hardly stretch at all. I keep track of fish using 3-D sonar technology that electronically monitors the position of fish and objects around me, and monitors water temperatures and pH using high-tech probes developed for the fisheries sciences. I jig Swedish Pimples, Marmooska Spoons, Jigging Rapalas, Marmooska Minnows, Cicadas, Fire-Eye Jigs, Water Fleas, and Rat Finkys in a repertoire of sizes and a rainbow of colors.

Wow. How did it ever get so complicated? I used to catch fish with none of this equipment available to me. What's even more amazing is I never questioned why I was using all this equipment—not until a cold evening last January, when a three year old taught me something.

The lesson began when one of my colleagues asked if I'd help his son ice a few bluegills after work. As always, whenever the opportunity to go fishing arises, I jumped at the chance. He suggested we try a nearby farm pond. I nodded in agreement.

Two days later, his three year old, Andy, took my hand as we walked toward the garage to get his sled. His little legs were working hard to move through the deep snow in his miniature snowsuit, and his gentle eyes were peeking out from between his scarf and stocking cap. I kept him from falling by simply lifting on his arm each time he would lose his balance.

On the way, we stopped to watch a cardinal fly from the bird feeder, and to look at the different shaped snowflakes. His eyes conveyed a mind at work, and reflected genuine fascination.

We finally reached the garage, where I sat him in his plastic sled, and, warning him to hold on tight, began pulling him down the hill toward the pond. So far as I could tell, that was the highlight of the trip for him.

We reached the pond, and I quickly drilled a hole, rigged a basic Little Jigger jig pole/ice reel outfit for him, and dropped the bait into the hole. Almost immediately, the bobber bounced, popped under the surface, and disappeared. I set the hook for him, showed him how to pull the fish up, and let him at it. Watching him land that four-inch bluegill, eyes wide, nose running, I

Father and son ice fishing

suddenly remembered why I began ice fishing in the first place and why I love fishing so much yet today. And I found myself smiling—laughing out loud, actually—almost as energetically as the three year old. One of those rare, genuine, real laughs.

The fun lasted an hour or so, until all too soon the attention span ended and we headed back home. But for me, the trip wasn't over. I still relive that trip in my mind time and time again.

Perhaps it was the way he grinned at me as his first fish lay flopping on the ice at his feet, covered with snow. Maybe it was the way he hesitated when I told him he could touch the fish, or the excitement in his voice when he asked if he could keep the fish to show Dad and Mom, and Grandpa and Grandma. Whatever it was, it stayed with me.

Later that week, I again found myself ice fishing on my favorite little bluegill lake near home with this wonderful three year old, a couple basic jig poles, and a sandwich bag full of cookies his mother made us. We caught about the same number of fish as the cookies we ate, I think. Somewhere, I lost count.

Upon cleaning the fish, I counted twenty-nine, but in Andy's mind, it might as well have been 3,000. At least, that's what he told his mom when we got home. From the looks of things, he will never forget those trips.

Neither will I.

Ask a couple serious ice anglers to recall their most cherished fishing memories, and many will likely mention a favorite trip to a remote Canadian lake, their biggest fish, a big one that got away, or the time their fishing buddy slipped on the ice while bragging about his or her huge catch that dramatically outranked their own. However, after a few laughs and more thought, they might reconsider and describe a childhood fishing memory, or a magic moment ice fishing with a child.

Unfortunately, such special moments seem to be falling by the wayside. Getting kids interested in fishing is a problem today. Fishing has serious competition. Kids are tempted by a myriad of recreational opportunities, most of which are commercialized and tend to dissuade, rather than promote, family participation. In a world where Mom and Dad both have to work overtime just to pay for that new pair of sport shoes the kids "need," time is also of the essence to many parents.

To complicate matters further, it seems even panfish such as perch and bluegill are becoming fairly well educated and more selective. Fishing is no longer as simple as taking the kids to a local ice fishing hole and threading a waxworm on a teardrop.

But no matter how you look at it, fish haven't changed. And when caught, fish have an uncanny ability to captivate. They're able to thrill young and old alike, providing challenging and satisfying fun if you carefully evaluate the right factors.

What factors are important to getting kids hooked on ice fishing? To start with, it has little to do with pH, water temperature, oxygen counts, microstructure, jigging speed, lure classification, and the like. You've got to consider these things in order to put the kids on fish, but once the trip starts, in my opinion, attitude, planning, fishing action, and fun are the most important aspects to children. Mix them together with a touch of love and understanding, and few other things will compete for your kids' time.

The best bet is to start with an attitude change, and I don't mean the kid's attitude. I'm talking about us—the adults—who need to change our outlook on things.

Whether I care to admit it or not, I'm all too often more worried about finding fish and patterning them than anything else. Patience and a willingness to deviate from my normally well-orchestrated fishing plans are critically important to successful kids' outings, which means I've got to make sacrifices. In fact, the smartest thing I ever did was leave my jig rod at home last winter and devote that special time to Andy. Guiding him through each step of how to hook a waxworm, find the depth, set the bobber, and reel in made the trip one of the most memorable excursions I had all year.

What if the fishing is slow or the kids seem to have had enough? Simple. Don't fight it! Set the jig rods down in exchange for making angels in the snow, playing in the portable ice shelter, sledding, or participating in snowball fights or on-the-ice football. If nothing else, you'll feel like a kid again, until the next morning, when your sore muscles remind you you're not seven anymore.

These trips won't be all fun and games. The barrage of questions will be endless, the tangles massive, the bathroom trips frequent, and the complaints of thirst, hunger, and cold constant.

Taking a child ice fishing can be a rewarding experience.

Panfish such as crappie are excellent for teaching tricks of the trade.

Be patient. Anticipate such actions. Show them this is their special time, during which your sole mission is to help them do something enjoyable and help them have fun. Most importantly, prove that you care through your actions. A person who baits their hooks, untangles their lines, points out favorite lures, and explains how to use them will be a hero in the eyes of children, inspiring future trips, and perhaps a lifelong fishing partner. Some kids may be fascinated with electronics—the outdoor version of a video game. Some may not. Feel the situation out, and do what you must to generate interest in fishing. Answer questions, and enjoy this precious time.

At the same time, if they get thirsty or hungry, feed them. If they need to use the restroom, head for shore. If they're cold, pack up for the day. Leave them on the ice just once for too long, and you're sure to foster a counterproductive lifelong disinterest in the sport.

Planning a Kid's Trip

Although it's important to forget about yourself, don't neglect to plan. Choose a lake that has a large population of panfish. It doesn't matter what size. A lake full of stunted bluegills, perch, or crappies is perfect. As long as there's action, the kids will be happy.

Remember that no lake, regardless of its fish population or reputation, is a certainty. Finding a few small panfish will not be difficult, but it does require planning. Call ahead to confirm the that ice conditions and fishing action are favorable before you go. Be aware of cold fronts, poor moon phases, and the different location patterns and factors of the period. Kids don't like slow fishing. You've got to do your homework before taking them out to do the best possible job of insuring success.

Once you've found a suitable lake and the right location, the next challenge is to provide the children with good equipment. Set up a portable shelter; kids love them, and they'll help keep everyone warm. Don't give a child equipment that is difficult to use. They don't need an expensive setup, but by all means, don't give them your rejected equipment either. Poor or damaged equipment only fosters frustration and ruins the fishing experience, creating an "I can't do this attitude," or at the least, disinterest in the sport.

Provide them with lightweight, reliable, easy-to-operate ice reels, or for older children, spincast or spinning reels. Ultralight versions of spinning reels work best, because the small size is easy for children to hold and operate. This may seem obvious, but I've seen many parents hand children their own larger rod and reel combinations, and the children can barely grasp them, much less fight and reel in a fish. Buy warm clothes, mitts and boots, too. It's a good investment in your child's ice fishing future.

Presentation? Simple. A #10 teardrop, a small split shot, and a tiny bobber or float work wonders. In my opinion, bobbers are the ice fishing teacher's best friend. I have yet to see a five year old able to hold an ultralight brim rod still enough to consistently sense the nibble of a sneaky bluegill. With a bobber, however, the kids can move around all they want, and still get a special kick out of watching it go under while feeling the excitement of hooking a fish.

Finally, don't expect a child's attention span to be any longer than it is in school, at

Avoid giving children difficult equipment to use.

When quantity is important for keeping one's attention, bluegill make a big impression.

piano lessons, at baseball practice, or in Sunday School. Kids don't like doing anything all day, so don't be discouraged if they fish successfully for an hour and then want to go home. Keep in tune with their attention span, be fun and flexible, and I guarantee they'll be bugging you to get back on the ice before it melts in spring.

There's no doubt that in today's world of ice fishing, it's easy to get wrapped up in the fancy toys we have available. I'll admit I enjoy using my GPS when I'm fishing big water. I'm convinced my

White bass are also willing to keep any child's line very busy.

$100 custom ice rod and reel combinations help me catch fish more consistently, and that comfortable seat in my heated portable ice shanty makes ice fishing truly comfortable.

Yet one doesn't need fancy equipment to get kids interested in ice fishing. In fact, it's better that you don't take a lot of expensive gear with you. It only confuses them.

Instead, bring just the basics, and a lot of patience. Be sure to follow the few general guidelines presented here to get things started. If all else fails, remember, nothing cures a bout of restlessness like munchies. Hide a few of their favorite treats among your equipment or in a concealed pocket, and in case of emergency, break glass.

Stopping for a burger and ice cream on the way home usually adds to the fun, too. Kids associate such foods with fun, and when these "fun things" are readily available, kids quickly determine that ice fishing trips are a pleasurable experience. I also rationalize that since it's for the kids, it's a legitimate reason to cheat on a diet, making it a pleasurable experience without guilt for us grown-up ice anglers, too.

If the kids want to play a few video games or something on the way home, by all means, do it. After all, kids aren't kids forever. These are the times you'll look back on someday and treasure.

And believe it or not, so will they.

Chapter 12

The Future: Ice Fishing Grows As An Industry

*I*ce fishing is a rapidly growing sport. As I see it, ice fishing equipment, gear, tackle, and tourism—the industry as a whole—is just in its infancy.

More advancements and developments for ice fishing applications are coming in electronics, tip-ups, rods, reels, lines, and lures. As more people become involved in the sport, use these advancements, refine them, and follow the system and methodologies outlined in this book, they'll learn.

Intentionally or not, they'll stumble across new, highly productive location and presentation patterns. They'll develop new techniques, tackle, and ideas that will improve our fishing and make it more productive.

Like other sports, ice fishing is dynamic, not static. Innovative inventors, manufacturers, anglers, and experts alike are coming up on an ice fishing heyday. Over the next several years, we'll all be able to sit back and enjoy the benefits of these innovations.

Left to right, standing, Paul and Joanna Grahl, seated, Ken and Nate Grahl, founders of HT Enterprises, Inc., pioneers in modern ice tackle

HT's lineup of ice tackle-not all shown here. The company offers over 1,000 items for ice fishing.

The industry built around this growth will benefit, too. In the past, many northern and high country restaurants, motels, resorts, campgrounds, guides, and other outdoor-oriented establishments and businesses closed for the winter and the owners headed south, windows boarded up until spring.

That's changing. More mobile ice anglers, armed with warm, comfortable clothing, knowledge, and sophisticated gear aren't just fishing the local lake from a permanent shack and fishing in an occasional club-sponsored fisheree. They're taking extended weekends and vacation time during the midst of the winter. They're loading up the family, the snowmobiles, the four wheelers, the winter camping equipment, the portable shanties, the electronics and the ice fishing gear, and enjoying the winter outdoors. Enterprising business owners, seeing this, are making a stronger effort to service winter outdoor enthusiasts like us.

It's about time. If I take the family into northern Wisconsin for an extended weekend in summer, for renting a cabin, many resorts throw in unlimited use of a boat. In summer, many resorts offer knowledgeable, well-equipped fishing guides, cookouts, fish fries, hiking, special events, and outings. I often wondered why they wouldn't offer unlimited use of an ice shanty in winter, well-equipped winter guides, cookouts, fish fries, skiing, snowmobiling, ice skating, and outdoor adventures.

Now they are. Those business owners and anglers capitalizing on this situation are pioneering something few others have done before, and anglers are enjoying some fantastic opportunities because of it. Many of these areas have lots of available ice fishing water, much of which has never been fished other than by a few local residents. The potential for catching many fish, and large fish, exists in these areas.

This is just the beginning. Communities located near ice fishing areas are capitalizing on this growth. Besides ice fishing, these same communities offer winter camping, snowmobiling,

Forest Lane resort, open year-round

The author is shown here presenting a seminar at the annual Midwest Ice Fishing Show in Waukesha, Wisconsin.

cross country and downhill skiing, dogsledding, wildlife watching, snowshoeing, and relaxing evenings in front of warm fires.

Consequently, sports shows devoted to winter sports, even entirely ice fishing, are also popping up across the country. One of the innovators of such concepts is Doug Reuter, who put on the annual Midwest Icefishing Show, held in Madison, Wisconsin, for the first time in 1989. The show continues, now expanded to two cities, Waukesha, Wisconsin, and St. Cloud, Minnesota. The show includes displays from various ice tackle manufacturers, resorts, and guide services, and even has a "pro booth" where anglers can meet modern day ice pros. The same folks also provide seminars and information on modern day ice fishing.

Other ice fishing shows are held in popular ice fishing areas across the Midwest, somewhat centered around the core of the ice fishing belt but now spreading beyond this nucleus into new realms throughout the northern United States. Many television shows have also noted the increasing popularity of ice fishing, and begun filming ice fishing shows.

Booking a Winter Guide

If a winter ice fishing vacation sounds good, but you're not sure of ice conditions or winter fishing patterns on your intended fishing lakes, a good winter guide might be your answer. They'll show you the ins and outs of the sport, organize and prepare all the equipment, arrange the transportation, and make fishing strategies and plans. All you'll need to do is show up with warm clothes, a fishing license, and a desire to fish. To pursue this effort, stop in at an ice fishing show and speak with a few sport shop and resort owners, guide services, and tourism agencies. You'll find winter guide services are becoming increasingly common.

Last winter I had the pleasure of fishing with several winter guides in Minocqua, Wisconsin, Hayward, Wisconsin, and Nashwauk, Minnesota. All proved to create memories I will not soon forget. And so the daydream begins...

The author filming an ice fishing television show

Winter guide services are becoming more popular each winter.

There is a variety of information available for nearly any winter adventure or destination you would like to enjoy.

Dawn is just breaking as Steve Heem of Jawbreak'r Guide Service in Nashwauk, Minnesota, finishes tying a train of Winter Fishing Systems' portable Fish Trap shelters stuffed with ice tackle to the back of his snowmobile. I'm busy hitching up my unit, the last in line, just as Steve turns the key on his machine's electronic ignition. The scent of two-cycle exhaust wafts through the air and greets me as Steve warms the engine, and when I look up, Steve motions me to hop on.

"Are you ready to catch some fish?" Steve asks over the thrumming drone of the snowmobile engine, knowing all too well I've been overanxious to dip a jig into the hidden depths beneath the ice. I flash Steve a smug grin, which I see returned as I throw a leg over the snowmobile seat. No sooner do I sit, and the snowmobile track catches. Churning snow, the machine begins inching forward.

In two days of fishing, we catch numerous bluegills, crappies, and perch. A large number of the bluegills top eight inches and one bull goes an honest ten inches, 1-1/8 pounds. Several crappies top fourteen inches! In between, we cook out, snowmobile, and enjoy the winter.

This winter guide service, appropriately named "Jawbreak'r," is really one of the pioneers of modern day, multi-species ice fishing guide services. The concept started four years ago, when Steve, who ice fishes frequently—and quite successfully, I might add—decided that as long as he was out fishing so often anyway, he might just as well guide and share his knowledge and enjoyment of the sport with others.

While Steve has guided groups of up to twenty-one, to ensure a shelter for everyone, groups of fifteen or less are best accommodated. If you plan to fish several days, Steve also operates a bed and breakfast, where you can plan the next day's fishing outing and strategies, including the review of various lake maps, equipment, tackle, and rigging. While preparing your tackle and strategies, you can enjoy friendly company, unsurpassed hospitality, and fantastic food. My prediction is that you'll see more, similar services available in the near future.

State parks, fisheries offices and Chamber of Commerce facilities offer a variety of different ideas for the outdoor enthusiast to explore.

Of course, more and more folks are getting into winter guiding each year. Some specialize in a particular species, certain lakes, or specific methods. Most are very good at what they do. Some offer elaborate "permanent" shelters with heaters, stoves, bathrooms, and bedrooms set up over fish—a cabin on the ice, if you will.

If you want to learn a variety of true multi-species techniques, be sure to ask how long has your guide been fishing, what species he primarily catches, how long he's been fishing the target area, how many lakes he fishes, and what kind of equipment and tactics he uses. A good winter guide shouldn't hesitate to provide satisfactory answers to such questions.

Finally, and perhaps most importantly, ask if you're going to catch fish. This may sound a little outright and unruly, but the answer supplied will often reveal a great deal about the guide's personality, honesty, attitude, and confidence. So don't hesitate to ask.

Ask enough questions, and you'll get answers that will help you catch more fish. Don't be afraid to check around. Time was when you'd have to scramble to find one available winter guide service. Today, most popular fishing areas have several good ones available. By checking around, you'll find the one that matches your intentions and pocketbook.

Put this altogether, and you'll notice a growing sport offering more products for helping you catch fish. Just as new tactics and techniques are springing up, so are winter guide services. More travel and trip related businesses are also now catering to ice anglers, converting the winter wonderland into a winter vacationland.

Those anglers who are first to capitalize on these developing opportunities are sure to create successful experiences, and a lifetime of memorable trips.

Chapter 13

The Recipe For Modern
Ice Fishing Success

*I*ce fishing is a unique sport. Through the years, innovative ice anglers have constantly come up with a variety of new, specialized fishing techniques and styles that improve and change our fishing. This trend will continue.

Yet the basics outlined here are eternal. They will help get you started and provide a foundation for ice fishing success on virtually any water body that freezes. If you use the proper combination of lake maps, electronics, and knowledge of the species you're seeking to decipher and match the best lures, equipment, and methods to the given situation, your ice fishing productivity is sure to show improvement and greater consistency.

I was thinking about this one day recently, while visiting with my grandfather, awaiting a fresh tray of grandma's secret recipe oatmeal raisin cookies with the crisscross icing on top to pop from the oven. I reminisced how it seemed only yesterday I was five, awaiting a chewy batch of Grandma's warm cookies, and I commented how things change.

"Consider the changes in my eighty years," Grandfather explained. "I came from a farm with no electricity, no running water, refrigerator, or radio, much less a television, microwave, or home computer. We've sure come a long way."

I sat there looking into his eyes, nodding. I was thinking about the changes I'll reflect back on when I'm eighty—and grandma's secret recipe, too—because both remind me of developments in ice fishing methodology over the last decade.

Ten years ago, few ice anglers referenced lake maps to find primary fish holding structure. LCRs were virtually unheard of. GPS wasn't marketed for fishing use. For the most part, micro and ultralight ice tackle wasn't commercially available. Seldom did ice anglers strategically approach ice fishing, or follow a secret recipe if you will.

Today, we have all the ingredients necessary to mix up recipes for winter fishing success. Lake maps depict precise lake bottom topographies. In-depth, species-specific, fisheries management studies provide data that not only allow fish managers to

An angler walks into the sunset.

increase production and grow more fish, but provide anglers with clues for locating primary winter fish holding features, migration routes, and location patterns.

Blend this knowledge with modern electronics, such as Global Positioning Systems, that allow anglers to electronically mark fish holding features, and with precision sonar devices for learning exactly how fish are moving and relating to these structures, and simmer the potential.

While this simmers, stir in today's lighter, smoother, and faster power and hand ice drills; comfortable portable shelters; virtually trouble-free, freeze-proof tip-ups; heavy, medium, and light action graphite ice rods; balanced, precision tapered micro ice rods; smooth, lightweight ball-bearing multi drag setting reels; non-stretch, low diameter braided monofilaments; thin, limp wispy monofilament lines slimmer than the diameter of a human hair yet many times stronger; and thousands of revolutionary new designs in swimming, flashing, darting, vibrating, jiggling, and plastic ice lures in a vast array of styles, sizes, and a rainbow of colors. Mix these together with just the right measure of each, and you'll have all the ingredients necessary for cooking up a batch of savory winter fishing trips.

Just remember to plan carefully before you begin. Even gourmet chefs with years of experience follow recipes, although they likely ad lib slightly, adding unique touches of this or that to make standard recipes special. Still, even the best chefs inventory the proper ingredients, then follow premeditated guidelines.

So it is with ice fishing. Successful ice anglers plan carefully prior to fishing, but versatile anglers also ad lib and add unique touches to their methods. Just as experience teaches a cook how to use a variety of spices and properly blend them to attain unique and special qualities, experienced anglers can experiment with today's equipment and presentations, modifying them to stay ahead of the crowd. Carefully blended with just the right measures, each recipe becomes unique, and hopefully, successful.

Even with experimentation, both chefs and anglers follow basic guidelines, but both can also make mistakes. A cook substituting salt for sugar makes an obvious blunder. Adding too much or too little of the wrong spice won't have the same dramatic implications, but does influence the end result. The same goes for the ice angler. Each piece of electronic technology, and every rod, reel, spool of line, and lure style, size, weight, and color plays a specific role in the end result. Making a major mistake such as fishing the wrong location is an obvious blunder. Using the wrong lure size or color, or hooking your live bait incorrectly won't always have the same dramatic implications, but can and often will influence the end result.

This winter season, plan your outings. Like a chef, follow a recipe, but don't hesitate to experiment with modifications and details. There will be successes and failures. That's ice fishing.

Even so, we're living in an exciting, opportune time, filled with more advanced refinements in knowledge and tackle than ever before for improving our odds on the ice.

Yes, grandpa, we have come a long way. We'll go further yet. I know we will, because as long as there are people, there will be a need for the outdoors; an incessant craving for the wild; a desire to explore the unknown and take what we know one step further. We will always need a chance to be challenged, to have fun, and to experience quality time with friends and family, especially with our children and our children's children, the future generations who will carry on this ice fishing tradition. They will build on the knowledge we pass onto them, and be the benefactors of our decisions that monitor and protect our waters and fisheries. Perhaps, someday, they will teach us something new about the sport. Children have a way of doing that.

Ice fishing will always provide such opportunities, while also offering a chance to relax and enjoy life, and to gain, if not be instilled with, an enthusiastic appreciation for the outdoors, nature, and all the God given things we're blessed with in it.

To some, none of this may be important, and I pity them. There are many equally unimportant, unquestionably trivial ways people can spend their time, their days, and their lives. Many of these ways are more frivolous and insignificant, but not nearly as challenging, fascinating, intriguing, fun, or enjoyable as ice fishing.

Once into ice fishing—truly in touch, immersed, engrossed, or, like me, even on the verge of being obsessed with the sport—you'll find it healthy, clean, inviting, and refreshing. If I can truly enjoy and feel refreshed by ice fishing, and see it as a chance to be rejuvenated, to get in touch with my life, and to grow closer to God, then the same opportunity exists for you, too.

To quote Psalms, "This is a day that the Lord hath made, let us rejoice and be glad in it." Life is a precious gift, a blessing, something we should lavish in and hold onto with a clean heart. For me, one way to relish the full, true, rich taste of life is to spend a day of sharing the fun and fascination of ice fishing with family, friends, and you.

Join me, if you will, on this great cathedral on ice, and experience the rebirth winter and ice fishing can provide. I think you'll find an understanding of the winter outdoors, of nature, and of ice fishing and all its complexities worth a life of inquisitive seeking. As I see it, life is but a lighted match in the winds of eternity, and I, for one, don't wish to waste it.

Index

N

O

P

Q

R

S

Zero in on successful deer hunting with these four exciting new books!

WHITETAIL: THE ULTIMATE CHALLENGE
by Charles J. Alsheimer
6"x9", softcover, 228 pg., 150 photos
Learn deer hunting's most intriguing secrets from America's premier authority on using decoys, scents and calls to bag a buck. Find insight on the whitetail's rut cycles, where and how to hunt whitetails across North America, rubs, scrapes, the impact of weather conditions and much more! Plus, many spectacular black and white photos.

$14.95

Available June 1995

HUNTING MATURE BUCKS
by Larry Weishuhn
6"x9", softcover, 256 pg., 80 photos
Learn how to take those big, smart, elusive bucks. Excellent blend of scientific knowledge and old-fashioned "how-to" gives you the information you need. Also learn behind the scenes management techniques that help balance doe/buck ratios to produce bragging-size whitetails.

Available February 1995

$14.95

AGGRESSIVE WHITETAIL HUNTING
by Greg Miller
6"x9", paperback, 208 pg., 80 photos
Learn how to hunt trophy bucks in public forests and farmlands from one of America's foremost hunters.

"Hunter's hunter" Greg Miller puts his years of practical experience into easy-to-understand advice that will help both bow and gun hunters bag that trophy. Ideal for busy outdoorsmen that have neither the time nor finances to hunt exotic locales.

$14.95

Available February 1995

SOUTHERN DEER & DEER HUNTING
by Bill Bynum and Larry Weishuhn

These two popular southern hunters and DEER & DEER HUNTING field editors join forces to bring you the history of deer in the south, plus techniques that work below the Mason Dixon line as well as anywhere whitetails are found. Understand terrain, firearms, equipment, rattling and calling along with much more firsthand experience that's guaranteed to bring you success in southern climates.

Available June 1995

$14.95

ORDER TODAY! BUY ALL FOUR BOOKS AND GET FREE SHIPPING!*

Please send me:

____ copy(ies) WHITETAIL: THE ULTIMATE CHALLENGE...$14.95 $ _____

____ copy(ies) HUNTING MATURE BUCKS...$14.95 $ _____

____ copy(ies) AGGRESSIVE WHITETAIL HUNTING...$14.95 $ _____

____ copy(ies) SOUTHERN DEER & DEER HUNTING...$14.95 $ _____

Shipping ($2.50 for first book, $1.50 for each additional book, FREE if you buy all four) $ _____

WI residents add 5.5% sales tax $ _____

Total Amount Enclosed $ _____

Name _____

Address _____

City _____

State _____ Zip _____

☐ Check or money order (to Krause Publications)

☐ MasterCard ☐ VISA

Credit Card No. _____

Expires: Mo. _____ Yr. _____

Signature _____

Mail with payment to:
KRAUSE PUBLICATIONS
Book Dept. WFB1, 700 E. State St., Iola, WI 54990-0001

*Books shipped upon publication

For faster service MasterCard and VISA customers dial toll-free
800-258-0929 Dept. WFB1
6:30 am - 8:00 pm, Sat. 8:00 am - 2:00 pm, CT